Inter-Actions

Relationships of Religion and Drama

Nelvin Vos

UNIVERSITY PRESS OF AMERICA,® INC.

Lanham • Boulder • New York • Toronto • Plymouth, UK

Copyright © 2009 by
University Press of America,® Inc.
4501 Forbes Boulevard
Suite 200
Lanham, Maryland 20706
UPA Acquisitions Department (301) 459-3366

Estover Road
Plymouth PL6 7PY
United Kingdom

Library of Congress Control Number: 2008944381
ISBN: 978-0-7618-4469-3 (paperback : alk. paper)
eISBN: 978-0-7618-4470-9

⊗ ™ The paper used in this publication meets the minimum requirements of American
National Standard for Information Sciences—Permanence of Paper for Printed Library
Materials, ANSI/NISO Z39.48-1992.

Contents

Preface

I once heard the Swiss theologian, Karl Barth, comment that "and" (he actually said a guttural German "und") is one of the most important words in any language. He continued by speaking of both heaven and earth, both male and female, and in the greatest act in the Christian tradition, Jesus Christ came to earth, both human and divine.

"And" is both similarity and difference, connection and disjunction, counterpoint and tension.

This book is an exploration of the relationship of drama and religion. Within that "and" are both the complexities as well as the richness of human experience.

The study is not an attempt to sacralize drama so that drama becomes a substitute for religion. Neither is it an attempt to reduce religion to its aesthetic dimension. Instead, its purpose is to maintain the integrity of both areas of human experience while attempting to illustrate that the two phenomena in our Western history are inextricably connected and inherently related in their very nature and at the same time, always in tension with one another.

In brief, what does religion tell us about drama and what does drama tell us about religion?

The book is divided into three sections. The first, after an introductory chapter, is an exploration of "Drama and Religion: Their Languages" with a brief excursus into the relation of the Scriptures and the dramatic. "Drama and Religion: Their Structures" constitutes the second section with chapters on ritual, play, and worship. The major part of the volume is devoted to "Drama and Religion: Their History" with seven chapters explicating the intersections of drama and religion with specific plays from the Greeks to the present. A coda suggests some connections between drama and life.

This study therefore engages in at least five ways of seeing:

- Seeing as if through a microscope. An enlarged view of objects is invaluable for analysis and insight. The dominant portion of this book is a careful examination of specific plays. Such a perspective gives one knowledge of the particular and the concrete.
- Seeing as if through a telescope. To view the whole in panoramic gaze may give one the detachment of distance. Thus the book takes the wide scope from the Greeks to a play in 2003 in order to discern similarities and differences in religion and drama over the centuries.
- Seeing through a periscope. From the depths, we survey what is visible at the horizon, far and near. What has been happening in religion and drama within history over the centuries? What do we see more recently?
- Seeing through a kaleidoscope. Etymologically, the word implies beautiful form. It is to see the familiar in an endless variety of patterns. It is a way of seeing reality which relies on juxtaposition, montage, collage. The combination of two or more seemingly dissimilar objects or ideas such as religion and drama may give one insight into both areas.
- Seeing through a cinemascope. This is the gift of imagination, what Shakespeare calls "the mind's eye." Imagination and faith cannot really be distinctly separated. To imagine and to make a leap of faith are very similar acts. We do not abandon the rational in religion and drama, but we allow ourselves the risky adventure of being open to other worlds.

This undertaking is more than ambitious; it may be seen as presumptuous. But religion and culture, specifically Christianity and drama, is rooted deep within my Reformational religious background and my love and knowledge of the theater. My education at Calvin College, with its emphasis on the sovereignty of God in all spheres of life, and at the University of Chicago, both in the English Department and the Divinity School, opened up wide vistas to explore in both theology and drama. And my teaching and writing as well as my longtime involvement in the Society for the Arts, Religion, and Contemporary Culture the past four decades as well as my earlier membership in the Conference of Christianity and Literature have provided opportunity for many forays into specific areas of the relationship of religion and drama.

But the journey did not begin so positively. I grew up in a strict Dutch Reformed community that, amid its rich heritage which I continue to affirm, was very negative about theater. In fact, I did not see my first movie until age nineteen, and my first professional production until age twenty-three in 1955. A trip to the newly-opened Guthrie Theatre at the Stratford Shakespeare Festival in Ontario, Canada, provided an epiphany of the power of drama. To see the young Christopher Plummer play Hamlet and to experience Ophelia's funeral procession come down the amphitheater's aisle next to me meant that I not only knew the definition of the catharsis of pity and fear, but I had experienced it deeply. The centrality of the Christian faith and my love of theater and the tension and interaction between them are deeply imbedded.

This volume by its very nature and purpose is not definitive, but rather intends to be evocative and provocative. The book is a hypothesis and an argument in progress in that it raises questions, points toward directions for possible answers, and urges others to join the conversation.

For the conversation between religion and culture, drama and Christianity, needs to be ongoing. This undertaking is a modest contribution to the dialogue.

This book was long in the making and I am grateful to Muhlenberg College for a sabbatical leave in 1993–94 during which time I sketched out the topic and began my research. The staff of Trexler Library at Muhlenberg College was very helpful at many points in the undertaking. John Trump gave good advice about the manuscript. And Mrs. Elsie Schmoyer was invaluable in her patient reading of my messy hand-written copy and many drafts in order to put these words into print.

My greatest debt is to my wife, Beverly, who continues to be the mainstay in my life.

N.V.

Acknowledgments

Grateful acknowledgement is due for permission to quote from the following works:

Euripides. *The Bacchae*,tr.William Arrowsmith from *The Complete Greek Tragedies*. Volume IV, ed. David Grene and Richmond Lattimore. The University of Chicago Press. Copyright 1958, 1959 by The University of Chicago. Used by permission of the University of Chicago Press.

Henrik Ibsen. *Ghosts* from *The Complete Major Prose Plays of Henrik Ibsen*, tr. Rolf Fjelde, copyright 1965, 1970, 1978 by Rolf Fjelde. Used by permission of Dutton Signet, a division of Penguin Group, (USA) Inc.

August Strindberg. *A Dream Play* from *A Dream Play and Four Chamber Plays*, tr. Walter Johnson, copyright 1973. Used by permission of the University of Washington Press.

Luigi Pirandello. *Henry IV*, tr. Edward Storer, from *Naked Masks: Five Plays*, ed. Eric Bentley, copyright 1922 by E.P. Dutton. Renewed 1950 in the names of Stefano, Fausto and Lietta Pirandello. Used by permission of Dutton, a division of Penguin Group (USA) Inc.

T. S. Eliot. *The Cocktail Party*. Copyright 1950 by T.S. Eliot. Used by permission of Harcourt, Inc.

Samuel Beckett. *Endgame*.Copyright 1958, by Grove Press, Inc. Used by permission of Grove/Atlantic, Inc.

Tom Stoppard. *Rosencrantz and Guildenstern are Dead*. Copyright 1967 by Tom Stoppard. Used by permission of Grove/Atlantic, Inc.

Introduction: Places of Seeing:
Religion and Theater

I am sitting in the warm April sun. Surrounding me are the low hills of Argos, and far below me is the orchestra, a circular area about fifty feet in diameter. Rows and rows of tiered stone seats (I count sixty-five rows as I climb to the topmost one) are arranged in a perfect half circle. The guide lights a match as she stands in the center of the orchestra; I can hear the match strike in the top row. She chatters on while I imagine Oedipus or Orestes striding in front of the proscenium. For I am sitting in the amphitheater at Epidaurus, built in the fourth century B.C. On this hollowed-out hillside, some twelve thousand people view each performance of the Greek plays produced here during the summer months. The power of the ancient ritual of Dionysus is still present.

A dramatic tradition impresses itself upon us, said a recent critic, not first of all as a series of dates or plot outlines, but as a cluster of images, a montage of particular persons. To think of a play is to see a person in action.

A powerful hulk of a man, shackled to a rock, shouts defiance to the heavens; an avenging queen persuades her returning conqueror-husband to walk in pride upon the red carpet; a king with the nobility of a demigod exclaims:

It was true! All the prophecies! Now—
Light, may I look on you for the last time.

Near all of these persons within the acting area is an altar for sacrifice to the gods. The community, the polis, is visibly present in the chorus. Most important, all of what takes place is completely open; the brilliance of the sun illumines all of the action. The spectators in the theater are thus confronted with the principal symbols, the ultimate foundations of their world—the social and the heavenly order, the city, the palace, the temple, the abode of the mysterious gods. The Greek dramatist saw the heroes and heroines as directly

1

related, connected, if you will, with the *communitas*, the world of Nature, and the arena of the gods. The Greek actor-doers are affected by all of reality, and when they fall, the repercussions affect the whole of the universe.

It is no coincidence that the Greeks bequeathed the word "cosmos" to all of civilization. The roots of the term "cosmic"—vast, grandiose, orderly, the universe as a whole—are apparent, for when the spectator is in the theater, the mountains, the sea, and the sky are all visibly present. The ritualistic actions of the protagonist take place within the pattern of the cosmos as a whole.

The theater was from its beginnings what its etymology conveys, *theatron,* "a place of seeing." Theory (*theorein*) derives from the same source and thus the kind of seeing involved in the theater is a looking at with a distinctive intensity. It is not first of all a coming into the range of vision or staring, but a process by which the mind inspects, and by which the imagination is open to a new world, to all infinite possibilities. What is happening in my mind and imagination as I experience a drama is a rich and complex process of seeing the relationship between the "theory" (the play as a hypothesis, a way of seeing) I am beholding and the practice of my day-to-day existence.

Religion claims that its perspective opens up our ways of seeing. When one enters a religious space for worship, the space becomes "a place of seeing" and looking with distinctive intensity. Like religion, drama also provides a perspective which may see one's self, others, the world, and the presence of the transcendent.

Both religion and drama prompt us to see within, for both may initiate a struggle within the depths of one's being which has always been characterized as a quest for meaning. Such an experience encourages a process by which the mind and the heart scrutinizes its longings and desires, its fears and hopes.

Both religion and drama also prompt us to look beyond, to point toward and to open to the transcendent. We engage in a search to see the intangible in the tangible, the mystery within the ordinary, to be aware that the holy, the awe-ful (full of awe) is something around and within us, if only we risk opening our eyes. For a period of time, we enter, while remaining rooted in the here and now, a timeless world which permits us to transcend, at least for a moment, the temporal limitations of our condition.

The chief function of theater, wrote Gabriel Marcel, is "to awaken or re-awaken in us the consciousness of the infinite which is concealed in the particular."[1] We at all times sense the paradox—and the frustration—of our finite existence within an infinite universe. Such a perspective reminds us that in the here and now is the extraordinary, that within the immediate is the transcendent. The genius of theater and religious rites is their ability to put people in touch with the mysteries of the universe we inhabit and to the mysteries beyond.

The stage is thus the locus where the horizontal and the vertical meet. Peter Brook, one of the most noted names in theater in the last several decades, has commented that, for audiences and actors alike, a theatrical experience may give "a burning and fleeting taste of another world in which our present world is integrated and transformed."[2] In another work, *The Empty Space*, Brook speaks of "the Holy Theatre," "The Theatre of the Invisible—Made—Visible . . . the yearning for the invisible through its visible incarnations. . . ."[3]

Tom F. Driver who has devoted much scholarship to the relationship of religion and drama accurately perceives the theater as the infinite bound with a finite space:

> The theater, like dance and unlike cinema, is the art of the use of finite space. It requires a space that does not move, that is fixed, limited, that imposes re-straints. The aesthetic of theater is in large part built upon the imaginative over-coming of fixed space, just as the aesthetic of painting is largely built upon the imaginative overcoming of a two-dimensional limitation. When the theater is at its height it binds infinite space into a nutshell, as Hamlet said:
>
> > O God, I could be bounded in a nutshell and count myself a king of infinite space, were it not that I have bad dreams.(II. ii. 260)
>
> Hamlet was speaking, to be sure, of his mind, but the image was theatrical. His was a theatrical understanding of consciousness: an infinite abound concen-trated into a finite arena.[4]

A play in performance is a fusion of the fixed with the elements of the liv-ing reality of the actors and audience. Every performance can thus be seen as an act of resurrection: the inert words are reincarnated by the living presence of actors and members of the audience.

We all know that moment, that moment when the theater darkens and ev-eryone is hushed. And then out of the darkness appears on the stage another world. The participants in the drama, both the actors and the audience, are joined together not only by particular words and actions, but they also form for a few hours a community who enters a unified suspension of disbelief. We are open to believe the world created on stage. Drama requires for its maximum fulfillment a high degree of social cohesion, a common under-standing of values, symbols, and myths. "A play exists, really exists, lives and really lives only when its life-spark leaps from the stage and from the playwright's soul across to the audience in a moment of vital contact,"[5] writes the playwright Henri Gheon. He adds: "Dramatic art is an art of barter, of interchange."[6]

Above all other arts, drama is thus the art of shared response. "In drama," wrote critic Harold Clurman, "the community is talking with itself."[7] Or, as Brooks Atkinson, another New York drama critic, wrote: "A successful production has to beguile several hundred strangers every performance into being a community of believers."[8]

Since the dawn of history, human beings have experienced the interaction between the finite and the infinite, human and divine, in particular spaces. In Christianity, the Garden of Eden, the tower of Babel, the stone at Bethel and the hill of Golgotha are specific places of seeing. In Western dramatic history, the orchestra in the amphitheater, the altar in the cathedral, the processions on the streets became spaces to enact the ways of the human and the divine. More recently, in the last several hundred years, specific buildings have been set aside for performances of drama.

But no matter what and where the spaces, "all play," as Eric Bentley has suggested, "creates a world within a world—a territory with laws of its own."[9] Because the world created on the stage has its own life, we experience a drama differently from the way in which we experience ordinary life. In the theater, space and time take on a coherence that in "real life" we find almost impossible to perceive—time becomes destiny and space becomes a world. In that finite space, the infinite and the particular are made concrete.

In William Saroyan's play of 1957, *The Cave Dwellers*, a strange little commune of out-of-work actors have staked themselves to living quarters on the stage of a deserted theater condemned to be demolished. As they wait for the wreckers to come, an old man, called the King, delivers a final soliloquy that becomes a string of stunning metaphors for the theater:

Farewell, then—womb, cave, hiding place,
home, church, world, theatre—a fond and loving farewell.[10]

This rag-tag family saw the theater not simply as a deserted and condemned building, but as their very ground of being, and to leave it was to leave the world. To them, the death of the theater was emblematic of the death of the soul. They had lost not only a particular space; they could no longer see.

NOTES

1. Gabriel Marcel, *Homo Viator: Introduction to a Metaphysic of Hope*, trans. Emma Craufurd (Chicago: Henry Regnery, 1952), 19.

2. Peter Brooks, *The Shifting Point: Theatre, Film, Opera 1946–1987* (New York: Harper and Row, 1989), 235.

3. *Brook, The Empty Space* (New York: Atheneum Publishers, 1969), 42, 71.

4. Tom F. Driver, "The Loss of the Histrionic and the Modern Quandary of Theology," *Soundings*, LI, Number I (Spring 1968): 216.

5. Henry Gheon, *The Art of the Theatre*, tr. Adele M. Fiske (New York, Hill and Wang, 1961), 18.

6. Gheon, 19.

7. Harold Clurman, *Lies Like Truth* (New York: Macmillan, 1958), 42.

8. Brooks Atkinson, *Broadway* (New York: Macmillan, 1970), 418.

9. Eric Bentley, *The Life of the Drama* (New York: (New York, Atheneum Publishers, 1970), 150.

10. William Saroyan, *The Cave Dwellers* (New York: G. P. Putnams' Sons, 1959), 120.

Part One

DRAMA AND RELIGION:
THEIR LANGUAGES

Chapter One

Drama: Where the Action Is

Drama is act. It is a doing (dran = to do) a happening, an event, or as Aristotle described tragedy, as "an imitation, not of men, but of action" (*Poetics*, 1450a). Drama is mimetic action, action in imitation or representation of human behavior. Drama occurs, as Bernard Beckerman states, when "one or more human beings isolated in time and space present themselves in imagined acts to another or others."[1] The presentation of drama is a presentation of an imagined act. Earlier, Beckerman had written that "the medium of a play is *not* language but human presence."[2]

Drama is thus the most concrete form in which art can recreate human situations, human relationships. To think of a play is to see a person in action. The essence of drama is not an idea, although certainly a drama always has ideas, but ideas put into action, dramatized ideas. Drama is neither philosophy nor even poetry. To go searching for philosophical or religious ideas apart from the action of a play or to talk glowingly about the poetic verse apart from the action of a play is to violate the nature of drama.

The following lines are frequently cited, for example, from *King Lear*:

As flies to wanton boys, are we to the gods
They kill us for their sport. (IV, I, 38–39)

To isolate these lines as Shakespeare's religious philosophy, on the one hand, would be to imply that *King Lear* is an essay, an exposition of ideas that Shakespeare is speaking to us directly. To ignore the depths of skeptical fatalism in these lines by talking only about their fine poetic power, on the other hand, is to imply that Shakespeare's play is primarily a lyric poem, an evocation of moods and feelings by means of metaphorical language. But the dramatic understanding of the play would best be achieved by focusing on the action of the scene. A particular man in a particular situation utters these lines. Who is this man from what we have observed about him earlier in the play? When does he say these lines? Where does he say them? To whom? How are they received? In brief, what is the relationship of these lines to the whole of this man and to the whole action of the play? We begin to catch the action of the scene by observing that the speaker is the Earl of Gloucester whom we have seen in action as a naïve and gullible but nevertheless a loving father of two sons, and as a highly superstitious and extremely mercurial man of moods and temperaments who at present is contemplating suicide in the blind depths of his despair of losing his son, Edgar. That his enemies have recently blinded him in their sportive abuse and that Edgar is actually guiding him at this time and will only have him pretend to leap from the cliff—all this and more is part of the dramatic immediacy of the scene.

The first questions for a drama therefore are not these (although both must be part of the total understanding of the play): What are the philosophical or religious themes of the play or what is the language of the play? The primary focus is: What's happening here? What's going on in this world of people? What kind of actions, inner and outer, are the people performing? A play-reader by looking analytically at the philosophy or the poetry of the play may have the advantage of detachment and of close attention to the text, but may miss what the spectator cannot ignore: to become caught up in the action on stage. Francis Fergusson in his excellent book, *The Idea of a Theater*,[3] helpfully points out that the action of a play or scene can best be indicated by the use of an infinitive phrase. He suggests that Oedipus's action is "to find the culprit,"[4] and out of this action flows the conflicts, inner and outer, of the whole play, for both Oedipus and the audience are caught up in this action.

The pivotal term "action" does not refer to events, deeds, or physical activity but rather, as Robert Corrigan wrote in several helpful phrases, to action as "the play's all-encompassing purpose, the source of the play's higher meaning," and "the governing motivation that shapes the thoughts and feelings of all the characters in the play, the choices they make, and the deeds they both commit and react to."[5]

Drama is not only the most concrete artistic imitation of actual human behavior; it is also the most concrete form in which we can think about human situations. Drama, by being a concrete representation of action as it actually takes place, is able to show us several aspects of that action simultaneously and also to convey several levels of action and emotion at the same time. And the action of the drama as Martin Esslin suggests, "is happening in an eternal present tense, not there and then, but here and now."[6]

Because drama is essentially "act," its greatest weakness and at the same time, its greatest strength is that it is the least didactic of the verbal art-forms.

The essay, of course, is most amenable to teaching. It presents an idea, and in its rhetoric, essayists can make the presentation as didactic as they wish. The form of almost all sermons, although they need not be, is therefore the essay, the exposition. Lyric poetry also interprets reality rather directly through its evocation of moods and feelings, less so than the essay, but more so than narrative, whether in poetic or prose form. The narrative poem as well as the novel or short story possess direct interpretation. The fiction writer intersperses the dialogue of the characters with his own commentary; the reader is told that this character speaks "haltingly," the next "boldly," and so on. Thus essayists, poets, and novelists all have in varying degrees ways of directing the reader's attention to their point of view.

Drama, on the other hand, is people in action. True, the directions in the text to the actor and reader give clues to the interpretation of the dialogue, but unless the actor or the reader's imagination conveys this interpretation, the action is dead, inert, inactive. Propaganda reveals its inauthenticity very quickly in drama; neither the actor nor the audience can hear the ring of truth in the words. Neither can enter the action. And if authors use characters too obviously as their own mouthpieces, the dramatic conflicts are lost, for there is no inter-action.

The dramatic form of expression leaves the reader-viewers to make up their minds about how they interpret the actions portrayed on stage. It puts them in the same situation as the characters to whom the words are addressed.

Drama therefore possesses inherently the risk of induction; the reader-viewers are given only the bare bones of a happening, of people in action; we are to imagine, that is, dramatize in our inner selves, the rest. Such an entering into the play is what the dramatist attempts to evoke from the members of the audience. What a member of the audience sees is filtered through the individual's sensibility and thus again it is evident that the theater is "the place of seeing."

In 1925, Martin Buber, in a little-known essay entitled "Drama and Theatre," suggested that drama is "the formation of the word as something that moves between beings, the mystery of word and answer. Essential to it is the fact of the tension between word and answer."[7] For that is where the action is.

NOTES

1. Bernard Beckerman, *Dynamics of Drama* (New York: Drama Book Specialists, 1970), 20.

2. Beckerman, 18.

3. Francis Fergusson, *The Idea of a Theater* (Princeton: Princeton University Press, 1949).

4. Fergusson, 48.

5. Robert W. Corrigan, *The World of the Theatre* (Glenview, II: Scott Foresman, 1979), 74.

6. Martin Esslin, *An Anatomy of Drama* (New York: Hill and Wang, 1976), 18.

7. Martin Buber, *Pointing the Way*, tr. and ed. by Maurice Friedman (London: Routledge and Kegan Paul, 1957), 63.

Chapter Two

Biblical Revelation:
The Mighty Acts of God

A director, the stage, actors, masks, plot, script, audience—all the elements of drama are present within the Scriptures.

The Bible is presented as a drama. To be sure, this figure of speech is not found anywhere in the Bible itself, but characteristics of a drama spring to mind immediately. The Bible has a unity which runs from beginning to end, from Creation to the New Creation. The story portrays humankind's hopes and fears, their joys and sorrows, their ambitions and tragedies. God is not only behind the scenes prompting and directing the drama, but, according to the Christian tradition, in Jesus, God enters the stage of history as the chief actor, the participant. The plot is the working out of God's purpose in spite of all efforts to oppose it. The denouement is reached when the Crucifixion and Resurrection are proclaimed as the sign of his victory, and in the light of this climactic event, the earlier stages of the story are understood with deeper meaning.

The Bible then is the record of "the mighty acts" of God (Psalm 145), for the concept of "act" is central in the Biblical drama. Professor C. Ernest Wright has pointed out that "the focus of the Bible's main attention . . . was on what God had done and was yet to do according to his declared intention."[1] Thus Professor Wright entitles his study, *God Who Acts*, in order to point up the contrast with the customary expression, *God Who Speaks*.

Emil Brunner goes still further in asserting that the "act" is the dominant motif of the biblical witness:

The decisive word-form in the language of the Bible is not the substantive, as in Greek, but the verb, the word of action. The thought of the Bible is not substantival, neuter and abstract, but verbal, historical and personal. Its concern is not with a relation which exists in and for itself, but with a relation with men. He deals with them, for them and in a certain sense also against them; but He acts always in relation *to them*, and He always *acts*.[2]

In his mammoth work, *Theo-Drama*, Hans Urs von Balthasar asserts that

. . . the revelation of the Old and the New Covenants . . . in its total shape is dramatic. It is the history of a struggle between God and the Creature over the latter's meaning and salvation.[3]

The cosmic drama as the Biblical narrative unfolds begins with God as author (creation) and as director (providence). "The plots of God are perfect,"[4] wrote Poe, and one of the reasons for this assertion is that God not only is spectator and audience but also participant and director of the world's drama. Hagar in her powerful encounter called the Lord who spoke to her, "You are the God who sees me" (Gen. 16:13, NIV). The images of God in scripture often are those of an Oriental king in which the whole universe is his court: "Heaven is my throne and the earth is my footstool" (Isaiah 66:1); "The Lord looks down from heaven; he sees all the drama of men; from where he sits enthroned he looks forth on all the inhabitants of the earth." (Ps. 33:13–14)

God has already taken the drama of existence which plays on the world stage, and inserted it into a quite different "play" which, nonetheless, God wishes to play on our stage. It is a case of the play within the play: our play "plays" in God's play.[5]

The earth is the theater of God's play. Calvin in his *Institutes of the Christian Religion* speaks of man as he "contemplates God's works, since he has been placed in this most glorious theater to be a spectator of them."[6] Later, Calvin writes of "the works of God open and manifest in this most glorious theater."[7] Tom F. Driver explicates such a perspective:

The roots of theology lie in the Biblical witness to the divine activity and in the religious experience of the community of faith created by that activity. For they rest upon man's sense of himself as an occupant of space, an actor in ritual, one capable of going out of himself by imaginative reach and returning to himself by the incorporation of his imaginative adventure.[8]

Thus when we read the Scriptures, what makes it drama is that we as audience know more than those in the story do. Job, for example, has little insight into what is happening to him and why; yet, we are aware of God's action in relation to Job's suffering.

At the beginning of the Scriptures, we see the dramatic encounter of God and Adam and Eve. The two must listen to directions or else, a bad scene will result. Then Satan in the mask of a serpent introduces deception and sin. This episode in the Garden, as Erich Auerbach in *Mimesis* suggests is "presented to us in dramatic form [as] the starting point of the Christian time of redemption."[9] The dramatic tension is real, for Adam and Eve possess a potentiality of their own. They are not completely independent in the sense of being able to devise their own plot or improvise their own lines. But they are emphatically not puppets. This limited freedom reveals itself in the relationship of dialogue. God speaks with particular persons in the situation; the people are creatures who speak with God. The relationship of God and human beings is not that of a jerk of a string but the address through a word, not the mechanical reflex but the personal response through a word. God is known as one who speaks, addresses, calls, initiates agreements or covenants; in brief, God acts, God invites mutual conversation and understanding. God says: "Come now, let us reason together" (Isaiah 1:18), or "Son of man, stand upon your feet, and I will speak with you" (Ezekiel 2:1).

The divine-human dialogue in the Bible is not static. The relationship between God and human beings is constantly changing according to their capacity for obedience and God's capacity for initiating new opportunities for humankind.

The Biblical drama therefore becomes a conflict of loyalties. Adam and Eve, Cain and Abel, Noah and his family, Moses and Aaron, Samson and the Philistines, Saul and David, David and Absalom, Elijah and Jezebel, Job and his friends—all are depicted as torn between various allegiances. In its basic structure of call, temporary success, downfall, and restoration, the Old Testament is a play about love, about the wooing and winning of stubborn Israel by gracious Jehovah.

The foundation for the relationship between God and Israel was laid in the Covenant, the on-going dialogue between human kind and God, as von Balthasur notes:

> . . . at the very center of the biblical events lies the Covenant between God and man, in which God gives man, whom he has created and endowed with freedom, an area of independent being, an area where he can freely hear and answer and ultimately cooperate responsibly with God.[10]

Martin Buber's comment that "all real living is meeting,"[11] is the recognition that the relationship between God and humanity becomes concrete in the encounter of word and action.

This focus on word and action is in keeping with the Biblical centrality of history. Instead of a religion based upon nature in which life is recorded in cycles, the Old Testament portrays God as revealing Himself in historical acts. The chief sources of meaning came not from isolated spiritual experiences but from the certainty of God's working in every event.

Thus each religious festival of Israel was a re-enactment of an historical event, for example, the Feast of Tabernacles remembered the journey through the wilderness, and Purim commemorated the rescue of the Jews under Esther. By re-enacting the historical event, the participants enter ever more deeply into the significance of the redemptive acts of God.

God acts in history—this affirmation of faith finds its dramatic fulfillment in two acts of redemption which are the central core of Biblical revelation.

In the Jewish faith, the central action of God is found in the deliverance of His people from Egypt, and in the Christian faith, the drama of the Incarnation is the action of God on earth. In the drama of the Passover and the Exodus, it is not first of all that God said something, but that He did something. The almost unbelievable escape and rescue were experienced as "mighty acts of God," in and through which the participants knew that they had been chosen for a divine purpose. This liberation from slavery, this struggle between Moses and Pharaoh for the liberty of a whole nation was the starting point of the corporate faith of the house of Israel. Throughout Jewish history, the Exodus drama was not only celebrated regularly but was recalled with particular vividness whenever an historical crisis called for another mighty act of deliverance. The commemoration of this act of God was not first of all the recital of an historical record but the presentation in symbolic form of the events accompanied by appropriate dramatic ritualistic action. Thus each man and woman and child had a responsibility to be a participant in the drama. The action was played out by a whole people.

The Jewish people look back to the mighty acts of God in ancient history to find the reality which gives coherence and unity to all subsequent developments. Christians see in Jesus Christ the reality which provides meaning for the drama of humankind. Both Judaism and Christianity conceive of history in a linear structure. Thus history has movements and plots, characters and settings, climaxes and denouements.

The Incarnation of Jesus Christ is God's use of the dramatic form in human history: God appearing in human flesh in the person of Christ. One of the early Church fathers, Clement of Alexander, provides the image of drama to describe the work of Christ:

> Without divine providence the Lord would not have been able to complete such a gigantic task in such a short time; on account of his external appearance he was not despised, but because of what he achieved he was worshipped . . . For neither did the message meet with unbelief when his coming was first announced, nor did he remain unknown when he adopted the human mask and clothed himself in flesh in order to perform the drama of mankind's redemption. For he was a genuine combatant (*agonistēs*), striving with his creature.[12]

It is not first of all that Christ said something, but that he did something; he was born, he died, he was buried, and he rose again. When we follow the drama of the life of Christ, we know and are aware that he is born a babe in Bethlehem and that he will suffer on the cross. When he is on the cross, we are aware that the resurrection and ascension will come later in the unfolding action.

Biblical revelation does not present us with an idea, but with God revealed in action. The center of the Christian faith is not revealed in a painting or a sculpture or even an essay or poem or a novel, but in a drama: the act of reconciliation and atonement of Jesus Christ and the resurrection.

As G. K. Chesterton comments, the life of Jesus Christ, was above all things dramatic. It did above all things consist in doing something that had to be done. It emphatically would not have been done if Jesus had walked about the world forever doing nothing except tell the truth.[13]

It had to be lived, acted out, among those who could personally witness his presence among them. God allowed Himself to be known in time and space, for this earth became the stage for his action. Particular places, from Bethlehem to Calvary to Mount Olivet, are the settings. The life of Jesus Christ was one long participle: "The light that . . . was coming into the world." (John 1:9)

Thus the new movement of the Gospel was not first of all to be identified with a new teaching, but with an action, the work of Christ. The earliest Christian writings after the Gospel, the Acts of the Apostles and the Epistles, say little about the teaching of Jesus, but focus totally on the actions of his suffering, death, and resurrection: "By this we know love, that he laid down his life for us" (I John 3:16a). The opening of the first letter of John sets the frame for the response of the believing community:

> That which was from the beginning, which we have heard, which we have seen with our eyes, which we have looked upon and touched with our hands, concerning the word of life—the life was made manifest, and we testify to it, and proclaim to you the eternal life which was with the Father and was made manifest in us—that which we have seen and heard we proclaim also to you . . . (I John 1:1–3a)

It is clear that the writer has been part of a drama, and now he wants to have others join in the action and become part of the cast as the drama continues to unfold.

Christianity perceives not only the life and death of Jesus Christ as a drama, but also that the very earth itself, all of creation, is involved in a cosmic drama. "The creation waits with eager longing for the revealing of the sons of God" (Romans 8:19), as if all non-human action were the audience.

But the creation is transformed from audience into actor as it joins all mankind in the act of waiting:

> We know that the whole creation has been groaning in travail until now; and not only the creation, but we ourselves, who have the first fruits of the Spirit, groan inwardly as we wait for adoption as sons, the redemption of our bodies. (Romans 8:22,23)

What happens in the redemptive and cosmic scale also takes place in the individual's inner experience. Paul frequently employs the same image of Israel involved from slavery to liberation as that of the action of salvation for the believer. (Romans 8:15–17) The new participants in the Christian drama are not to be passive spectators, but active and spirited players who attempt to recruit others in the action.

The writer of the Letter to the Hebrews catches the whole of the drama by citing the Old Testament figures as people cast in leading roles in the divine action. That is the power of the eleventh chapter of Hebrews, that pantheon of faithful pilgrims: "By faith Abraham and Sarah and Isaac and Jacob and Moses and time would fail me to tell of. . . ." Such a procession inspires the writer to see the continuation of the drama to the present: "Therefore, since we are surrounded by so great a cloud of witnesses, let us also lay aside every weight, and sin which clings so closely, and let us run with perseverance the race that is set before us." (Hebrews 12:1)

A Lutheran church in the Midwest has inscribed this passage near the ceiling in its circular worship sanctuary. Following the passage as it circles the sanctuary comes the names of Adam, Eve, Abel, Noah, other Old Testament figures, then the New Testament disciples, early Christian believers, through the Reformers, and the more recent heroes of the faith with Dietrich Bonhoeffer as the last name. But space is left in the circle at the end. That space affirms that the drama of the Christian faith continues with new actors in each time and place. Those earlier saints serve as audience to cheer and encourage those who are now on stage, the participating actors in the drama of history from the Creation to the Last Day.

NOTES

1. Ernest Wright, *God Who Acts* (London: SCM Press, 1952), 25.

2. Emil Brunner, *The Divine-Human Encounter*, tr. Amandas W. Loos (Philadelphia: Westminster Press, 1943), 47–49.

3. Hans Urs von Balthasur, *Theo-Drama: Prologomena*, Volume I, tr. Graham Harrison (San Francisco: St. Ignatius Press, 1988), 125.

4. Edgar Allan Poe, *Eureka: A Prose Poem* (Hartford: Transcendental Books, 1973), 120.

5. von Balthasur, 20.

6. John Calvin, *Institutes of the Christian Religion*, tr. Ford Lewis Battles (Philadelphia: Westminster Press, 1960), Book I, VI, 2.

7. Calvin, Book I, XIV, 20.

8. Tom F. Driver, "The Loss of the Histrionic and the Modern Quandary of Theology," *Soundings,* LI, Number 1 (Spring 1968): 222.

9. Erich Auerbach, *Mimesis*, tr. Willard R. Trask (Princeton, NJ: Princeton University Press, 1953), 151.

10. von Balthasur, 35.

11. Martin Buber, *I and Thou*, tr. Ronald Gregor Smith (New York: Charles Scribner's Sons, (1958), 11.8.

12. *Protreptikos* X, 110, quoted in von Balthasur, 95–96.

13. G. K. Chesterton, *The Everlasting Man* (London, Hodder and Stoughton, 1927), 20.

Part Two

DRAMA AND RELIGION:
THEIR STRUCTURES

Chapter Three

Ritual: The Act Re-Done

"Drama only flourishes in the neighborhood of its shrine"[1] wrote William Butler Yeats early in the twentieth century, and in those words, the rich and complex relationship of drama and religion is both suggested and still further entangled.

The ceremonial patterning of an action through dialogue, incident, and physical movement indicates the action of ritual in both drama and religion.

In its incantation of word and its use of appropriate gesture as well as in the vestigial observances of sacrifice and feast, ritual dimensions can be discerned in both drama and religion. In sacrifice, we give 'it' up, and in feast we live 'it' up. In both, that which takes place are re-enactments of fundamental rituals. Rituals, in their broadest sense, says Northrop Frye, are "recurrent acts of symbolic communication."[2] Each of these words is crucial in understanding ritual.

Ritual, according to Ronald Grimes who has written extensively on the subject, is "idealized activity performed in a special place at a special time."[3] Another scholar, Rainer Friedrich, identifies mimesis as central in ritual in its three main aspects of imitation, representation, and expression and further comments that "ritual is partly the imitation, partly the stylized representation of an action through which collectively felt emotions are collectively expressed and cathartically discharged."[4] And Martin Esslin describes several important characteristics of ritual in both drama and religion:

. . . collective experiences with the three-cornered reinforcement of feed-back from performer to audience, from audience to audience.

. . . all ritual has a mimetic aspect; it contains an action of a highly symbolic, metaphysical nature . . .

. . . ritual abolishes time by putting its congregation in touch with events and concepts which are eternal and therefore infinitely repeatable.

. . . the aim is an enhanced level of consciousness, a memorable insight into the nature of existence, a renewal of strength in the individual to face the world. In dramatic terms: catharsis; in religious terms: communion, enlightenment, illumination.

. . . the use of heightened language or verse, song, music, rhythmical chanting, spectacular visual effects: costume, masks, dance, spectacular architecture.

Esslin concludes that "theater can be described as secular cathedrals and cathedrals as secular stages."[5]

When rituals take place in theaters or cathedrals, they are actions which tacitly are metaphors of much larger worlds. The communal experience in ritual is an attempt to belong, to seek unity with another and with meaning beyond one's self, and to be bonded to the past, the present, and the future. Others have re-acted this ritual before, others are performing it somewhere else, and still others will engage in this action in the future. Ritual is a way of preserving our contact with such moments.

Why are we attracted to ritual? First of all, we are constantly aware of the incompleteness of our physical existence. Throughout human history, life has seemed ultimately mysterious, and our persistent efforts have been to identify and define the nature of that mystery. We are creatures who sometimes find meaning through order, and ritual is one way of ordering an apparently chaotic and sometimes hostile environment. Ritual attempts to make the mysterious concrete by identifying it in a fixed sequence of acts. We have always sensed the paradox of our finite existence within an infinite universe. In ritual, we participate in a timeless world, permitting us to transcend, at least for the moment, the typical conditions of our finitude.

"In ritual, we enlarge our being," writes Bruce Wiltshire, and adds that the result is "discovery, and we come home to ourselves as we believe we are: beings of inexhaustible particularity as well as indefinitely extendable horizons of human concern and identification."[6]

To participate in ritual is to engage in a collective transforming.

Thus both time and space are transcended in ritual. And the whole person is involved. Ritual, according to Richard Schechner, is an event upon which its participants depend.[7] The participants experience re-integration, or, as Hanna Scolnicov describes the response:

The catharsis experienced in tragedy, according to Aristotle, is not far from the religious experience of purification and rebirth. Like ritual, a performance brought the community together on religious festivities, and was an occasion for the reaffirmation of shared ideas and beliefs.[8]

She later adds: ". . . the theater does not belong to the 'profane sphere', but is a special secular development of the sacred space . . ."[9]

The history of drama reflects this desire to connect to the sacred. Greek drama was not merely a poet's presentation of a story, but a ceremony in honor of the god. The priests in these ancient rites of Thespis had special seats, like canons at a cathedral. Sophocles and Aeschylus and Euripides accepted without question the faith-evoking ritual which celebrated each year the resurrection of the wine-god and assured the audience of its spiritual rebirth. Greek drama occurred, according to Wiltshire, at "a holy place on a holy day . . . and probably it was felt that the actors were vehicles possessed by a god, or by the mythic heroes, at least for that time and at that place."[10]

Drama still conveys the fundamental mysteries of life and death and life after death. In the tragic falls of Macbeth and Willy Loman are reflected rituals of sacrifice. The deaths of Shakespeare's Desdemona in *Othello,* of O'Neill's Brown in *The Great God Brown*, and of Eliot's Becket in *Murder in the Cathedral* are all carefully patterned for ritualistic action. Comedies, whether Shakespeare's mistaken identity plays or current Broadway musicals, are reenactments of renewal in their rituals of celebration and feast.

But just as some religious rituals become routine and therefore meaningless, ritualistic actions in drama sometimes became distorted. Francis Ferguson, for example, speaks of "maimed rites" in Hamlet: marriages that are false, funerals that are truncated, entertainments that are stratagems.[11]

Religious rituals such as confession, forgiveness, and sacrifice are present in outline form in many plays, but their inner authenticity is frequently missing. The characters in Albee's *Who's Afraid* of *Virginia Woolf?* and in *A Delicate Balance* constantly confess their shortcomings and ask each other for forgiveness, but little is accomplished by these actions. The pupil in Ionesco's *The Lesson* and the Old Man and the Old Woman of *The Chairs* die in sacrificial martyrdom, but nothing is gained.

Such characters are engaged in rituals that have lost contact with the life that produced them. They are unable to explain why they are doing what they are doing; they have forgotten the substance of the ceremony. The figures who should arrive to help them are only parodies of saviors: Lucky and Pozzo in *Waiting For Godot*, the Fire Chief of *The Bald Soprano,* and the Orator of *The Chairs*. Instead of presenting salvatory messages, they only narrate incoherent fairy tales and stammer in their muteness. When ritual is emptied of meaning, like Richard II without the divine right of kings, the action turns to farce. By concentrating on the empty outward motions, dramatists expose the terrifying nullity within.

Yet the power of ritual will not be denied. Tyrone Guthrie, the noted director and designer of theaters, speaks of the energy which is manifested in

> . . . the prescribed recreation of significant words and acts which the audience knows to be Ritual, and from which it seeks not merely relaxation but inspiration and wisdom. Such a theater will be an altar where Rites in honor of an Unknown God, but not on that account an unworthy God, will be performed with the purposeful intensity of prayer.[12]

Religious ritual attempts to confront us with God. Dramatic ritual confronts us not only with another and with gods sometimes recognized and sometimes unknown. In both ritualistic actions, we gain self-knowledge and insight and experience renewal and restoration.

NOTES

1. William Butler Yeats, quoted in Donald R. Pearce, "Christianity and the Form of Western Drama," *Shenandoah Review*, 22 (Spring 1971): 69.

2. Northrop Frye, *The Anatomy of Criticism* (Princeton: Princeton University Press, 1957), 105.

3. Ronald L. Grimes, *Marrying and Burying: Rites of Passage in a Man's Life* (Boulder, Colo, Westview Press, 1995), 216.

4. Rainer Friedrich, "Drama and Ritual," in *Themes in Drama: Drama and Religion*, ed. James Redmond (London: Cambridge University Press, 1985), 163.

5. Martin Esslin, *An Anatomy of Drama* (New York: Hill and Wang, 1976), 27–28.

6. Bruce Wiltshire, *Role Playing and Identity* (Bloomington: Indiana University Press, 1982), 10.

7. Richard Schechner, "From Ritual to Theatre and Gods" in *Ritual, Play, and Performance*, eds. Richard Schechner and Mady Schuman (New York: Seabury Press, 1976), 211.

8. Hanna Scolnicov, "Theatre Space, Theatrical Space, and the Theatrical Space Without," in *Themes in Drama 9: The Theatrical Space*, ed. James Redmond (London: Cambridge University Press, 1987), 13.

9. Scolnicov, 15.

10. Wiltshire, 61.

11. Francis Fergusson, *The Idea of a Theatre* (Princeton: Princeton University Press, 1968), 132.

12. Tyrone Guthrie, "Is Lady Macbeth Really Walking in Her Sleep?" *New York Times,* 28 August 1966, 3.

Chapter Four

The Play's the Thing
in Drama and Religion

The house lights go down and the curtain opens. Liberated from human space, we observe beyond the invisible fourth wall a boxed-in world that does not recognize our existence. From this vantage point, we can observe the "real." We join in the illusion that there is no illusion. We are attending a play.

Drama—theater—is play. It is an imitation of the actual world as make-believe. "The presentation of drama is the presentation of an *imagined* act,"[1] writes Bernard Beckerman. Theater is a manifestation of the play instinct—to pretend—for both the actors and the audience enter a world of make-believe. Making believe is deep within the human. Children pretend to play house and fireman. In a game such as Prisoners' Base, several children act as if they are captured in jail and others as if they are rescuers.

Latin has one word to cover the world of play and illusion: *ludus* from *ludere*. To play is to imitate, to pretend, to make-believe. The audience enters the world of the play with a contract to participate in this experience. For theater is a participating act. It occurs solely in the meeting of the imagination of actors and audience, with the paradoxical mixture of the hope that insight will be gained and the fear that too much of ourselves will be exposed. That is the magic and power and risk of entering the illusion of a play.

Art, including drama, cannot happen without risk. Neither can faith. Making believe, constructing belief out of things unseen, envisioning, imagining, requires risk.

The audience, if the performance is effective, is "taken out" of where they are to another world. Both time and space are suspended. The actors are pretending they are someone else and the audience suspends belief. To create an illusion implies presenting characters, events, and ideas in such a way that the audience believes they are present. We enter the world of "as if."

A play is action which is self-contained, its aim being achieved in its performance. And every performance can be seen as an act of resurrection; the dead words of the text are re-incarnated by the living presence of the actors.

We can thus distinguish three levels in theater as Diana Devlin has suggested:

(1) the reality of here and now where the audience and actors are united;
(2) the illusionary reality, the fiction that is built up by the arts of theater;
(3) the reality beyond, the truth that the play or the whole event is about.[2]

For within the illusion of theater is the possibility of exploring and discovering truth. As the playwright Edward Albee has said, "A play is a fiction—and fiction is fact distorted into truth."[3]

In the theater we can engage our imagination in the re-visioning of ourselves and our world. Another playwright, David Mamet, points out that

As in our dreams, the law of psychic economy operates. In dreams we do not seek answers which our conscious (rational) mind is capable of supplying, we see answers to those questions which the conscious mind is incompetent to deal with . . . Only if the question posed is one of whose complexity and depth renders it unsusceptible to rational examination does the dramatic treatment seem to us appropriate, and the dramatic solution become enlightening.[4]

David Cole, drama theorist, is direct:

Theater, and theater alone of human activities, provides an opportunity of experiencing imaginative truth as present truth. In theater, imaginative events take on for a moment the presentness of physical events; in theater, physical events take on for a moment the perfection of imaginative form.[5]

The presence in theater is not only the presence of the actions, but, as Cole writes, "what distinguishes theater from the other arts is that it makes imaginative truth present, or rather makes it presence."[6]

When we enter a theater, we come to play with our hopes and anxieties, our fears and desires. Thomas Whitaker helpfully describes what takes place, for example, when we participate in a performance of *Rosencrantz and Guildenstern Are Dead*:

We relax for an evening of flirting with the void. We play with our anxieties, secure in the fiction that we are even brighter than our brothers in motley. We share buoyantly in the play's ruthless control of its action. We have become Shakespeare. We have become Death. We are the ones who *play* those players.[7]

Thus we again see that play not only takes place on stage but also in the participants. The play-contests (*agons*) in Greek culture involved not only the dramatists who vied for honor in competition but also the members of the audience as each wrestled inwardly with the deep conflicts portrayed on stage. Theater's intrinsic function is to be a place where we can look in a mirror in order to recollect ourselves and remember who we are.

What moves us as an audience is that we see what we had not seen before, or had not seen in this way. "Ah! That is it!" we sense when a moment in theater becomes a mirror of insight. For a play to touch an emotional nerve or to bare a hidden fear or evoke a deep joy is to know that this action illumines the inner self in astonishing and unexpected ways.

Don Quixote was accurate: "Nothing, in fact, more truly portrays us as we are and as we would be than the play and the players." And that image also illumines the relation of God and humankind. Gerhardus van der Leeuw, the Dutch scholar, agrees:

> The meeting of God with man, of man with God is holy play, *sacer ludus*. The theological nature of the dance . . . lies in movement; that of the drama, in movement and countermovement. God moved; he came down to earth. Then the puppets on earth moved also; or, if one prefers, the bones in the dry valley of Ezekiel. God began; we followed. For we are only 'God's masques and costume balls,' as Luther says, or 'God's toys,' as Plato puts it. The most ancient drama, the drama that rules the world, is the drama of the meeting of God and man. God is the protagonist. We are only his antagonists . . . Play is the prerequisite for those forms of existence which strive toward a communion with the other, and finally for a meeting with God.[8]

Other theologians, as David Miller has noted, speak of play and theology:

> Gregory Nazianzus wrote in this mode of a *theologica ludens*:
>   For the Logos on high plays
>   Stirring the whole cosmos back and forth, as he wills,
>   into shapes of every kind.

> Maximus Confessor wrote:
>   'For this earthly life compared with the life to come, the true divine archetypal life, is but a children's game.'

> And he followed it with:
>   '. . . truly we deserve to be looked upon as a children's game played by God.'

> Clement of Alexandria spoke of the Christian life as a 'divine children's game.' And he spoke of *mustikē paidia* ('mystical play'). The Venerable Bede and Bernhardt both spoke of the life of faith as a game Christians play.

Jerome spoke of the church as a bit of religious play. And in order not to omit the usually solemn, unfestive Protestant tradition from this listing, we should mention that Luther once said that 'all creatures are God's masks and mummeries.'[9]

A contemporary theologian, Jürgen Moltmann, writes that creation has "its ground not in itself but in God's good will or pleasure. Hence the creation is God's play, a play of his groundless and inscrutable wisdom."[10]

The Puritans, often slandered as overly-serious and straight-laced, after all, began their description of the Christian life in the Westminster Catechism of 1676 by asking: "What is the chief end of man?" and answering: "Man's chief end is to glorify God and enjoy Him forever." They understood that their relation to God was one of being surrounded and surprised by God's grace.

Even liturgy, according to the noted Roman Catholic scholar, Romano Guardini, is not work, but play. To be a play, or to fashion a work of art in God's sight—not to create, but to exist—such is the essence of the liturgy. From this is derived its sublime mingling of profound earnestness and divine joyfulness.[11]

Earlier, he had cited a prayer from the Benedictine Breviary, Lauds (i.e., the prayer at daybreak) of Tuesday:

Laeti bibamus sobriam
Ebrietatem Spiritus . . .
[Literally, 'Let us joyfully taste of the sober drunkenness of the Spirit.'][12]

Such a stance implies, as Robert Neale suggests, that each of us is a play-filled "adventurer with the playtime and playground of the play world."[13] For faith has its base in make believe, not in the meaning of pretending but in the sense which David Miller helpfully terms "faith-ing into."[14] We live in the drama of God's action, and when we hear the Gospel, we enter, are caught up in, "faith into;" we begin to "make belief" that this gracious offer of salvation is meant for us. Within the play of God's plan, we are free to enjoy, to play joyfully as we find our roles in our vocational callings. Such is the drama in which we play, as Robert Bridges expressed:

They that in play can do the thing they would,
Having an instinct throned in reason's place
—And every perfect action hath the grace
Of indolence or thoughtless hardihood—
These are the best . . .[15]

NOTES

1. Bernard Beckerman, *Dynamics of Drama* (New York: Drama Book Publishers, 1979), 18.

2. Diana Devlin, *Mask and Scene* (Metuchen, New Jersey: Scarecrow Press, 1989), 201.

3. Edward Albee, quoted in David L. Miller, *Gods and Games* (New York: World Publishing Company, 1970), 145.

4. David Mamet, *Writing in Restaurants* (New York: Viking Press, 1986), 8–9.

5. David Cole, *The Theatrical Event* (Middletown, Conn.: Wesleyan University Press, 1975), 5.

6. Cole, 6.

7. Thomas K. Whitaker, "Notes on Playing the Player," *Centennial Review*, 16:1 (1972); 6.

8. Gerhardus van der Leeuw, *Sacred and Profane Beauty*, tr. David E. Green (New York: Holt, Rinehart and Winston, 1963), 111–112.

9. Miller, 109–110.

10. Jürgen Moltmann, *Theology of Play*, tr. Reinhard Ulrich (New York: Harper and Row, 1971), 17.

11. Romano Guardini, *The Spirit of the Liturgy*, tr. Ada Lane (New York: Sheed and Ward, 1925), 181.

12. Guardini, 130.

13. Robert E. Neale, "Religion and Play," *Crossroads* (July-September 1967): 86.

14. Miller, 166.

15. Robert Bridges, "The Growth of Love," *Poetical Works* (London and New York: Oxford University Press, 1913),187.

Chapter Five

Worship: The Drama Re-Enacted

At 8:00 a.m. and 10:45 a.m. each Sunday at 5th and Maple Streets in Allentown, Pa, a drama takes place.

The pastors have been working on their scripts the past week; the chorus has had a rehearsal on Thursday night. The sextons have gotten the stage ready, the Altar Guild has furnished the properties, and ushers have been enlisted. The office has prepared programs which detail the roles of the main participants as well as that of the chorus and the audience.

St. John Evangelical Lutheran Church is ready for worship, ready for the drama to begin. And in worship spaces throughout the world this drama with variations is being enacted every hour.

Worship is indeed a matter of the heart and the spirit but it is only through words and actions that worship happens. The very term, "liturgy" derives from two Greek words, *laos* and *ergon*, meaning "people" and "work." Worship is the *ergon*, the action, of the *laos*, the people of God.

And certain words and actions will be enacted by the people of God at worship—

lighting:	to illumine the altar with candles
processing:	to enter the area, the main characters and the chorus in appropriate costume form a pattern of march with accompanying music and with candles and symbolic cross
standing:	to praise in music and to affirm basic beliefs in creed
responding:	to engage in chanting dialogue with psalms and other liturgical texts
kneeling:	to pray and confess with humility in a position of utter vulnerability

closing eyes:	to concentrate during prayer
reading:	to present sacred texts to the gathering
speaking:	to interpret sacred texts on behalf of the people
offering:	to express gratitude and share with others by contributing sacrifice
processing:	the entering people exit with music and symbols

Such actions imply that the worshipers are participants in the drama, not merely spectators. They are not wearing masks, but come naked before God. And the whole action is not a performance but a drama in which the whole self is engaged: the sincere spirit, the inquisitive mind, and the active body— eyes, ears, mouth, and limbs.

This description is based on liturgical worship in church bodies such as Catholic, Lutheran, and Anglican in which the formal elements are indebted to the Old Testament priestly tradition and medieval royal rituals. Other traditions reflect their heritage and their purposes of worship. Worship in the Reformed tradition, flowing from the scholar, John Calvin, has a dramatic form analogous to a classroom—a catechism organizes the liturgical year and the pastor is often in academic robe. The Quakers, amid their pure white surroundings, act in worship by listening and meditating in silence. Free churches insist that informality and business suits are crucial to identify with the worshipers and to symbolize the open invitation to join the fellowship. Black churches are often similar to an emotional family gathering in which shouts of Brother, Sister, and Amen are punctuated by laughing, crying, clapping, and rhythmic movements. Pentecostal gatherings close their eyes and raise their arms to the Holy Spirit in a frenzy of enthusiasm, literally being filled by a god.

What all these traditions have in common is that when the participants enter the place of worship, they enter the drama of salvation—the drama which proclaims the mighty acts of God, celebrates and sets forth what Christ has done, and is guided by the Holy Spirit. All of the traditions set forth the same pattern of action: from fall and sin to newness and restoration.

Thus the three levels of theater as Devlin described them in the previous section have analogies in religious life:

(1) "the reality of here and now where the audience actors are united;" the life of the religious here and now as they gather in worship united with one another and with God;
(2) "the illusionary reality, the fiction that is built up by the arts of theater," the Biblical story which they enter in belief and imaginative faith
(3) "the reality beyond, the truth that the play or the whole event is about," God, the truth which the whole play is about.

The worship year of the liturgical churches begins with Advent, a time of anticipation of hope and judgment that Christ has come in the Incarnation and will come again on the last day. Then comes the celebration of the nativity at Christmas. Epiphany, the time of revealing, of illumination, follows the twelve days of Christmas and extends to Lent: forty days of preparation and self-sacrifice and renewal. The dramatic climax is Holy Week, beginning with procession of palms and later with the washing of feet (very prominent in Moravian worship), the initiation of Christ's Supper, and Good Friday with its black somberness (Tenebrae—its movement from light to total darkness). Holy Saturday is the day between, both one of hope and fear, of waiting in the vigil and the baptism of the newly converted members. Easter morning finds the jack-in-the-box (a medieval phrase for Jesus) not being able to be contained but breaks out with a party-balloon bang. Forty days later, the act of Christ's ascension is celebrated and followed ten days later by the flaming speaking tongues and the rushing of the wind on Pentecost. And after a long season centering on the Trinity, the drama begins again.

Although various Christian traditions differ on the number of sacraments, most, if not all, see as central two dramatic acts: baptism and the Supper.

In baptism, in highly ritualistic action with water as the basic element, the new member, whether infant or adult, is initiated into the fellowship. One is now signed on and one is listed as a member of the active company.

In the Supper, variously named the Mass, the Eucharist, Holy Communion, with actions of eating bread and drinking wine, the people of God are both renewed in forgiveness and united with one another. Christ said: "Do this . . ." and the early Church spoke of "doing the Eucharist." John A. T. Robinson states: "It is Christ's *command* performance."[1] Earlier, Robinson perceptively connects the action of the Supper with Christ's acts on Good Friday and Easter:

> The action of Jesus at the Last Supper when he took, and blessed, and broke, and gave, is what ever since has shaped the structure of the Eucharist. But this action was itself in the first instance but the acting out, for the disciples' comprehension and subsequent participation, of what Jesus was about to do in the 'finished act' of Good Friday and Easter. And it is to this decisive act that the Eucharist goes back.[2]

The Eucharist is the action of what Christ has done so that believers may be renewed and forgiven to go forth and be active in sharing the compassion of Christ in the world.

The drama of worship involves both the divine and the human, both the church and the world. Thus when the bread and wine are brought forth, they are products both of God's creation and human endeavors. In the loaf of bread representing Christ's body has gone the work of many hands and in the wine representing God's blood is the symbol of life's joy and freedom. In such an action we bring the world into the church just as at the end of the service, we are ready to share the message of Christ in the world.

The Roman order of the Communion, the Mass, takes its name from the *Ite, missa est*: you can go now; the gathering is over. The instinct which led in the Middle Ages to carrying the Blessed Sacrament through the streets is still true today. The worship service is over; let the service in the world begin. The point of the action really begins when it finishes.

All worship, like drama, is shared response, is communal. Worship is corporate action, "body" action, for in the Christian view, each is a member, a part of the body of Christ. Christian worship is *koinonia* which is usually translated as community, fellowship, participation. When Christians are at worship, they are, as Robinson has suggested, "cast for an active part in this great dramatic company, which one of the early Fathers called the *plebes sancta Dei*, the holy common people of God."[3] To worship is to be a member of this dramatic company in time and space.

NOTES

1. John H. T. Robinson, *Liturgy Coming to Life* (London: A. R. Mowbray and Co., 1960), 61.
2. Robinson, 21.
3. Robinson, 64.

Part Three

DRAMA AND RELIGION:
THEIR HISTORY

Chapter Six

Dionysus: Lord of the Greek Theater

Very seldom in the history of Western drama has the presence of *sacer ludus*, holy play,[1] been more dominant than in the Greek theater of antiquity. Every fifth century play that is known contains either a prayer, hymn, a thanksgiving to the gods or a ritual action such as a funeral procession. Many have more than one instance of worship. Some commentators such as Aylen assert that the theater was "the center of Athenian worship"[2] and Kitto reminds us that all the Greek plays are plays about the ways of the gods.[3] The Greek audience attended the theater, as all participants do, to be instructed and delighted, but at the same time, to experience communion with the gods. The space was filled with spirits who the Greeks believed influenced human action. To re-enact, to re-present, to re-live, to imitate—all of these actions within the plays were an attempt to participate in the beings of the gods. And the deity central to this drama was the god in whose honor the theaters of Greece were named, the god Dionysus. In the center of the dramatic space was an altar on which incense burned to this lord of the theater.

With Dionysus as the reigning presence, this chapter explores the relationship between religion and Greek drama, particularly looking first at the god himself, then to the beginnings of drama within the festival of Dionysus, thirdly to the space including its participants of the chorus and actors and concludes with comments on the play in which Dionysus appears on stage, Euripides' *The Bacchae*.

I

The Greek Dionysian rite, as was true of many other ancient rites, was a very elaborate and complex religious ceremony. Not only did the rite itself develop in different ways but the location of the rite, whether rural or urban, influenced the celebration. The essential element in all the rites was the central figure, the god Dionysus.

The origin of the Greek Dionysian myth, as almost all authorities agree, was from the area of Thrace.[4] The cult spread rapidly in Greece because as Nilsson states:

> In reality it [Dionysian religion] was an epidemic of psychopathic religiousity which seized upon mankind. . . . The rising tide of religious feeling seeks to surmount the barrier which separates man from god, it strives to enter the divine, and it finds ultimate satisfaction only in that quenching of the consciousness in enthusiasm which is the goal of all mysticism.[5]

Thus, Dionysus in his cultic origins was associated with spiritual impulse and vitality.

Still more pivotal in the understanding of Dionysus was his birth. His mother was Semele, the Thracian Earth-Mother. But since Semele was one of the thundersmitten gods, she became discredited. Thus Dionysus became the adopted child of the God of the Thunderbolt, Zeus. The name of Dionysus shows his adoption: "Zeus-Young Man,"[6] but it is significant that the god is the offspring of the Earth-Mother and the chief of the Olympian gods. His origin is not only auspicious but also therefore directly related to the Sacred Marriage of the Sky-God and Mother Earth.[7]

At the core of the Athenian drama then is a being of terrifying power, known by more than one name, and apparently with several contradictory characteristics. Although our too-quick associations of Dionysus is with wine, to the Greeks, he was far more. Dodds cites Plutarch, who gives the god various titles: the Power in the tree, the blossom-bringer, the fruit-bringer, and most comprehensively, the abundance of life.[8] Another commentator asserts that "Dionysus was identified with liquids—blood, sap, milk, wine" and adds "the Dionysian is nature's enthonian fluidity."[9]

Dionysus was thus the incarnate life force itself, the uncontrollable chaotic eruption of nature in individuals and communities, generating awe and vitality. He was lord of fertility and growth, says Aylen, as well particularly the god of the dance.[10] Women danced in honor of Dionysus on the mountain in midwinter each alternate year. The women were possessed, having become drunk with wine. The dancers were clearly enthusiastic, in the root sense of that word, filled with a god, god-possessed. They were beside themselves, but at the same time, in a state of *in vino veritas*. Madness, yes, but the madness of incisive perception as well as of insanity.

To be in the presence of Dionysus therefore was to be in a state to be cultivated and not simply to be condemned. The intention was to identify one's self with the god, to praise and honor the gifts from the god. Dionysus had given humankind all the good things of the earth. These good things—symbolized by wine—enabled his worshippers to transcend themselves, to go out of themselves, to go beyond reason. But beyond reason, there is not only ecstasy, but also dark and blind forces ready for blood.

"One is the Lord of Death, and Dionysus of the raving maenads," wrote Heracleitus (Fragment 15).[11] Aylen, building on the evidence that the Dionysian festival was in winter, the dead time of the year, insists that Dionysus is the lord of death as well as of life and fertility.[12]

Such an understanding confirms that the Greek perspective of worship was indeed cosmic, that Dionysus personified the entire cycle of birth, growth, decay, death, and rebirth or resurrection. And if Dionysus incorporates the total life-death cycle, he also signifies the entire spectrum of being—from divine (his most common manifestation) to human (as he appears in *The Bacchae*) to nature (the vine) to bestial, as the Chorus of *The Bacchae* prays:

O Dionysus, reveal yourself as bull! Be manifest,
A snake with darting heads, a lion breathing fire!

(lines 1016–1017)[13]

All the manifestations of Dionysus are inextricably tied to one another. Is he then beneficent or malevolent, praiseworthy or terrifying? He is all of these. He is, in the words of Walter Kerr, who reviewed a production of *The Bacchae* in London's National Theater, Dionysus is "the awful absolute."[14]

II

Although no consensus exists on the exact date of the birth of drama nor on the specific development of the origin of theater, the most accepted hypothesis is that the Greek drama was the outgrowth of the rites of worship of Dionysus.[15]

The relationship between religious ritual and drama is complex and intricate. Both are actions in which human beings participate in order to confront the mysterious. Both are actions to attempt to understand and identify with forces and powers beyond the visible. Usually with appropriate words and gestures so that the whole self is involved, we both want to approach such forces and to flee from their powers in fear. Thus we participate in religious rites and dramatic actions to assist us in dealing with the mysterious.

One dimension of ritual is anticipatory: to prepare for a future event, as before a battle or a journey or in the Christian tradition, the rituals of Advent and Lent. One prays for strength and the tone is one of hope and promise.

Another dimension of ritual is remembering: to look back at an event, as a death or a victory, and engage in the appropriate response of sorrow or joy. The observance of Easter is such a religious ritual. One remembers what God has done in the past.

But basic to all ritual is re-imitating, re-enacting, re-presenting, of participating in an action which is here and now, but at the same time, aware of the past and the future. The rituals of Passover and the Eucharist not only remember what God has done in the past and anticipate the hope one has in such a saving God in the future, but re-present that God is saving and redeeming the very people who are participating in the ritual at this very moment.

The fundamental conflict within ritual is between life and death, between decay and renewal, between dying and rebirth. The ritual is re-enacted to confront this central struggle and to discern the ways in which life is renewed and death is given meaning. For even in the presence of death, the hope of life is affirmed and celebrated.

Thus the hypothesis is not surprising that in Greek culture the rituals in honor of Dionysus provide the roots for drama.[16] The worship of Dionysus was introduced into Greece as early as the thirteenth century B.C. By the sixth century B.C., there were four festivals in honor of Dionysus: the Rural Dionysus (in December); the Lenaia (in January); the Anthesteria (around the end of February); and the City or Great Dionysia (about the end of March). With the exception of the Anthesteria, plays came to be performed at each of these festivals. Plays were not given at the festivals in honor of any of the other many Greek gods.

The first record of a performance of drama is in 534 B.C. when the Athenian tyrant, Pisistratus, re-organized the festival of the Great Dionysia and established a contest for tragic plays. Thus instituted and supported by civil edict, the attendance at the plays was mandatory for the citizens of Athens.

All evidence points to the fact that the festivals were a combination of lively carnival and a display of the city to the world (outstanding citizens were honored), but primarily they were religious rites to honor the god of vitality and life. In the performing area of the sacred precinct, for example, in view of all, stood an ancient statue of the deity, a constant reminder that Dionysus was indeed the patron of the highly competitive set of ritual contests.

The festival began with a procession in which the old revered statue of Dionysus was taken from its temple from the theater into the Agora (the marketplace), followed by dancing in the front of the statue, and then the procession moved out of the city. After dark, the procession returned by torchlight to the precinct of Dionysus. A dominant part of the procession was a phallus, an obvious symbol of fertility. And a leading role was played by an animal, namely, a bull on its way to be sacrificed, escorted by the *epheboi*, the young men of military age.

Both the subject of the bull and the action of sacrifice have deep ritualistic implications. Dionysus, as we saw earlier, often took the form of a bull, as he is described in *The Bacchae*.

The participation of the bull in the Greek Dionysian rite is in keeping with the kind of symbol a civilized agricultural people would have. The bull is connected with the richness and the fatness of the earth as well as linked with the sun, the greatest procreative power in nature. The appropriateness of Taurus as the Zodiac sign ushering in the productive season of spring is obvious. The bull therefore represented the active energizing principle of the universe.

Not only the bull itself, but what is done with the bull has significance. The bull is so holy that he has powers to make others holy.[17] By moving the bull from house to house, everyone partakes in the sanctity. So holy is the bull that nothing unlucky may come near him. The people who lead the procession of the bull must have both parents alive. They must not have been under the infection of death.

A prayer was given aloud for "the safety of the city and the land, and the citizens, and the women and the children, for peace and wealth, and for the bringing forth of grain and of all other fruits, and of cattle."[18] The bull was then devoured by tearing at the raw flesh or it was sacrificed. But either case, the flesh was eaten. Harrison describes the action: "When they shall have sacrificed the bull, let them divide it up among those who took part in the procession."[19]

The bull dies just because he is holy, that he may give his holiness, his strength, his life, just at the moment it is holiest, to the people. The flesh is eaten so that each person may receive a share of the strength of the bull. Nilsson suggests that the Dionysian "sacramental meal is the supreme mystery, through which the worshippers received the god and his power into themselves."[20] The bull dies for the people that they may have new life from his life-blood. Participation in the cosmogonic myth assures the worshipers of the renewal of life in himself and in the world of nature.

In some of the rites, the death of the bull was followed by a resurrection. In Athens, after the people have slain and eaten the animal, according to Porphyry, "They sewed up the hide and stuffed it out with hay and set it up just as it was when it was alive, and they yoked a plough to it as though it were ploughing."[21] The worshippers had to kill the bull in order to receive its strength and life. But it was not to give him up to the gods that they killed him, not to sacrifice him in a sense, but to have him, keep him, eat him, live through him. Their strongest hope was that he had not really died. This intense desire resulted in the resurrection rite. If he did not rise again, how could they plow again next year? He must live again.

Great was the sanctity of the bull for the Greeks. On the bull was focused the desire of the whole people. He was sacred because his strength was intensely desired. He died that he might be eaten, and above all, he died that he might live again.

In this setting of death and resurrection, the entire festival of Dionysus took place and provided the ritualistic action for the drama. The particular literary roots of drama were to be found in the dithyramb, the choir dance-song performed in honor of Dionysus. Several sources, including Plato (*Zeus*, Book III, 700b) and Aristotle (*Poetics*, 1449a) speak of the dithyramb as pivotal.

One of the functions of the dithyramb, as Pindar notes, was to drive the bull:

> Whence did appear the Charites who sing
> To Dionyse their king
> The dithyramb, the chant of Bull-driving?[22]

Plutarch's dithyramb has the same perspective:

> In Springtime, O Dionysos,
> To thy holy temple come,
> To Elis with thy Graces,
> Rushing with thy bull-foot, come,
> Noble Bull, Noble Bull.[23]

But the dithyramb represented more than a chant to drive the sacred animal. The song also celebrated the new birth of the god, Dionysus. However, Dionysus was not represented as an infant, but as a young man. Therefore, the emphasis is as the etymology of the word, *Dithyrambos*, indicates, on the second birth of Dionysus, his adoption by Zeus. He was twice-born, once of his mother, like all men, once of his father's thigh, like no man.[24] This aspect of the dithyramb is shown clearly in a paean to Dionysus discovered at Delphi:

> Come, O Dithyrambos, Bacchos, come
> Bromios, come, and coming with thee bring
> Holy hours of thine holy spring.
> All the stars danced for joy. Mirth
> Of mortals hailed thee, Bacchos, at thy birth.[25]

Therefore, one can see that the birth of Dionysus and the coming of spring are intimately connected. As Jane Harrison summarizes: "The Dithyramb . . .

is not only a song of human rebirth; it is the song of the rebirth of all nature, all living things; it is a Spring song ' for the Year-Feast.'"[26]

Scholars have been unable to discover any information about the dance of the Dionysiac rite except that it was in the form of a circle. But this phenomenon does aid us in seeing the cosmogonic structure of the rite. The dancing worshippers of Dionysus, according to Brown, "typified the grand cosmic circular dance-movement of material phenomena. . . ."[27] The idea of a circular nature-dance arose from a perception of the cyclic movement in surrounding phenomena. Drawing from Brown's inferences, one can enumerate some of the possible implications of the circular movement, all of which are closely connected with generative power such as the vault of the sky, the rainbow, and the shape of the sun and the moon.[28] To dance in a circle is to participate in the cyclic motion of the cosmic structure.

"The center of Athenian drama," Aylen insists, "was an interconnection of dance and worship so absolute that the two were indistinguishable"[29] and later adds that dance is "not just an element in the staging of fifth-century plays like costumes and music. It is the central flavor of the culture . . ."[30] His point is that "the Greek drama are dance dramas."[31]

Van der Leeuw's discussion of the interpretation of the dance is relevant:

> It (the dance) is the service of the god, and generates power: the rhythm of movement has a compelling force. . . . In the dance life is ordered to some powerful rhythm and reverts to its potent primeval motion, and thus it is possible to attain to all manner of things 'by dancing', from one's daily bread to heavenly bliss.[32]

Van der Leeuw suggests that the Dionysian dance was of the ecstatic type, in which "superfluous power is released, cast away in recurrent movement."[33] Participation with the god is the keyword, for "the dance may even become the symbol of mystic unity with God."[34]

III

It is significant that the entire festival, whether in the procession or the word or the dance or any other element, that all is done collectively by a group of persons experiencing the same emotion. The individual's actions and reactions gain importance only in so far as they express what the group believes is sacred. By one's self, one may make excited movements, one may leap for joy, but unless these movements are made by the group, they will not become rhythmical and they will lack intensity. The foundation of the rite, therefore, is to be found in a desire and emotion expressed by means of common participation.

Thus the festival underlined the communal dimension of existence, that each individual is related to the god and to one's fellow beings, a theme which *The Bacchae* echoes:

> Bless'd is he who hallows his life in the worship of god,
> he whom the spirit of god possesseth, who is one
> With those who belong to the holy body of god.

(lines 73–75)

The presence of the spirit of Dionysus not only releases the individual which results in a sense of freedom but also binds together to draw the individuals into community with one another.

And it is in that tension between the individual and the community that the history of drama in ancient Greece took place. Herodotus (5th century, B.C.), for example, reports that in the mid-seventh century B.C. the poet Arion "was the first of men known to us to compose ['poetize,' or reduce to set, written, metric form], the dithyramb and to give it a title and to represent it at Corinth." (Book I, 23) The dithyramb consisted of Dionysian subjects with satyr performers. The form was responsive singing between satyr chorus and leader, lyric in character.

In the 6th century, Thespis, poet of Icaria, in taking his role as leader of the satyr chorus performing his dithyrambs, chose to impersonate Dionysus and to regard his chorus as impersonating satyrs. This action is pivotal. Prior to that time, men told stories and called them epics. Now someone is impersonating a character and we have entered the dramatic. Thespis took performances of his dithyrambs from place to place in wagons; he likewise experimented with varieties of mask for facial disguise. Since he is the first known actor, performers to this day are often called thespians.[35]

Once Thespis had set one member of the chorus apart from the others, essentially creating a form of monologue with the leader addressing the audience directly, the next step was to add another actor. Aristotle stated: "Aeschuylus first introduced a second actor: he diminished the importance of the chorus and assigned the leading part to the dialogue." (*Poetics*, 1449a)

We now have dialogue and with Sophocles contributing three actors (*Poetics*, 1449a), we have full-blown drama. The third actor for example, such as Jocasta in *Oedipus Rex*, silent but present listening to all that is being reported by the messenger to her son about his fateful past, provides the audience with identification not only with Oedipus but also with Jocasta. The *agon* has become a deep and complex struggle.

We have moved from ritual to art, from religion to drama. But the religious is still deeply infused in the action of the drama. Not only does ritual continue to form the major structure of the plays, but also the participants, both actors and spectators, are exploring the forces that surround them and their awe toward and struggle with the great events of life: love, war, peace, freedom, justice, fate, and death. As one commentator accurately suggests, "the plays thus spring from life itself, giving form and expression not only to what a human being is, but to what he or she aspires to be."[36]

Thus the theater is a crucible for experiencing ethical struggles, a space where the individuals within the community participate in moral dilemmas which sometimes are irreconcilable and sometimes lead to a purged catharsis.

But the difference between the rituals of the Festival of Dionysus and the later dramatic performances of the fifth century, B.C. should not be minimized. In the ritual dance to Dionysus, the whole body of worshippers participated; only the uninterested, women, and children were spectators. All are actors; all are doing the thing done; there is no distance between actor and audience. The common action, the common emotion is the core of ritual. As Jane Harrison comments, "No one at this early stage thinks of building a *theater*, a spectator place."[37] The dance and the story are not only danced and sung, but the action is observed from a distance. She adds: ". . . the *dromenon*, the thing actually done by yourself has become a drama, a thing also done, but abstracted from your doing."[38]

The most obvious location to have spectators observe the action is on a hill, a slope. Thus the prototype of all Greek theaters, the theater of Dionysus in Athens, is located on the south slope of the Acropolis. It was for such a setting that Aeschylus, Sophocles, and Euripides created their tragedies.

The emphasis in the construction of the theater was primarily a seeing, but listening was also important. As one recent scholar who has carefully studied the sound waves of the extant theaters has asserted, its shape "matches almost perfectly, the direction followed by the human voice."[39]

The various elements of the theater—the circle of flat ground, the orchestra (literally "Dancing place"), the *skene* (the building from which the actors made their entrances and exits and which eventually was decorated with simple painting)—have all been described rather clearly based on archaeology as well as literary evidence. Scholars agree that the presence of Dionysus was pervasive.[40] The cult statue of Eleathereus, a pillar-shaped idol of Dionysus, was erected at the foot of the Acropolis. An altar to the god was located in the center of the orchestra. The principal spectator was the priest of Dionysus whose seat was in the middle of the front row of the *theatron*. This splendidly decorated priest's throne was decorated with cocks, as symbols of the contest among the dramatists, being urged to fight by young boys.

Within the action, the major presence of the spiritual forces was revealed in the Chorus. Ranging in numbers from twelve to fifteen to fifty,[41] the Chorus was on stage during the entire drama and contributed visually, aesthetically, rhythmically, and dramatically to the action.

Visually, the Chorus in their turning and counter-turning (*strophe* and *antistrophe*) provided beauty of dance and movement. Originally, all the choral interludes were accompanied by music and thus were both sung and danced. Such color and spectacle provided powerful visual appeal.

Aesthetically, the Chorus set the mood of the play and echoed the images present within the action. High lyrical and emotional intensity was conveyed by the Chorus. They amplified the agony and the exaltation.

Brockett explicates well the rhythmical functions:

> Greek drama without its choral passages . . . [would make] the action move too fast. These retardations—these pauses in which to look backward and forward—contributed enormously to the over-all emotional effect; they are part of the design without which the whole would be incomplete or unsatisfying.[42]

Dramatically, the members of the Chorus informs us of the past, connects in the present, and foresees the future. They interpret, give advice, express opinions, and sometimes threaten to become involved in the action. In brief, they furnish the ethical framework of the play. At the same time, they are representatives of the community (Argive elders, for example, in Aeschylus' *Agamemnon*) as well as ideal spectators who respond as if they are observing the action *sub specie aeternitatis*. They are both bridge between author and drama as well as link between drama and audience.

Although the Chorus was the central focus in Greek drama, the role of the actors gradually became more dominant. In the earliest plays, the actor, according to Jacques Burdick, was "something of a priest. He was deputized by the officials to a play in 'place of the people,' just as the athlete was chosen to compete in 'place of the people' and to represent them at the games."[43] For every play was produced for a serious competition and Burdick adds that ". . . their very composition, pitting the individual against the elements—against fate, against society, and other individuals—depended upon competition, and was the force of this basic and pervasive struggle that gave vigor to every line of dialogue."[44]

Much of the mystery and power of this conflict was captured in the mystery and power of the mask. The masks of comedy and tragedy are the emblems of all theater, a legacy the Greek drama provided to the present. The mask portrays a double intent: both escape from the self and self-disclosure. The wearer of the mask both hides and reveals the self.

Masks were not just a disguise, but often expressed forces which were activated and released through the medium of the mask. Robert Corrigan affirms that "the mask is the emblem of our condition of otherness" and adds:

> The mask, then, symbolizes both the nature of the theatrical event and also our response to that event. It embodies the power of the other world of mystery which the theater makes present for us and also the excitement, awe, and fear we feel when we experience that presence.[45]

Such an experience for both actor and audience took place in the Greek theater. The actor's mask was identical with the character in the play, and both were referred to as *personae* (from *sonare*, to sound through). The actor gave up his own identity in honor of the god in order to let another being speak and act through him. Dionysus was indeed the god of ecstasy (standing outside oneself) and thus again the renunciation of individuality is revealed in the wearing of the mask.

But the practice of masks points toward the moral dilemma inherent in acting and drama. For the Greek actor was known as the answerer, the *hypocrite* (one who answers), since his function was to answer questions about the world of the gods. Corrigan describes the actor:

> As the envoy from this other world he was set apart, someone different; yet he was also a member of the community (as represented by the Chorus of singers and dancers) pretending to be someone else.[46]

One notes the implication of dissembling and insincerity (to be a hypocrite) present in the use of mask. It is indeed ironic that at the *theatron*, the place of seeing, men wear masks which keep secret the particular self behind the mask.

IV

Euripides' last play, *The Bacchae*, is not only a drama of masking and unmasking but also a return to the origins of theater. This final vision of the last of three great playwrights of fifth century Greece dramatizes the coming of Dionysus, the godhead, in person to the theater of his name. The title of the play may well mark the central experience of Dionysiac religion, the transformation of the initiates into the worship of Bacchus, a later name for Dionysus. Michael Goldman asserts:

> Like the shaman in his trance, the Dionysiac celebrant in his ecstasy is a prototype of the actor. His transport carries him into impersonation. He abandons

his own personality and adopts another, expressing this by radical changes in dress, carriage, expression and behavior. He acts the god and acts his followers and enemies; eventually he is likely to act the god's story—of mutilation and resurrection, persecution and triumph . . .[47]

Partly because of the primitive starkness, the drama is not produced frequently; notable exceptions are Richard Schechner's re-interpretation (*Dionysus in '69*), Wole Soyinka's version at the National Theatre in London in 1973 and a production at Canadian Stratford Festival which I saw in 1993. The elemental forces and fears—all these were vivid to the participants in Stratford for we were forced to be involved in the rather small and three-sided Tom Patterson Theater.

We were more than participants, that is, persons vicariously experiencing the ritualistic action. We, like Pentheus, were spies and voyeurs who viewed the scenes of sensuous and dancing mothers secretly and perversely. At the same time, we, like Teiresias, were witnesses and seers who observed the unfolding events and now testify to their power.

Indeed, the imagery of seeing is dominant in the play, as it is many Greek plays (one thinks immediately of Sophocles' *Oedipus Rex*). Dionysus arrives incognito, not seen by others. Cadmus, the father of Pentheus, asks of Teiresias: "Are we the only men/who will dance for Bacchus?" and the prophet responds: "They are all blind./ Only we can see." (lines 195–196) The messenger comes to Pentheus and informs him:

Sir, I have seen the holy Maenads, the women who run barefoot
and crazy from the city . . .
If you have been there and seen those wonders for yourself,
you would have gone down on your knees and prayed
to the god you saw dancing. (lines 664–666, 717–714)

Then in the temptation scene, Dionysus, still in disguise, asks Pentheus: "Would you like to see their revels on the mountain?" (line 811). Pentheus as spy and voyeur now disguised in his female costume sees, as the Messenger later repeats: "so we might see and not be seen." (line 1050) Then suddenly the Messenger states, "The Maenads saw him [Pentheus] more clearly than he saw them." (lines 1074–1075) The voice of the god Dionysus thunders from above, screaming for vengeance. The women including his own mother, Agave, see the intruder but do not recognize him as they begin to pull apart his body. Pentheus pleads to be recognized: "I am Pentheus,/your own son/ the child you bore to Echion!" (lines 1118–1119). Later, all look upon Agave, who bearing the head of her son, does not yet see the depths of her tragic situation. But the time of *anagnorisis* (self-discovery, to see one's self truthfully) does come for Agave: "Now, now I see: Dionysus has destroyed us all" (lines 1296–1297). She accepts her exile:

> Let awful Cithaeton never see me again.
> Let me never set my eyes on Cithaeton again.
> And let me never see another thyrsus,
> To bring this back to me again.[48]

The most theatrical scene focuses our attention on the entrance of Dionysus at the end of the play (Arrowsmith introduces him stating: "Above the palace Dionysus appears in epiphany"). He takes human form in order to reveal himself to mortals. An alternate translation conveys the divine origin of Dionysus:

> I am the god Dionysus, son of Zeus,
> the son of Semele the Theban,
> come back to Thebes, where I was born,
> to make you face what madness blinds you to:
> the power I hold as your god.[49]

This theme of vengeance pervades the play. A mere mortal has doubted Dionysus' godhead; a human being has defied him. His revenge is that the women will be driven out of their minds, an action that precipitates all the events following. The drama insists that the revenge of Dionysus is just. R. P. Winnington-Graham, the author of an entire book on *The Bacchae*, points out that the play itself recognized that "the vengeance is not only just, it is fair, honourable, glorious,"[50] and according to this classicist's translation, not only the Chorus but even Agave affirms that justice has been achieved:

> 'Fair is the contest—to clasp a child with a hand dripping with his blood!' [the Chorus] sing when the whole story has been told to them 'What is there here that is not fairly done?' asked Agave.[51]

But revenge and justice demand that a sacrifice be made. Pentheus is made the scapegoat, as Jan Kott states in his book, *The Eating of the Gods*:

> The scapegoat is the image of the One to whom he is sacrificed. The ritual is a repetition of divine sacrifice. Pentheus is torn to pieces because the Other had also been torn to pieces. Pentheus' body is put together from the torn fragments because the dismembered fragments of the Other had also been joined together.[52]

All the elements of the Dionysian festival are present. The *sparagmos* (tearing the body into pieces) and *omophagia* (consuming the raw flesh) are foreshadowed by the devouring of the fat calf by the women which later becomes the ritual sacrifice of Pentheus. And his own mother serves as "priestess" within the rite (line 1114).

In contrast to *Oedipus Rex* in which the slaying of the father is the killing of the past, Agave's destruction of her son murders the future. The final word describes the ways of the god, as the Chorus ends the play:

> Many forms are there of the divine.
> Many things the gods accomplish unexpectedly,
>   for what remained undreamed the god finds ways,
> Just such doing was this doing.[53]

The "doing" of the god has become the drama, "the thing done." To his believers and followers, Dionysus is still the lord, not only of the theater, but of life itself.

NOTES

1. The phrase is from Gerhardus van der Leeuw, *Sacred and Profane Beauty*, tr. David E. Green (New York: Holt, Rinehart and Winston), 1963, 77ff.

2. Leo Aylen, *The Greek Theater* (Cranbury, NJ: Associated University Press, 1985), 74.

3. H. D. F. Kitto, *Greek Tragedy* (London: Methuen, 1961).

4. Lewis R. Farnell, *The Cults of Greek States*, Vol. V (New York: Clarendon Press, 1909), 86, J. G. Frazer in *The Golden Bough*, (Vol. 1 (London: Macmillan, 1912), 3 and Gertrude R. Levy in *The Golden Horn* (London: Faber and Faber, 1948), 281ff. One dissenting voice is Carlo Kerenyi (*Diogenes*, 20 [Winter 1957], 1020), who argues eloquently that the Thracian origin of Dionysus owes more to Nietzsche than to scientific evidence. Kereni suggests a Cretan origin of Dionysus.

5. Martin P. Nilsson, *A History of Greek Religion*, tr. F. J. Fielden (Oxford: Clarendon Press, 1925), 205.

6. Jane Harrison, *Mythology* (Boston: Marshall Jones, 1924), 134.

7. Mircea Eliade, *The Sacred and the Profane*, tr. Willard R. Trask (New York: Harcourt, Brace, 1959), 145.

8. E. R. Dodds, *Euripides' Bacchae* (Oxford: Clarendon Press, 1960), xii.

9. Camille Paglia, *Sexual Personae* (New Haven: Yale University Press, 1990), 30.

10. Aylen, 41.

11. Quoted in Aylen, 41.

12. Aylen, 41–43.

13. All quotations from *The Bacchae*, unless noted otherwise, are from the translation of William Arrowsmith, *Euripides V*, eds. David Grene and Richmond Lattimore (Chicago: University of Chicago Press, 1958, 1959).

14. Walter Kerr, "Will We Ever See '*The Bacchae*' as Euripides Wrote It?" *New York Times*, 19 August 1973, Section 2, 3.

15. This study concentrates on dramatic tragedy. The origins and history of Greek comedy are well documented in Francis M. Cornford's *The Origin of Attic Comedy* (New York: Doubleday, 1961). An excellent summary of the hypotheses concerning the origins of Greek tragedy is found in Michael Hinden's essay, "Ritual and Tragic Action: A Synthesis of Current Theory," *Journal of Art Criticism and Aesthetics*, 31 (1974): 357–373.

16. The work of the British scholar, Sir Arthur Pickard-Cambridge, is our major source of information, *The Dramatic Festivals of Athens* (Oxford: Clarendon Press, 1968), and his earlier study, *Dithyramb, Tragedy and Comedy* (Oxford: Clarendon Press, 1927).

17. Harrison, *Ancient Art and Ritual* (Oxford: Oxford University Press, 1913), 86–89.

18. Harrison, 88.

19. Harrison, 89.

20. Nilsson, 206.

21. Jane Harrison, *Themis* (Cambridge: Cambridge University Press, 1912) 143.

22. Quoted in Harrison, *Prolegomena*, 437.

23. Harrison, *Themis*, 205.

24. See Harrison, *Themis*, 33–38.

25. Harrison, *Prolegomena*, 438.

26. Harrison, *Themis*, 202.

27. Robert Brown, *The Great Dionysia Myth*, Vol. I (London: Longmans, Green, 1877–1878), 105.

28. Brown, Vol. II, 46–49.

29. Aylen, 19.

30. Aylen, 114.

31. Aylen, 143.

32. Van der Leeuw, *Religion in Essence and Manifestation*, tr. J. E. Turner, (New York: Harper and Row, 1963), 374.

33. Van der Leeuw, *Religion,* 375.

34. Van der Leeuw, *Religion*, 375.

35. A full study of this pivotal figure is Theodore H. Gaster's *Thespis* (Garden City: Doubleday, 1961). The name of the student dramatic club at the church-related college from which I graduated was The Thespian Society.

36. Spiros Mecouris, "The Ancient Theater and Its Values" in *A Stage for Dionysos: Theatrical Space and Ancient Drama* (Athens: Kapon Editions, 1998), 17.

37. Harrison, *Ancient Art*, 126.

38. Harrison, *Ancient Art*, 127.

39. Emanuel G. Trekakis, "Theaters Worth Listening In," in *A Stage for Dionysos*, 173.

40. Another strong voice in the understanding of Greek theater to whom I am indebted is that of Erika Simon, *The Ancient Theatre*, tr. C. E. Vafopoulou-Richardson (London: Methuen, 1982).

41. Oscar G. Brockett discusses this issue in *The Theatre: An Introduction* (New York: Holt, Rinehart and Winston, 1969), 67.

42. Brockett, 68.

43. Jacques Burdick, *Theater* (New York: Newsweek Books, 1974), 21.

44. Burdick, 21.

45. Robert W. Corrigan, *The World of the Theater* (Glenview, IL: Scott, Foresman, 1979), 37.

46. Corrigan, 46.

47. Michael Goldman, *The Actor's Freedom* (New York: Viking Press, 1975), 13–14.

48. Euripides, *The Bacchae*, tr. C. K. Williams (New York: Noonday Press, 1990), 86.

49. Euripides, *The Bacchai*, tr. Robert Bagg (Amherst: University of Massachusetts Press, 1978), lines 1846–1850.

50. R. P. Winnington-Ingram, *Euripides and Dionysus* (Amsterdam: Hakkert, 1969), 24.

51. Winnington-Ingram, 24.

52. Jan Kott, *The Eating of the Gods*, tr. Boleslaw Taborski and Edward J. Czerwinski (New York: Random House, 1973), 193. Kott goes on to trace the analogies between the action within *The Bacchae* and Christ's passion and resurrection (207–222). So too Camille Paglia in *Sexual Personae* briefly exegetes this comparison (103–104). However, in my view, the analogy breaks down: Dionysus is not sacrificed; Pentheus is. In this narrative, humankind becomes the sacrifice; there is no divine redeemer who dies for the guilt of humankind.

53. C.K. Williams, 86–87.

Chapter Seven

Religion and Drama in Opposition: Two Instances

Twice in Western history, religion and drama have been in particular opposition to one another. The early Christian fathers and the English Puritans of the late 16th and early 17th centuries both raised serious objections to the theater. Although some scholars have written off these conflicts as aberrations of ascetic minorities, a close exploration of the issues involved will illumine both the nature of drama and religion as well as their possible relationship to one another.

The charges should be taken seriously for they reflect inherent tension between the religious and the dramatic. In fact, disapproval of theatrical activity may be observed not only in such major philosophers as Plato, Rousseau, and Nietzche, but also in our very use of language, as Jonas Barish points out in the opening sections of his major study, *The Antitheatrical Prejudice.*[1] While many terms describing the arts are laudatory (a landscape is "poetic," a struggle is "epic," beauty is "lyric"), terms derived from theater tend to be hostile or belittling: "theatrical, melodramatic, stagey." One could add a wide range of phrases: acting, play acting, playing up to, putting on an act, putting on a performance, making a scene, making a spectacle of oneself, playing to the gallery, and so forth.[2] The world of theater has frequently been regarded with suspicion.

Specifically, in the 2nd and 3rd centuries and the late 16th and early 17th centuries, Christian leaders wrote and spoke against the theater with articulate vigor.

This chapter will examine these two periods to set forth the major objections and then conclude with a discussion of the elements inherent in the Christian tradition which have been and continue to be in tension with the dramatic.

55

I

The Church was born in a period of theatrical spectacle. A playgoer in first century Rome would have been able to choose among the following: productions of old and new comedies or tragedies, assorted popular mimes of low life, or some rough topical farces, consisting for the most part of bawdy and slapstick, the actors in all probability wearing grotesque masks and large leather phalluses.

The basic form of Roman theater was satire and caricature which produced a tone of irreverence and anti-authoritarianism. Mimes particularly flourished and since they almost always dealt with recognizable material, they were enthusiastically received by the public. The curious mysteries of this new belief called Christianity became the target of farce and ridicule.

Some of the most sacred rituals, for example, baptism by immersion, were the standard butt of ridicule in the popular mimes and farces. It is hardly surprising therefore that we find Christian writers attacking the public theaters as "inventions of demons"[3] (the phrase is from St. Cyprian) and "honey drippings from the bowels of a toad" (Tertullian).[4]

The most vociferous attack was struck in the uncompromising treatise *De Spectaculis* (200 A.D.) of Tertullian (c. 160–230).[5] He articulated twelve major objections to the theater, citing evidence and argument to support each of them. These allegations ranged from the argument against vanity (encouraged by the stage) to the objection against men in women's clothes. He held that Christians had explicitly forsworn spectacula when they renounced the devil and all his works at baptism. What are these but idolatry, and where is idolatry, if not in the spectacula, which not only minister to lust, but also take place at the festivals and in the holy places of Venus and Bacchus? He vehemently calls the theater, "the devil's church."[6]

Tertullian saw the basic conflict as one of pretense versus truth. The theater not only encourages filth but through its use of mask and makeup promotes hypocrisy:

> Masks and makeup are lies. A Christian must be sincere. He who condemns every hypocrisy cannot approve any disguise of evil, or false tears, pretended moans, feigned love, outbursts of anger . . .[7]

He is particularly concerned about masks:

> And in regard to the wearing of masks, I ask is that according to the mind of God, who forbids the making of every likeness, and especially then the likeness of man who is in His own image? The Author of Truth notes all the false; He regards as adultery all that is unreal.[8]

To have men appearing as women is forbidden by the law of God. Thus he appeals to Deut. 22:5: "The woman shall not wear that which pertaineth unto a man, neither shall a man put on a woman's garment: for all that do so are abomination unto the Lord thy God."

If Christians need *spectacula*, they can find them in the exercises of the Church. Here are nobler poetry, sweeter voices, maxims more wise, melodies more comforting than any comedy can boast, and besides, here is truth instead of fiction. [9]

For Christians is reserved the last great *spectaculum* of all. The final chapter of the treatise points in glowing colors a picture of the greatest spectacle the world will ever see, the "new Jerusalem," when God will come to judge the living and dead. "Then," says Tertullian, "will be the time for tragic actors to be heard, more vocal in their own tragedy, whose lamentations will be more poignant and the players to be seen, lither of limb by far as comedians turn and twist, render nimbler than ever by the sting of the fire . . ."[10]

It is with St. Cyprian (200–258), Bishop of Carthage, that the attack on the *histrio*, the actor ("the chief purveyor of vice to the general public"), found its most rigorous spokesman. In a sweeping polemic, St. Cyprian lambasted the theater:

> Men are emasculated, and all the pride and vigour of their sex is effeminated in the disgrace of their enervated body; and he is most pleasing who has most completely broken down the man into the woman. He grows into praise by virtue of his crime, and the more he is degraded, the more skillful he is considered to be. Such a one is looked upon—oh shame! And looked upon with pleasure . . . Can he who looks upon such things be healthy-minded or modest? Men imitate the gods whom they adore, and to such miserable beings their crimes become their religion.[11]

A century later, Chrysostom (c. 345–407), Archbishop of Constantinople, maintained that stage play is deceitful, and that the stage causes the destruction of man's character and the doom of his soul. "Truly," wrote Chrysostom, "it is not for us to pass our time in laughter, in light entertainment, in trivial delights; that is good only for the stage players, for the indelicate actresses, above all for the parasite and flatterers . . . for those who execute the will of the devil."[12] On Easter Day, 399, he preached an impassioned sermon which repeated many of the attacks he had used over the past years. He spoke of the inevitable corruption bound up with things theatrical, and ended with a threat to enforce the sentence of excommunication, prescribed only a few months before by the Council of Carthage, upon whoever would join the processions and go to the theater on Sundays or holy days or during Holy week. Such actions were necessary, felt Chrysostom, because Christians "were so intent upon [plays] that they stayed whole days at those infamous sights, without going one moment to church."[13]

Augustine (354–430), Bishop of Hippo, both condemns and was very aware of the theater's influence on him. He censures theaters, for actors indulge fake emotions and audiences relish the "repulsive" imitation of suffering and imbibe the licentious atmosphere of bawdy comedy.[14] In a well-known passage of *The Confessions*, Augustine records the powerful influence exercised by tragedy, and particularly erotic tragedy, over his tempestuous youth. "The scenic spectacles," he admits, "enraptured me. In my time I had a violent passion for these spectacles, which were full of the images of my miseries and of the amorous flames of fire which devoured me. "[15] In *The City of God*, he draws a careful distinction between the higher and the lower forms of drama, and if he does not approve, at least does not condemn, the use of tragedies and comedies in a humane education.[16]

The whole of Augustine's writings are marked by references to the theater, thus revealing how deeply the stage had influenced his mind. And he expressed the well-known image from classical writing that "we too are acting in life this mime of ours."[17]

The judgment of the Fathers also found its expression in the disciplinary regulations of the Church. An early formal condemnation of actors is included in the so-called *Canons of Hippolytus* (c. 225)[18] and the relation of converts to the attendance at the theater was discussed by the councils of Elvira (306) and of Arles (314). These councils determined that any person connected with the circus or any pantomimic actor must positively abandon his profession before he could be received into the fold. They also spoke of keeping actors from partaking of Holy Communion.

After the Edict of Milan (313), the state met the views of the Church on several points: performances were forbidden on Sunday and during sacred periods of the church calendar as well as the strict caste laws which forbade actors and actresses to quit their profession were somewhat relaxed.[19]

The very fact that future councils (for example, the Council of Trullo in 692 passed a resolution forbidding all mimes and other theatrical spectacles, including popular festivals and over-lavish weddings) continued to make pronouncements indicates that it appeared impossible to stamp out the interest in the theater.[20] And yet one cannot and should not overlook the fact that the theater of that time and place did not contribute to the general good of individuals or the community. Even the Emperor Julian (331–631), the great enemy of the Church, charged that "the theater is the most noxious activity, the most reprehensible manner of spending time."[21] No one of the Christian Fathers discussed earlier could have put the matter more clearly. Thus throughout those early centuries, the Church's objection to the theater was a complex intermingling of motivations, as von Balthasar summarizes:

The original "No" to the theater remains a burdensome legacy throughout Church history right into modern times; it weighs all the heavier since in part it had a theological basis (in the opposition of myth and revelation), and in part it arose out of the state of the theater at that time, the social position of the actors, and continued the pre-Christian criticism of everything to do with the stage.[22]

II

The second period of opposition between drama and religion, the mid-seventeenth century in England, shares much in common with the earlier controversy of the Church Fathers. Just as the Patristic leaders recognized moral grounds on which to condemn the spectacles, so the Puritan divines called attention to the abuses of both the actors and the plays themselves.

As in the rise of Christianity, so in the rise of Protestantism, the believers were insistent on distinctiveness and purity. It is crucial to remember that the Puritans were more than stone-faced, irrational idol-smashers dressed in black. They spoke, as E.N.J. Thompson in his major study of this period of theater history insists, as "earnest, practical men against a real and growing abuse . . ."[23]

Indeed, the theater of the Jacobean period was in great contrast to Elizabethan drama. Rather than exploring penetrating questions of human nature, the Jacobean playwrights attempted to mirror the decadence of the age. Plays such as John Webster's *The White Devil* (1614) and John Ford's *'Tis Pity She's a Whore* (c. 1628) were seen by many of their contemporaries as titillating their audiences with portrayals of incestuous love amid crude humor and political intrigue.

The proponents of theater insisted that drama was a form of moral instruction. Humanists, rediscovering the classics, viewed the plays of Terence, satirical and iconoclastic as they were, for example, as a means of inculcating pure classicism and sound moral precepts. William Montanus Bavande (1559), a lawyer, defended the theater by writing that "such pastimes must be set forth in a commonweal as to minister unto us good examples wherein delight and profit be matched together . . ."[24]

Furthermore, a number of the Reformers saw the plays of their day as possessing characteristics of Roman Catholicism. Therefore the liturgical drama as well as the feast days of Corpus Christi at which time plays would be performed were all part of the popishness which must be eliminated. This new generation demanded a clean sweep of the medieval past and a return to simple Biblical Christianity. They did not intend to reform the drama of the 17th century; they hoped to abolish it.

On September 2, 1642, the theaters were closed. An *Ordinance of the Lords and Commons* was published which stated: ". . . that while these sad causes and set times of humiliation continue, public stage-plays shall cease and be forborne."[25] Although performances were held sporadically, particularly in 1648 when the Ordinance was not renewed at its expiration, only with the restoration of Charles II did the theater receive official sanction to continue.

Such an enumeration of dates indicates that the opposition to the theater in that day had as many political nuances as moral implications. The Puritan opposition to the theater had become increasingly identified with their hostility toward the Stuart cause. The playwrights of the period were notorious Puritan baiters, and as the Puritans gained political strength, they began to retaliate. When the predictable split between the established church and the dissenters took place, the theater was therefore in double jeopardy. For the theater was not only held by the Puritans to be an occasion of sin and the devil's tool, but was also attached by royal decree to the monarch, the church's nominal head and the Puritan's arch foe.

The acting companies were also caught between the conflicting authorities of the city of London and the court. On May 16, 1559, an ordinance was passed by the city which forbade any performance unless it had the licensed approval of the Lord Mayor. By 1572, the law stated that any actors not in the service of some noblemen were regarded as vagrants, and thus a penalty was imposed on them. Such pressure led to two results: (1) Since the strictness of the law was limited to London, the theater moved out of the city into the fields and (2) the theater became more and more attached to the royal court and looked for its patronage from the reigning monarch.

In addition to the use of civil authorities to rid the state of actors ("caterpillar(s) of the Commonwealth" and "a very superfluous sort of men"[26]), preachers and pamphlet writers condemned the theater.

A sermon preached as early as 1375 by a Lollard or a follower of Wycliff foreshadowed the arguments which were later to be set forth more fully. This sermon first presented six reasons in support of plays:

I.   They (the plays) are played to the worship of God and for his glory.
II.   They do not pervert, but, by force of example, turn men to God.
III.   They move men to tears and this in turn leads them to compassion and devotion.
IV.   They often lead to God those men whose hearts have been proof against all other approaches.
V.   Men must have some sort of relaxation and miracle plays are better than other japes.
VI.   It is lawful to paint pictures of miracles, therefore, it is lawful to act them, and the dramatic method is more effective for teaching Holy Scriptures.

To these bold claims, the preacher replied:

I.   They are played not to the worship of God, but to the approval of the world.
II.   It is true that men are converted by miracle plays, just as evil can be the cause of good, i.e., Adam's evil was the cause of Christ's coming. But more people are perverted than converted. Moreover, plays are condemned by the Scriptures.
III. Men weep, not for their own sins, not for their inward faith, but for their outward sight. It is not therefore allowable to give miracle plays, but reprehensible.
IV.   Conversion is an act of God, therefore not true conversion can come from miracle plays, but only feigned conversion, for if he were truly converted a man would hate such playgoing.
V.   Recreation should consist in doing works of mercy for one's neighbor, not in false vanity. The wicked deeds of the actors and spectators of miracle plays prove their worthlessness.
VI.   Painting, providing it is true, Christian and restrained, may be a book to discover truth. But acting is an appeal to the senses. Good men, seeing that the time is already short, will not want to spend it in idle playgoing.[27]

The main lines were drawn: drama and religion were inherently in opposition; the pulpit and the stage were enemies. In brief, a Puritan objector stated, "enterludes weare the divells sarmons."[28]

A sermon preached by John Stockwood in 1578 tied his objections to the wicked theaters of Rome:

> I know not how I might with the godly learned especially more discommende the gorgeous Playing place erected in the Fieldes, then to term it, as they please to haue it called, a Theatre, that is, euen aftr the manner of the old heathenish Theater at Rome, a shew place of all beastly and filthie matters.[29]

A similar tone is set in a sermon by William Crashawe, father of the poet, in 1607:

> The ungodly *Playes and Enterludes* so rife in this nation, what are they but a bastard of Babylon, a daughter of error and confusion, a hellish device (the devils own recreation to mock at holy things) by him delivered to the Heathen, from them to the Papists and from them to us.[30]

Since the theater was "a bastard of Babylon," natural disasters such as an earthquake (April, 1500) or a fall of a scaffold (January 1583) or even the

Great Plague seemed to the devout to show the Almighty's wrath on the existence of playhouses as a sermon of that day expresses:

> The cause of plagues is sinne, if you look to it well: and the cause of sinne are
> playes: therefore the cause of plagues are playes.[31]

Pamphlets increased the tempo and volume of the various voices raised
against the theater.[32] A writer such as Stephen Gosson published *The Schoole
of Abuse* (1579) whose title page included the statement: "Containing a pleasant invective against Poets, Pipers, Plaiers, Jesters, and such like caterpillars
of a commonwealth . . ."[33] Gosson is particularly harsh on the entertainment
offered in the theater:

> . . . straunge consortes of melodie to tickle the eare, costly apparrell to flatter
> the sight, effeminate gesture to ravish the sence, and wanton speache to whette
> desire to inordinate lust . . .[34]

The Anatomie of Abuse, a pamphlet written by Phillip Stubbes in 1583,
has a brief section entitled, "Of Stage-Playes and Enterludes with their
wickedness." To patronize the theater is "to worship devils and betray Jesus
Christ."[35] Interestingly, the first edition of the work deliberately commended
"honest and chast playes" as "a Godly recreation of the night" and as "a good
example of life."[36] It is not known why this section did not appear in later
editions.

A final example is that of William Prynne's pamphlet of 1633 whose very
title page in its length and vociferous language reflects this time of extreme
controversy:

> Histriomastix. The Players Scourge, or, Actors Tragoedie, Divided into Two
> Parts. Wherein it is largely evidenced, by divers Arguments, by the concurring
> Authorities and Resolutions of sundry texts of Scripture: of the whole Primitive
> Church, both under the Law and Gospell; of 55 Synodes and Councels; of 71
> Fathers and Christian Writers, before the yeare of our Lorde 1200; of above 150
> foreign and domestique Protestant and Popish Authors, since: of 40 Heathen
> Philosophers, Historians, Poets; of many Heathen, many Christian Nations, Re-
> publiques, Emperors, Princes, Magistrates; of sundry Apostolicall, Canonicall,
> Imperiall Constitutions; and of our owne English statues, Magistrates, Univer-
> sities, Writers, Preachers. That popular Stage-playes (the very Pompes of the
> Divell which we renounce in Baptisme, if we beleeve the Fathers) are sinfull,
> heathenish, lewde, ungodly Spectacles, and most pernicious Corruptions; con-
> demned in all ages, as intolerable Mischiefes to Churches, to Republickes, to
> the manners, mindes and soules of men. And that the Profession of Play-poets,
> of Stage-players, together with the penning, acting, and frequenting of Stage
> plays, are unlawfull, infamous and misbeseeming Christians. All pretences to

the contrary are here likewise fully answered; and the unlawfulness of acting of beholding *Academicall Interludes*, briefly discussed; besides sundry other particulars concerning Dancing, Dicing, Health-Drinking, etc. of which the Table will informe you.[37]

His writing, says Thompson, "represents the extreme of intolerance and unreason which the Puritan argument ever reached."[38] Prynne particularly cited the pernicious effects of the waste of time and money: "the prodigall mispence of much precious Time" and "the prodigall, sinfull, vaine expence of money."[39] Ironically, the "pamphlet" of some one thousand pages is organized in two *Tragic Parts, Acts, Scenes, Prologues*, and occasionally a chorus of reflection.

Prynne's central point, as it was for all those who opposed the theater in the late 16th and early 17th centuries, was that a religious sensibility which emphasizes simplicity and honesty cannot but judge theater to be evil and devious.

III

What were the elements in the Christian tradition which were (and still are, to some observers) the sources of opposition to the theater? Some half-dozen areas will be identified but permeated throughout these objections are two reasons which are rooted deep in the Christian tradition's tension and quarrel with drama: distrust of the body and distrust of the imagination. The two historical areas discussed earlier in this chapter reflect these elements and point towards the root hostility between the religious and the dramatic.

The first element in the Christian tradition is its emphasis on purity. To be moral, to lead a clean and wholesome and stable life comes in direct opposition to the acting profession. Although in particular instances such an accusation is often inaccurate, nevertheless the unstable economic status of actors frequently means that the bourgeois emphasis on thrift and respectability is not and cannot be a high priority. Both the Church Fathers and the Puritans articulated in strong language and objections which even today's liberal parents set forth when one of their children declares he or she is off to New York to become an actor or actress.

Solemnity is a second element in the Christian tradition which finds difficulty in relation to drama. The comic and the satirical were and are some of the major forms of theater, and the Church has always been uncertain where the lines of irreverence and blasphemy are crossed. Should laughter be trusted, especially if the laughter is mocking sacred matters? Do the individual Christian and the Christian community have enough self-confidence to allow biting critique and satirical commentary to be dramatized? The spectacles of the early Christian era and the Jacobean drama of the Puritan period played fast and loose with beliefs and practices of believers. Most of all, how can Christians distinguish between solemnity and seriousness? Seriousness is to be affirmed, but solemnity—is that the essence of the Christian faith?

Christians, thirdly, emphasize truth, honesty, and sincerity, and thus the pretense, illusion, and role-playing present in drama is contrary to the deep conviction of believers. W. H. Auden put the matter directly: "If a man is called to be an actor, then the only way he can be 'true' to himself is by 'acting,' that is to say, pretending to be what he is not."[40] To act is to seem, to impersonate, to lie. To wear a mask, either literally or figuratively, is to disguise and deceive. And certainly, for a male to portray a female is to engage in gender confusion. God is unchanging and the devil is the epitome of disguise. But what is too frequently overlooked is that not only is Satan in the disguise of a serpent but also Jesus Christ on earth is God made flesh in disguise. The Incarnation overcame the plan of the serpent. And yet a part of all of us affirms what Iago, the most Machiavellian of all literary characters, stated: "Men should be what they seem."[41]

Fourth, prodigality is sometimes a characteristic of Christianity. To waste time and money in such trivial and superficial entertainment as theater is to show a lack of commitment and loyalty to the Christian faith. A more serious objection is that the Sabbath is profaned by Christians attending theatrical performances. This practice, forbidden by the Fourth Commandment, was condemned by both the early Christians and the Puritans and continues to be discouraged in various religious communities today.

In the fifth place, the theater and the church were in many ways rival religions, each with its myths, symbols, and rituals. The opposition between drama and religion in the early Christian era lies in the fact that two different religions are in conflict: the new religion of Christendom and the ancient fertility religion with its candor and sexual symbols. The confrontation between paganism and early Christianity was played out on the stage which was the Roman Empire. The pagan world was generally tolerant; therefore, so many gods were already worshipped that the presence of one more need not cause alarm. But the Christians insisted, as Paul did on Mars Hill in Athens, that God was the one true God and all other gods and shrines should not receive the worship of the people.[42] Pagan tolerance disappeared; bitter retaliation set in, and in amphitheaters the bodies of believers were attacked by lions and in theater, their beliefs were ridiculed and mocked. And some Christians counter-attacked with vehement sermons, treatises, and edicts. The state could destroy the body, but the church did have the power to excommunicate and therefore endanger the spirit. The rival religions battled and struggled to gain the loyalties of the populace.

Fundamentally, Christianity was in deep quarrel with drama and theaters because it, buttressed by Platonic arguments, has always found the use of the body difficult to accept and affirm. Music can be used to the glory of God; painting and even sculpture, though they may images of Christ, can be vehicles and instruments of devotion. But dance and drama with its direct and immediate presence of the body with all its earthiness as well as beauty is often perceived to be degenerating, let alone evil. How can the transcendent and infinite be revealed through the weak and coarse body of a human being? The spiritual is what is crucial; bodies are at best only frail vessels to house the soul. The interpretation of the Fall as sexual transgression and the erroneous exegesis of Jesus and Paul as ascetics who rejected the body have contributed to the arguments of those who have found drama essentially incompatible with the Christian faith.

Finally, Christianity has frequently been tempted to rely too heavily on reason and logic and doctrine and thus undermines and denigrates the use of the imagination, symbol, and ritual. The understanding of Logos is then associated with logic and doctrine, and loses much of the living drama of Jesus Christ. The importance of intellect and dissertation outweighs the place of the imagination and metaphor. The result was that the battles were fought in the early Church by scholiasts, metaphysicians, and the battleground became policy sessions and councils. What was frequently overshadowed was the drama that "the Word became flesh and dwelled among us."[43] Theology (the words about God) became expository prose (think of Aquinas, and the commentaries of Calvin and Luther), not dialogue and poetry and song. The understanding of religion as primarily doctrine and precept is the inheritance we have received. And as heirs, we continue to struggle with the arts, especially drama, as a unique way of knowing, as a form of perceiving the meaning of our lives.

NOTES

1. Jonas Barish, *The Antitheatrical Prejudice* (Berkeley: University of California Press, 1981).

2. Barish, 1.

3. Cyprian, "On the Public Shows," in *The Ante-Nicene Fathers*, ed. and tr. by Alexander Roberts and James Donaldson, Vol. V (Grand Rapids: William B. Eerdmans Publishing, 1986), 576.

4. Tertullian, quoted in Phillip A. Coggin, *The Uses of Drama* (New York: George Braziller, 1956), 34.

5. For a full discussion of Tertullian's view of the theater, see Victor Power, "Tertullian: Father of Clerical Animosity toward the Theater," *Educational Theatre Journal*, 23 (1971): 36–50.

6. Tertullian, quoted in Harold Ehrensberger, *Conscience on Stage* (New York: Abington-Cokesbury, 1957), 35.

7. Tertullian, quoted in Donald R. Pearce, "Christianity and the Form of Western Drama," *Shenandoah Review*, 22 (Spring 1971): 71.

8. Tertullian, *De Spectaculis*, Chapter XXIII.

9. Tertullian, Chapter XXIII.

10. Tertullian, Chapter XXX.

11. Cyprian, "Epistle to Donatus," 177.

12. Chrysostom, *Hom. VI in Matt.*, quoted in Allardyce Nicoll, *Masks, Mimes and Miracles* (New York, Cooper Square Publishers, 1963), 138.

13. Chrysostom, in Nicoll, 138.

14. Augustine, Book III, Chapter 2.

15. Augustine, Book II, Chapter 8.

16. Augustine, *The City of God*, Book II, Chapter 8. Barish insists that Augustine's approach to the theater is more subtle and complex than his predecessors, 52–65.

17. Augustine in Psalm 127; *Enarratio*, quoted in Nicoll, 140.

18. Hippolytus, *The Apostolic Tradition*, II, 16: "If a man is an actor or a panto-mimist, he must desist or be rejected [as a catechumen]" in *The Apostolic Tradition* of Hippolytus, tr. by Barton Scott Easton (Cambridge: Cambridge University Press, 1934), 44.

19. See E. K. Chambers, *The Medieval Stage*, Vol. I (Oxford: Oxford University Press, 1903), 12–17.

20. See Nicoll, 145.

21. Gerhardus Van der Leeuw, *Sacred and Profane Beauty*, tr. David E. Green (New York: Holt, Rinehart and Winston, 1963), 95.

22. Hans Urs von Balthasar, *Theo-Drama*, Vol. I. *Prologomena* (San Francisco: St. Ignatius Press, 1988), 93.

23. Elbert N. J. Thompson, "The Controversy Between the Puritans and the Stage," in *Yale Studies of English*, II, ed. Albert S. Cook (New York: Henry Holt, 1909), 107.

24. *A Work of Johannes Ferrarius Montamus* touching the Good Ordering of the Common Weal, tr. W. Bavande, 1559, cited in Coggin, 56.

25. Cited in Coggin, 105.

26. J. Dover Wilson, "The Puritan Attack Upon the Stage" in *The Cambridge History of English Literature*, Vol. VI, eds. A. W. Ward and A. R. Walkers (New York: G. P. Putnams' Sons, 1910), 428.

27. Coggin summarizes the contents of the sermon, 50–51.

28. Sir John Harington, *Nugua Antiqua*, Vol. I., cited in Wilson, 424.

29. Quoted in Frances A. Yates, *Theater of the World* (Chicago: University of Chicago Press, 1969), 94.

30. Sermon, 14 February, 1607, cited in Wilson. 423.

31. Thomas White, Sermon, 1576, p. 47, cited in Wilson, 424.

32. For more detailed discussion of the three pamphlet writers discussed (Gosson, Stuffs, and Prynne), see Thompson, 62–85 and 159–78.

33. Wilson, 550.

34. Stephen Gosson, *The Schoole of Abuse* (London: Shakespeare Society, 1841), 22.

35. Wilson, 445.

36. Thompson, 81–2.

37. Wilson, 552–3.

38. Thompson, 162.

39. Thompson, 168–9.

40. W. H. Auden, Foreword to Henrik Ibsen, *Brand*, tr. Michael Meyer (New York: Anchor Books, 1960),30.

41. *Othello*, III, iii, 126.

42. Acts 17: 16–31.

43. John 1:14.

Chapter Eight

The Medieval Stage:
The Inherent Drama in the Mass

While the classical civilizations of Greece and Rome cultivated drama and some of the early Christian leaders opposed the theatrical spectacles, believers continued to be aware of the Biblical understanding of the drama of God and humankind. In the Middle Ages, participants, whether in the early liturgical drama or the later play of Corpus Christi, saw themselves as part of the grand drama of the actions of God in past, present, and future history. As we explore the drama inherent in the Mass which finds expression in liturgical drama, and later in mystery, miracle and morality plays, one question is dominant: how is the revelation of God in Jesus Christ to be made vivid, real, and visible?

In the Middle Ages, the whole cosmos was theatrical space, time all of salvation history, and action the intersection of God and humankind. Both the conception of time and of space in the Middle Ages reflect a full sense of the cosmic. Time was of one piece; no sharp distinction, for example, was made between Holy Day and holiday. Therefore, the great festivals of the Christian calendar, Easter, Christmas, and all the rest, including various days to celebrate individual saints, prompted both praise to God and celebration of life. At such a moment in time deemed to be special, the normal activities of living were suspended. The community, released from its mundane preoccupations, would assemble together for religious renewal and social interaction. Spiritual time and temporal time joined as the community re-enacted the festival ritual.

The most significant space within the community was the interior of the cathedral. No building could have provided a more suitable setting for drama than the cathedral, for it was, as Otto von Simpson has suggested "at once a 'model' of the cosmos and an image of the Celestial City."[1] The worshippers were surrounded and enhanced by the symbolism of the decorative arts of sculpture, painting, and stained glass windows which everywhere in the cathedral pointed to the eternal and the invisible. The architectural framework of the space also served to associate individual parts and locations with spiritual meaning. If "stage right" for example came to signify a place of honor in the mystery plays, iconography within the cathedral based on Biblical precedent made this association very evident. Paintings and sculptures all over Christendom reinforced the idea that St. Peter sat at the right of Christ at the Last Supper and the Virgin to his right at the Last Judgment. And the vastness of the cathedral itself prompted reflection on the mighty cosmic acts of God.

There were of course many other influences that contributed to the making of the drama.[2] Secular pageantry was an important part of medieval life. All public occasions—court and civic ceremonies, royal entries, Lord Mayors' shows, and tournaments—provided form and content, aesthetic satisfaction as well as significant action. The very presence of processions, whether down the long cathedral aisles or in the streets of the cities and villages, conveyed a drama of anticipation as well as of visual splendor.

Throughout the Middle Ages, traveling performers attracted crowds with pantomime, juggling, and comic interludes. Cities bustled with mummers, those who engaged in merry-making in disguise, especially during festivals. Folk plays featured figures such as St. George or St. Nicholas; other plays used classical models based on Terence and Plautus but with didactic content. All of this hurly-burly dramatic activity (think of our vaudeville, Marcel Marceau, musical comedy, Radio City Music Hall, and the 4th of July parade all rolled into one) is known to us only in fragments, but nevertheless was found all over Europe.

Yet it was the Church, and specifically, its liturgy, which provided both the seed and womb for medieval drama. Liturgy and worship possess inherently dramatic elements. One answer to the question: Why did drama begin in the church? is therefore, it was always there, or as O. B. Hardison notes: "Religious ritual *was* [his emphasis] the drama of the early Middle Ages. . . ."[3]

The first dramatic dimension is the Mass itself. Dialogue, antiphonal singing, and most of all, ritualistic action and movement are all present in the celebration of the Eucharist.[4] The "earthly [is] joined to the heavenly, [and] one thing is made of visible and invisible," as St. Gregory in the 6th century wrote about the sacrifice of the Mass.[5] Allegorical interpretations of the Mass such as that of Bishop Amalarius of Metz (780?-850),[6] provided the base to uncover dramatic significance in each of the major prayers and ceremonies. Definite roles are assigned to the participants, and the plot focuses on a conflict of rising action, renewal, and catharsis. As Honorius of Autun writes concerning the Mass in *Gemma animae* about 1100, the celebrant in the Church, like the actor in the theater, presents Christ's struggle through his action. The document is worth citing at some length:

> It is known that those who recited tragedies in theaters presented the actions of opponents by gestures before the people. In the same way our tragic author [i.e., the celebrant] represents by his gestures in the theater of the Church before the Christian people the struggle of Christ and teaches to them the victory of His redemption. Thus when the celebrant [presbyter] says the Orate [*fratres*] he expresses Christ placed for us in agony, when he commanded His apostles to pray. By the silence of the *Secreta* he expresses Christ as a lamb without voice being led to the sacrifice. By the extension of his hands he represents the extension of Christ on the Cross. By the chant of the Preface he expresses the cry of Christ hanging on the Cross. For He sang [*cantavit*] ten Psalms, that is, from *Deus meus respice* to *In manus tuas commendo spiritum meum*, and then died. Through the secret prayers of the Canon he suggests the silence of Holy Saturday. By the *Pax* and its communication [i.e., the "Kiss of Peace"] he represents the peace given after the Resurrection and the sharing of joy. When the sacrifice has been completed, peace and Communion are given by the celebrant to the people. This is because after our accuser has been destroyed by our champion [*agonotheta*] in the struggle, peace is announced by the judge to the people, and they are invited to a feast. Then, by the *Ite, missa est*, they are ordered to return to their homes with rejoicing. They shout *Deo gratias* and return home rejoicing.[7]

Such a description shows an understanding of the Mass as a living dramatic form, and confirms the idea that the central ceremony of Christian worship, the Mass, is indeed what Hardison entitles one of his chapters: "The Mass as Sacred Drama."[8]

The second dramatic dimension, particularly important to remember as we later discuss the Corpus Christi cycle, is that liturgical Christian worship revolves around the church year. This pattern, following the life of Christ and parallel to the seasonal cycle, is inherently dramatic in its sense of time and action. Beginning with the Advent, continuing through Christmas and Epiphany, then the forty days of Lent, culminating in the celebration of the Resurrection at Easter, the year concludes with the Ascension, Pentecost and finally, the Sundays of Trinity. Such a cycle has movements of birth and death, penance and celebration, and most of all, highlights the acts of Jesus Christ in such a way that the worshippers see their own lives with dramatic meaning. Their own births (both natural and spiritual), sufferings, death, and resurrection—these universal acts of the human—were analogical with those of Christ himself. All of these seasonal festivals were commemorative in essence and ritualistic in character. The earliest Christian drama therefore arose as part of a much wider process of elaborating and ornamenting the service appropriate to the principal commemorative festivals of the Christian year. And it is important to note, as Hardison comments, that the ritual structure characteristic of the Mass and the church year is essentially comic, not tragic:

> The mythic event celebrated is rebirth, not death, although it is a rebirth that requires death as its prelude. The experience of the participants is transition from guilt to innocence, from separation to communion.[9]

Every day, the Mass was enacted; each year, the drama of the liturgical calendar was experienced. Both conveyed the centrality of the life, death, and resurrection of Christ. The worshippers entered the acts of Christ, and beheld their own lives in this mirror. But with the major exceptions of the celebration of the Eucharist and that of baptism (often held in the opening moments after midnight on Easter morning), the worship is still primarily verbal. And the language is Latin which the worshippers do not understand.

To move from the verbal to the dramatic within the worship service meant the people could perceive graphically the powerful acts of God contained in the Scriptures. The movement to drama, first in the introduction of stained glass windows to portray Biblical scenes, was not only based on aesthetic rationale for both the windows and the drama enhanced the worship, but still more so, pedagogical. The Mass, in its breaking of the bread and the pouring of the wine, explicitly re-enacted the death of Christ in symbolic form. What could be better teaching devices than the actual representation of other events of Biblical history? The representational drama within the liturgy is a response to what all Christians at all times consider a very important challenge: the need to give visible expression to the relationship between the human and the divine, the need to make the presence of Christ real to the human mind and imagination. Such purpose governs the ritual of the Eucharist; such intentions nurture the growth of the seeds of medieval drama within the Church.

The earliest record of a written text in dialogue form is that of the tenth century *Quem quaeritus* trope from the Benedictine Abby of St. Gall in Switzerland. The trope (a turning),[10] words added as embellishment and interpolation to the regular sung parts of the Mass, follows the Gospel record of the meeting of the Angel and the three women on Easter morning. The dialogue in the earliest manuscripts consists of a question, an answer, and a reply:

Quem quaeritis in sepulchro, o Christicole?
Ihesum Nazarenum crucifixum, o celicole.
Non est hic, surrexit sicut ipse dixit; ite nunciate quia surrexit.

(Whom seek you in the tomb, O followers of Christ?
Jesus of Nazareth who was crucified, O Heaven-Dwellers.
He is not here, he has arisen as he said: go, announce that he has arisen.)[11]

This dialogue, chanted by antiphonal choirs as part of the Introit, foreshadowed the transition from narration to representation. Inherent drama is present in such an interchange: the form of question and answer and the antiphonal chanting, that is, voice or voices responding to the initiative of another voice or other voices. So brief, it hardly deserves to be called a drama, yet *Quem quaeritis* contains all the traditional elements. There is, first, the tension and the rising action; three people seeking something, troubled and uncertain in their quest. Next is the climax; the three are confronted by the unexpected news that Jesus is risen from the dead, and their hope is renewed. Finally there is the resolution; the three are called on to announce the good news.

In the Mass, the officiant symbolizes an eternal prototype; he makes the sacred event present to the congregation; he stands for Christ, who, to use doctrinal language, is "really present" during the rite. Thus, within the ritual, a play takes place. The belief that the bread and wine are transferred into flesh and blood insists that what is happening is not the illusion of reality but reality itself. The priest therefore is not an actor; the Mass, although it is highly dramatic, is not a play; it is not an imitation of an action but the mysterious reenactment of the death and resurrection of Christ. To confuse the two is to miss the significance of the *Quem quaeritis* which converts the officiant to actors and the ritual to drama. In the Mass, the priest represents Christ by virtue of his office, and not through any exercise of his individuality. In the *Quem quaeritis*, however, the participants represent the Marys and the angel.

Impersonation and action as well as elaboration of the sung dialogue are all present in the description of the *Quem quaeritis* which St. Ethelwold, Bishop of Winchester, set forth in the *Concordia Regularis* about the year 970:

> While the third lesson is being chanted, let four brethren vest themselves. Let one of these, vested in an alb, enter as though to take part in the service, and let him approach the sepulchre without attracting attention and sit there quietly with a palm in his hand. While the third respond is chanted, let the remaining three follow, and let them all, vested in copes, bearing in their hands thuribles with incense, and stepping delicately as those who seek something, approach the sepulchre. These things are done in imitation of the angel sitting in the monument, and the women with spices coming to anoint the body of Jesus. When therefore he who sits there beholds the three approach him like folk lost and seeking something, let him begin in a dulcet voice of medium pitch to sing *Quem quaeritis*. And when he has sung it to the end, let the three reply in unison *Ihesu Nazarenum*. So he, *Non est hic, surrexit sicut praedixerat. Ite, nuntiate quia resurrexit a mortuis*. At the word of this bidding let those three turn to the choir and say *Alleluia! resurrexit Dominus*! This said, let the one, still sitting there and as if recalling them, say the anthem *Venite et videte locum*. And saying this, let him rise, and lift the veil, and show them the place bare of the cross, but only the cloths laid there in which the cross was wrapped. And when they have

seen this, let them set down the thuribles which they bare in that same sepulchre, and take the cloth, and hold it up in the face of the clergy, and as if to demonstrate that the Lord has risen and is no longer wrapped therein, let them sing the anthem *Surrexit Dominus de sepulchro*, and lay the cloth upon the altar. When the anthem is done, let the prior, sharing in their gladness at the triumph of our King, in that, having vanquished death, He rose again, begin the hymn *Te Deum laudamus*. And this begun, all the bells chime out together.[12]

This miniature music-drama, bounded by altar, sepulchre, and choir, observes certain conditions of staging which underlie later stage practice.

The setting is the chancel. The most important property is the Easter sepulchre. Other properties are the palms held by the priest acting the part of the angels, the thuribles carried by those impersonating the three women, and the linen in which the crucified Christ has been wrapped. The costumes employed are the alb for the angel and the copes for the three Marys.

Singing marks the beginning, climax, and conclusion of this ritual-drama. The words of the angel's question, "Where is he?" leads to the women singing together "Alleluia! The Lord has risen!" And the ceremony ends the choir singing *Te Deum laudamus*.

The narrative is carefully choreographed. The angel proceeds to the place of the sepulchre as unobtrusively as possible while the three women make their way to the sepulchre. They turn to the choir to announce the Lord has risen. Then the angel lifts the veil of the sepulchre to reveal that only the wrapped clothes are remaining. They hold up the cloth for all to see and finally lay the cloth on the altar.

These moments dramatize the culmination of both the three women and the worshippers in their journey of faith. They begin "like folks lost and seeking something;" they are given evidence of Christ's resurrection; and they express their response in joy and praise. The pealing of the bells after their silence of during Holy Week announces to the community that Christ is alive among them. Indeed, the whole plan of redemption is re-presented here just as it is each time in the drama of the Mass, as Hardison states, "through the re-creation of the 'life, death and resurrection' of Christ."[13]

Historical time and ritual time are all now one; the temporal world and God's timeless world are continuous. We are in the present as well as transported back to Jerusalem on Easter morning in the year A.D. 33. We listen to what the angels and the Marys tell us; in our imagination we see the empty tomb; we are shown the empty shroud. We are invited to witness, as were the original disciples, to the actuality of the event, and thus urged to go out and announce the good news to others. The ringing of all the bells symbolizes this last expectation, as the message received within the church is carried out into the daily life of the people through actions and service.

The development of the dramatic within liturgical worship began with the celebration of the resurrection of Jesus Christ. The Word of God burst out of the liturgy into action at the most dramatic moment in the re-enactment of the life of Christ: the awareness of the glorious event of the Resurrection. The joy breaks forth at daybreak to commemorate the central act of the Christian faith. At the moment the three women enter the tomb and discover it empty, the greatest act of God is made manifest, for death itself has been conquered.

The Easter trope later became detached from its set place at the beginning of the Easter Mass, and reappeared as a separate little scene at Matins on Easter morning. This change was unquestionably of great significance, for it gave the trope opportunity to expand.

One development is by expansion; to the Gospel narrative of running to the tomb was added the extra-Biblical account of bargaining with the ointment seller. A further means of development is by analogy. The *Quem quaeritis* of the women at Easter is easily seen as parallel to the shepherds at Christmas:

> Whom seek you in the cradle, O shepherds, tell me?
> Christ the Lord and Savior, the infant wrapped in swaddling
> clothes, as the angel has said.
> The babe is here with Mary, His mother. . . .[14]

In both of these actions, the women at Easter and the shepherds at Christmas, the altar is central. In the first action, it symbolizes the sepulchre, in the second, the crib. In both events, the Incarnation and the Resurrection, the revelation is made real. In the frail form of a baby as Redeemer and in the victorious King who conquers death, Christ is visible, is dramatically revealed.

The plays also expand in relation to the time of ritualistic celebrations. The observance of Christmas was not confined to the day of the Nativity, but was a twelve-day holiday (holy days) starting on December 25 and ending on January 6, the day of the Epiphany. The Coming of the Magi therefore was dramatized on this day. In between lay four important calendar feasts, two of which were dedicated to the commemoration of saints: St. Stephen, the first martyr (December 26) and St. John the Evangelist (December 27). The other two were particular to children: The Day of the Massacre of the Innocents (December 28) and the Circumcision of Jesus (January 1). In the later Middle Ages, the whole twelve-day season came to be closely associated with inversion of status, and thus folly and misrule.[15] Two quasi-dramatic liturgies became associated with these two feast days: The Boy Bishop and the Feast of Fools. After the long preparatory meditations of Advent and the serious, if joyful, devotion of Christmas Day itself, a much more relaxed and informal celebration of the two other festivals followed.

Still other festivals of the Christian calendar called for attention. Because time is linear in representational drama, it extends backward and forward from the moment of the Resurrection, the most pivotal event in history. What events prepare for the Resurrection and what follows from it? From a Christian point of view, the answer is simple and inevitable. Ultimately, everything that has happened since the beginning of time is in some sense a preparation. The fall of Lucifer is the first preparatory event, and the fall of Adam the second. Between Adam and Christ, the sacred history of the Chosen People is crucial. The Old Testament is thus the primary scene for plays preceding the Nativity, and from it are selected episodes of special didactic or typological significance: Cain and Abel, the Flood, Abraham and Isaac, and the prophets. For the next part, the consequences of the Resurrection are portrayed by plays that foretell the final moments of human history: the Antichrist and the Last Judgment.

Wickham suggests convincingly that since the music-drama developed in close proximity to the *Te Deum*, this affirmation of praise influenced both the subjects (the apostles and prophets and later, the saints and martyrs) and the tone of thanksgiving in the plays:

> Holy, Holy, Holy: Lord God of Sabaoth;
> Heaven and earth are full of the Majesty: of thy glory.
> The glorious company of the Apostles: praise thee.
> The goodly fellowship of the Prophets: praise thee.
> The noble army of Martyrs: praise thee.
> The holy Church throughout the world: doth acknowledge thee;
> The Father: of an infinite Majesty;
> Thine honourable, true: and only Son;
> Also the Holy Ghost: the Comforter.
> Thou art the King of glory: O Christ.[16]

This glorious array of human and divine actors form the core of medieval drama. By the end of the twelfth century, as we shall see, the Church in Western Europe had developed a cosmic drama spanning from Creation to the Last Judgment.

The most important moments of human history are those in which God openly and decisively intervenes. He enters, He comes (*venio*) in dramatic form, and He acts in concrete ways. The drama's essential structure is described in a medieval sermon:

> Frendes, for a processe ye shall understand that I fynde in holy writt: iij [three] commynges of our Lord; the first was when that he com to make man; the secound was when he com to bie [redeem] him; and the iij shall be when he shall com to deme [judge] man.[17]

Advent is thus celebrated both ways in time, to the first coming and to the last. God acts as Creator, Saviour, and Judge, and He who made humankind in the beginning and will judge them in the end in the center of history and came as God incarnate in human form.

Medieval drama encompassed the complete action of God in time by portraying the drama of salvation in temporal time and by means of human bodies. And that is appropriate; the essence of Christianity does not lie first of all in its philosophical truth, but in its revelation in history, in what happened, does happen, and will happen. God acted and does act and will act.

As a means of conveying the drama of salvation, the medieval mass embodied in its form and content the drama inherent in the Christian faith. All of time is represented in the timeless present of ritual. All of space is represented within the walls of the cathedral. Within the liturgy is the microcosm of the visual representation of the whole cosmic drama.

NOTES

1. Otto von Simpson, *The Gothic Cathedral* (New York: Harper Torch Books, 1962), 37.

2. See Glynne Wickham, *Early English Stages 1300 to 1680*, Volume I (New York: Columbia University Press, 1980, especially Chapters II (*The Tournament*), III *Pageant Theaters of the Streets*), and VI (*Mummings and Disguisings*).

3. O. B. Hardison, *Christian Rites and Christian Drama in the Middle Ages* (Baltimore: John Hopkins Press, 1965), viii.

4. Karl Young, *The Drama of the Medieval Church*, Volume I (Oxford: Clarendon Press, 1933), 79–85. Young makes a careful distinction between dramatic elements in the Mass and the further step of actual impersonation, to pretend to be someone other.

5. Quoted in Hardison, 36.

6. Hardison, 37 ff. and Young, 81–82.

7. Quoted in Hardison, 39–40.

8. Hardison, 35–79.

9. Hardison, 284.

10. Young gives a more elaborate description of trope: "A verbal implication of a passage in the authorized liturgy, in the form of an introduction, an interpolation, or a conclusion, or in the form of any combination of these, 178. He also sets forth the sources of the term, 565.

11. Quoted in Hardison, 178–79.

12. Quoted in E. K. Chambers, *The Medieval Stage*, Volume II (Oxford: Oxford University Press, 1963), 14–15.

13. Quoted in Hardison, 39.

14. Quoted in Hardison, 297. Wickham discusses the Christmas trope in detail (Volume III, 1981), 31–4.

15. Wickham contrasts Christ's kingship with Herod's misrule (Volume III), 33.

16. Wickham, *The Medieval Theater* (New York: St. Martin's Press, 1974), 43.

17. V. A. Kolbe, *The Play Called Corpus Christi* (Stanford: Stanford University Press, 1966), 58.

Chapter Nine

From Liturgy to the Plays
of Mystery, Miracle and Morality

The liturgical music dramas from their beginnings in the tenth century through the twelfth century took place in church buildings with the clergy in the acting roles reciting and chanting in Latin. In the next two centuries, as the mystery, miracle and morality plays developed, all three elements—the stage, the actors, and the language—changed. And all three of these dimensions have religious as well as dramatic dimensions.

The location of the drama moved from choir to nave, from nave to churchyard, from churchyard to market place and street and court and much later to a building designated as a theater.

The actors in the early plays, no matter what the roles called for, were the clergy. Later, lay persons were in charge both in the production and performance of the drama.

The language, as was true for all the liturgy until rather recently in the Roman Catholic Church, was Latin. But by the thirteenth century, the vernacular was the common vehicle for the dramas.

At least two strands of speculative theory have attempted to account for these three changes. The first and more traditional approach by such scholars as E. K. Chambers (1903)[1] and Karl Young (1933)[2] has been to understand the changes as a general evolution toward secularization. The more recent interpretations have emphasized not the disjunction between the early drama (the sacred) and the later plays (secular), but has stressed the continuity in the whole process. Studies by O. B. Hardison (1965)[3] and V. A. Kolve (1966)[4] and Glynne Wickham, (1963, 1972, 1974, 1980, 1981)[5] have called attention to the fact that not only was there no such evolution (the liturgical dramas, for example, continued as late as the fourteenth century), but also that the Church recognized the changes as deliberate ways to take the sacred story into the world of the everyday. In brief, the first theory proposed that the Church wanted to push the drama out and it wanted to get out as well; the second implies that the Church saw the drama as a way of extending its message and mission into the world as well as making more clear what the message of Christianity means for believers.

The first approach stresses the purity of the Church (how can such elaborate scenes and such comic scenes be appropriate within the church?) and the second emphasizes the mission of the body of Christ (how can the Biblical story be made real and concrete and accessible to the person in the street and the marketplace?). And interestingly, both of these interpretations parallel the early seeds of the Reformation: to purify the church of its ostentation as well as to make the message relevant to all persons. In fact, each of the three changes—the location from church to marketplace, the dominant role from clergy to lay, and the language from Latin to the vernacular—all parallel significant dimensions of the Reformation.

The actual evidence indicates that both the purity and the mission of the Church are crucial in understanding the complex reasons of why the three changes—location, the actors, and the language—took place. As we trace the changes more carefully, the inherent tension between the religious and the dramatic will be self-evident. What happens in drama between the tenth and the fourteenth centuries therefore is a microcosm of the stresses and strains which Christianity and drama have at all times had with one another.

One of the major influences for the changes certainly was the increased number and the elaborate nature of the performances. The Church was not interested in increasing the resources—finances, personnel, as well as time—which were needed as the performances became more extensive. Instead of the clergy in their usual robes, costume became more important and therefore the cost became significant. The setting of the church also became confining. In order to portray the various locations (Hell, Heaven, the various earthly settings of the Biblical narratives), the space even within the largest cathedral was not large enough. And if machinery was wanted (for example, to have Christ ascend into the heights), the church building had not the space to construct such an apparatus. The audience wanted more: more action, more characters, more elaborate settings. And the Church was both unwilling and unable to provide more. As the performances moved from the liturgical music-drama to more realistic performances, the church building, the clergy, and the Latin language became less and less appropriate as the means to do so. As the drama became more dramatic, could the Church continue to be the vehicle?

A second development which influenced the changes was the consequences of placing unbelieving characters within the narratives. To portray the disciples and the women as they came to the empty tomb or to represent the Magi or Daniel or Noah could all be done in adoring reverence and seriousness. Such characters were serious and therefore good. Impersonators of such heroes and heroines have thus only to handle emotions ranging between joy and grief in a manner that fit the circumstances. With the possible exception of joy which could be expressed in ways that might be unseemly (dancing is an example), the imitation of conduct and emotion presented few problems.

But to introduce a Herod or a Belshazzar or Noah's wife or a foolish virgin was something else. There was then a need to contrast the behavior, both in word and deed, of the virtuous persons and their opposites: the Magi and King Herod, Daniel and Belshazzar, Noah and his wife, the wise virgins and foolish virgins. Such unbelieving characters necessarily must be portrayed as bad and ridiculous. The ranting of Herod or Belshazzar, the shrewish behavior of Noah's wife, the grumblings of the foolish virgins move the whole tone very quickly from reverence and seriousness to absurdity and ridicule and inevitably the comic and even the indecorous and ribald. The impersonation of non-believing characters carried within it an innate risk of moving toward entertainment. Any actor knows that if an audience responds warmly to the manner in which he executes an action on stage, this carries with it temptation to repeat or enlarge the same device. Thus, the lack of seemliness or appropriateness and not drama per se gave rise to ecclesiastical doubts and protests in the twelfth and thirteenth centuries since this indecorum was clearly at odds with the place and occasion which the ritual existed to illuminate. Moreover, since the best sources for the imitation of unseemly conduct were secular or pagan or both, this development could be construed as doctrinally dangerous and thus to be condemned.[6]

A still greater difficulty is, of course, the representation of the devil himself. Such an embodiment of temptation appeared "in orebyll a-ray" (horrible array), and he entered frequently "with thunder and fyre, cryeng and roryng." In medieval drama, Satan in various costumes appeared as an "Adder . . . with a maydens face" or with "a cote w[ith] hosen tayle for ye serpente . . ." or as an actor taking the part of a "werm with an aungelys face."[7]

The presence of the devil aroused not only mirth and merriment, but one commentator suggests, "fear and uneasiness."[8] The spectators were both attracted to temptation but at the same time, fearful, and repulsed by the evil portrayal. According to Christian belief, Herod and Noah's wife and even the devil himself are all within the dominion of God. Thus laughter becomes a teaching device to point out the folly of unbelief. What we laugh at, we reject. But what we laugh with, we accept.

Laughter, once begun, is difficult to restrain. The comic becomes raucous entertainment and even ribald. And thus the Church clearly was and still is ambivalent about the presence of the comic and of laughter within its precincts.[9] But in losing the comic (either by intention or by default), the

Church seemed to narrow the meaning of salvation to the ascetic and found itself unable to accept the diverse and often comic richness of humanity. The Church in confusing seriousness with solemnity, encouraged and in some ways forced the theater to become the arena to present a broader and fuller understanding of humanity.

Jane Harrison has suggested that drama in Greece emerged from ritual and dance only in the moment that the spectator was born.[10] When large numbers of people withdrew from participation in the communal rites to form an audience, ritual gives place to art. If this theory is accurate, when the ninth-century angels who first asked "*Quem quaeritus in sepulchro, o Christocole?*" and the three Marys to whom they spoke replied, at that point the other "followers of Christ" in the congregation that Sunday morning assumed the position of audience, of witnesses to an act. The second coming of drama in Europe was not unlike the first in its movement from religious ritual to dramatic art.

Half-ceremonial, half-art, the plays which developed outside the Church were poised precariously between ritual and art. The people who crowded about the pageant on the feast of Corpus Christi, as we shall see, were still actively involved in the performance of a community rite, a re-enactment of religious history.

For no idea, as Anne Barton has pointed out,[11] could have been more foreign to the medieval age than the Renaissance conception of the essentially self-contained play. In the Elizabethan theater, there is a clear line between the play and the actual world, between the actors and their audiences. The play is set apart in a specific area and the members of the audience are not seen as participants. In medieval drama, on the other hand, audience and actors shared the same ritual world, a world more real to them than the one which existed outside the frame. David or Mary, for example, spoke both at one moment to their colleagues on the stage and at the same time, to the on-lookers in the street, who depended for their salvation upon their participation within the cosmic drama. Christ Himself, Barton comments, speaks both to those spectators gathered at Golgotha who were actually responsible for his death, but also to fourteenth century Christians:

> I pray you pepyll that passe me by,
> That lede your lyfe so lykandly,
> Leyfe up youre hertys on hight! . . .
> My folk, what haue I done to the,
> That thou all thus shall tormente me?
> They syn by I full sore.
> What haue I greyvd thee, answere me,
> That thou thus nalys me to a tre,
> And all for thyn erroure.[12]

Such moments reveal the ritualistic melding between time present and time past upon which medieval drama is based. Both actor and spectator together, as it were, play Christ on the Cross. Even the most worldly member of an audience implicated so realistically in the events of the play, Barton affirms, would be forced to realize the immediacy of this drama, to feel personal involvement, to be a participant in sacred history.[13]

But this directness of the message of salvation was exactly what the Church desired. From the outset, the drama of the Biblical narrative was directed towards the people in an effort to portray that Christ died to save humankind so that they might live lives of Christian service. Such an effort only continued a perspective begun in the Gospels—to see within the mundane and the ordinary the presence of God. As Wickham asserts, this was not to "secularize" a drama that was distinctly religious, but the reverse: to be aware that every new manifestation of dramatic vitality could be re-molded into a form that was capable of a Christian interpretation and could be firmly tied to a Christian festival.[14] What the presentation of the drama in its direct and vernacular language and in its setting in the marketplace did was to remind Christians that the Church, the Body of Christ, embraced them in their daily lives as well as in their church-going.

To encourage laypersons to participate in such presentations made sense not only religiously (every person, not just the clergy, has a role to play in God's plan for salvation), but also practically. Medieval society was accommodating itself to the rapid growth to the new class of individuals—the merchant burghers and shopkeepers of the new towns—who occupied a middle ground between the landed aristocracy and the peasants. Thus when a new feast in the Christian calendar, the Feast of Corpus Christi, came to be instituted in the fourteenth century, these men with their trade associations, their brotherhoods and their quasi-religious guilds were already firmly established and would be able to offer the Church their assistance in organizing the celebration.[15]

The centers of dramatic initiative in fourteenth and fifteenth century Europe therefore shifted from the large monastic communities of St. Gall, Fleury, Limoges, and Winchester which had dominated the drama of worship in the tenth, eleventh, and twelfth centuries to the most prosperous centers of trade and industry such as Coventry, York, and London.

The new locus of the meeting of religion and drama was the street and the marketplace. In the well-ordered life of the Middle Ages, the Biblical plays came under the sponsorship of the trade guilds, for these groups had both the finances and personnel to undertake such a task. The guild plays at their height from about 1300 to 1450 presented in chronological order the Biblical drama from Creation to Doomsday. Such plays, usually called mystery plays,[16] could be more accurately called "Bible-histories," as the *Oxford Companion to the Theater* describes them.[17] Although cycles of mystery plays were produced in over one hundred English towns during the Middle Ages, most of the extant plays are from four cycles: the York, containing forty-eight plays; the Chester cycle, containing twenty-four; the Townsley manuscript, or Wakefield cycle, containing thirty-two plays; and the Coventry and the N___ Town plays (the blank was to be filled in with the name of the town where the cycle was being performed).[18]

In a major town such as York, each guild presented a particular segment of the Biblical drama. Frequently, the particular guild would be responsible for an appropriate scene, for example, the Shipwrights for the Building of the Ark, the Goldsmiths for the Coming of the Magi, the Bakers for the Last Supper, and the Butchers for the Mortification of Christ.[19] Thus the drama was a lively vehicle to convey that the Christian commitment of the participants was integrally tied to their occupation.

The plays were frequently performed on pageants, crude wagons which were drawn through the street from one place to another.[20] A late account (1594) by an Archdeacon named Rogers describes the setting:

> Every company has his pagiant, or parte, which pagiants weare a high scafolde with two rowmes, a higher and a lower, upon four wheels. In the lower they apparelled them selves, and in the higher rowme they played, beinge all open on the tope, that all beholders mighte heare and see them. The places where they played them was in every streete. They begane first at the abay gates, and when the firste pagiante was played it was wheeled to the highe crosse before the mayor, and so to every streete; and soe every streete had a pagiant playinge before them at one time, till all the pagiantes for the days appoynted weare played: . . .[21]

The effect therefore is that participants could, during the course of one day, experience the whole history of the world and by standing in one location, and see before them the places of Paradise, ancient Israel, and Jerusalem. Earth, heaven, hell—all of the cosmos were vividly before the audience. And all of this was conveyed through the ordinary bodies of fellow townspeople. Divine history is made incarnate through human form.

The cycle plays became linked in the late fourteenth century with one particular day in the church calendar, the Feast of Corpus Christi. The Council of Vienna in 1311 under Pope Urban IV designated that Corpus Christi, the Thursday after Trinity Sunday, should be strictly observed. The rationale for Pope Urban's Bull was, according to Wickham, to buttress a deteriorating Church which not only had eclipsed the Eucharist by allowing the other events of Passion Week to overwhelm the institution of the Supper on

Maundy Thursday, but also that another Thursday would be a time to explore faith and hope in the redemptive power of the Eucharist.[22]

We should not ignore that the context of this event is a festival: on the one hand, a time set aside in which a religious ritual was observed by the entire community,[23] and on the other hand, a time of festive celebration in which exuberance, joy, and communality reigned. It was a festival in which artistic, intellectual, and socio-economic life was inextricably linked with religion. This festival, as all other medieval festivals, combined sacred and ordinary time, both Biblical time and present time. Thus the participants saw themselves as participants in significant cosmic time.

Not only is that day one of the longest days of the year and one when the weather would most likely be favorable, but this celebration also marks the end of the annual cycle of historical events celebrated in the church year. After the sequence of the Advent, Passion, Resurrection, Ascension, and Pentecost, a time outside of these events is celebrated in which to remember the past year and to anticipate the coming year.

The feast day, celebrating the Body of Christ, does so in at least two ways. The first, emphasized by Thomas Aquinas, is the Corpus Christi as the Host. The sacrament is carried through the community in a procession. But the Corpus Christi is also the mystical body of Christ as the whole body of the faithful from the beginning to the end of time. This meaning expresses itself in the presentation of the history of the faithful from creation to judgment. Kolve suggests what is revealed in these pageants of sacred history is "the grandeur of God's continuous care for man, and the progress of His plan to redeem him."[24] Earlier, Kolve had discussed the celebration of the Feast of Corpus Christi both as a gift of God in the Sacrament's temporal power to work miracles and in its eternal power to alter the destiny of the human race.[25] All in all, the festival was a reminder that in the midst of life, Biblical revelation and especially the Eucharist are real, and are intertwined with ordinary human experience.[26]

The meaning of time within the Corpus Christi plays becomes important in order to understand its purpose, for the action encompasses the mimesis of total human time:

one day:	from 4:30 a.m. with the dawn of Creation to darkness with the Apocalypse[27]
one year:	the church calendar
Biblical history:	from Genesis to Revelation

In each of these, significant past and future time is emphasized. Kolve perceptively notes the figures and fulfillment with the Biblical cycle itself, for example, the figure of Noah in the flood looks forward to both the Baptism of Christ and to Doomsday, the saving and destruction of all humankind.[28] By staging all past action as if it were in the present, the Corpus Christi drama, says Kolve, "managed to hold a mirror to the times while imitating the structures of human time."[29] Within a short period of time, the audience is invited to contemplate the divine plan of human history presented in a temporal sequence. In a moment of time, all time passed before them.

Further, in ritual drama, an anachronism is perfectly legitimate. In the famous Second Shepherd's Play, for example, the idiom and the costumes are totally medieval. They quarrel, possess shrewish wives, and enjoy a good round of ale together. And at the same time, those rough men are already Christians who welcome the baby Christ at the crib in Bethlehem. For, as Murray Roston observes:

> Medieval drama should not be seen as a hotch-potch of buffoonery and solemnity, but, like martyrological art, as a deliberate blending of the spirit and the flesh, of mundane realism and expressionist stylization within the confines of a unified cycle.[30]

Nevertheless, the tension between past and present, between actuality and illusion is real. Lucifer plays God; the soldiers mock Christ. Then how do the actors avoid blasphemy? Two opposing implications were both held: first, that all the action, although serious, is a jest, a game. To understand the drama as play becomes a kind of protection for the actors. The second is the belief that all of human action, including that of playing the devil who plays God and mocks Christ, can and will be transformed by grace into worship and praise. Both the actors and the members of the audience still had the opportunity and time to be repentant and be forgiven. They are in Biblical time, but also in the present which was open to change and transformation.

Not only time is richly presented in the cycle plays, but also the manipulation of space conveys the progress of the dramatic action. Procession, with its implicit metaphor of journey, is the informing movement of the Corpus Christi plays. The journeys begin with the exile of Adam and Eve from the Garden, and continue with the Exodus. The birth of Jesus is surrounded by journeys: the holy family on its journey to Bethlehem, the Coming of the Three Kings, and the Flight into Egypt. And the death of Jesus includes the entry into Jerusalem and the Via Crucis and the pilgrimage to Emmaus, and later, the believer shares the geographic journeys of St. Paul and the imaginative journey of St. John as he beholds a new heaven and a new earth.

The action is multi-directional as well: horizontal-geographic and vertical-cosmic. Satan's fall from heaven to hell is the first great act. Thereafter, angels descend and rise again; the repentant climb upward and sinners fall. Christ harrows hell and is resurrected. Movement—divine, human and demonic—is everywhere. Nothing is left to the imagination and yet everything is. For the heaven-tower is, after all, only a scaffold, the ark but a decorated pageant-wagon, and the Exodus a turn once around the place. Particular space is transformed into universal space.

And this journey through time and space includes the very persons who are participating in the drama, either as actors or as audience. It is indeed fitting that in this ritual the people enact for themselves the drama of Christ coming into the world to save them. All of these persons see themselves as part of the Body of Christ. The Corpus Christi was incarnate in human form in the performance of the drama itself.

Concurrent with the cycle mystery plays but with few preserved were the miracle plays, the dramatization of lives of saints and martyrs. Perhaps staged on the day dedicated to the saint (for instance, the Play of St. Nicholas celebrated on December 6 was most likely one of the first), the plays demonstrate an example of how the believers in the past were faithful in their lives and death. All portray miraculous power at work or divine intercession in human affairs. The response of those who saw such plays must have been one of being encouraged to continue the challenge of Christian living. Again, the drama served to connect the saintly lives with the lives of the participants and members of the audience.

The third kind of play in which religion and drama met in the medieval period was the morality play. Flourishing between 1400 and 1500, the most well-known example is, of course, *Everyman* (about 1500). Other titles are *Pride of Life* (about 1410), *The Castle of Perseverance* (about 1425) and *Mankind* (about 1475). These moral interludes, as they were sometimes called, concerned themselves with the struggles of all human beings. The plays are dominated by ethics, or, in Anne Barton's words, are "a kind of sermon with illustrations . . ."[31] Whereas the mystery plays particularized the historical characters they presented, the morality plays attempted to universalize their characters as fully as possible.

This universality was usually achieved through the use of abstract and generalized names. The protagonist (such as Everyman or Mankind) is visited by personifications of good and evil (such as Mercy, Good Deeds, Ignorance, and Covetousness). Within the action of such a dramatized allegory, characters such as Conscience and Death contend for the soul's control. This battle becomes a test of the protagonist, that is, can he bring himself to submit to God's will and thus gain his grace and receive his mercy? The movement is not linear narrative, but a debate and battle over the control of the soul. The war between vice and virtue shows the soul wavering in the balance, attempting to choose between two courses of action, and in the climax, arriving at a decision. The action therefore is double, as Robert Potter carefully describes it:

> . . . a descent out of innocence into sin, and an ascent out of sin to salvation. The morality play . . . acts out and moralizes three interrelated stages of human existence. The life of humanity is seen to begin in a potential state of innocence but to lapse in the course of experience into an actual state of sin. This state of sin, in turn, is seen to lead by its own contradictions toward the possibility of a state of repentance.[32]

This ritual pattern of a fall from power followed by a reversal that opened the way to the regaining of lost grace is certainly parallel to the dramatic action of the cycle plays. Like the mystery plays, however, morality drama portrayed a reality greater than the one its audience could discern with their natural eyes. Principalities and powers were real; Vice and Virtue were tangible. But the cycle plays dramatize events that occurred within the microcosm of historical time. The morality play, however, as Hardison observes, "introduces two new elements: a method of constructing plays on the basis of doctrine (akin to Aristotelian *dianoia*) and a psychological concept of character portrayal."[33] In the morality plays, an individual as representative of all the race plays out the struggles that transpire within the microcosm of a human life.

By setting the drama in the present, not only is there closer identification, but also the here-and-now world becomes central. We are no more in ritual time; the performance is not tied to a sacred time such as Easter, Christmas, or Corpus Christi Day. What happens is that the world portrayed on stage and the spectator's own world are beginning to fuse. Instead of seeing their own lives in the light of Biblical reality as was true in the mystery plays, the morality dramas opened up the possibility that the stage is the world of illusion, and the audience lives in the real world.

What is crucial here is that the perspective is changing. Instead of a kind of God's-eye view of history which the mystery plays conveyed, the miracle plays and to a still greater extent, the morality plays assumed that human beings are viewing other human beings. The vertical dimension, the cosmic perspective, therefore, becomes less dominant both in the dramatic action as well as in the imagination of the audience. From perceiving that the whole cosmos and all of history, human and divine, is the arena of action, we are moving to an awareness that all the world's a stage and that each of us is a player.

NOTES

1. E. K. Chambers, *The Medieval Stage*, Volumes I and II (Oxford: Oxford University Press, 1903).

2. Karl Young, *The Drama of the Medieval Church*, Volumes I and II (Oxford: Oxford University Press, 1933).

3. O. B. Hardison, *Christian Rite and Christian Drama in the Middle Ages* (Baltimore: Johns Hopkins University Press, 1965).

4. V. A. Kolve, *The Play Called Corpus Christi* (Stanford: Stanford University Press, 1966).

5. Glynne Wickham, *The Medieval Theater* (New York: St. Martin's Press, 1974) and *Early English Stages, 1300 to 1660* (New York: Columbia University Press). Volume One (1980), Volume Two Part I (1963) Part II (1972), and Volume Three (1981).

6. But the comments of Harold C. Gardiner, S. J., "Mysteries' End", *Yale Studies in English*, Volume 103 (New Haven: Yale University Press, 1946): 19, should not be ignored:

> . . . never in legislation for the universal Church or in any appreciable numbers of local councils and synods, did the attitude adopted become one of opposition to the religious stage, as such; second, what few pronouncements can be shown to touch the *miracula* directly, reprobate not the *miracula* but entirely extraneous abuses; third, circumstances of time and place made it advisable not infrequently to restrict clerical participation in the plays and their production in churches, and that with increasing frequency as we move from the strictly liturgical drama to the more secular miracle plays; and, finally, where Church control of the drama was most absolute, the religious drama, far from being swept away, flourished into the most glorious drama of the nation, the drama of a Lope de Vega and a Calderon.

7. Quoted in Allardyce Nicoll, *Masks, Mimes, and Miracles* (New York: Cooper Publishers Square, 1963), 189. Nicoll discusses comic scenes and the devil in considerable detail, pp. 179–194.

8. Gardiner, 3.

9. Kolve devotes an entire chapter to "Religious Laughter," 124–144.

10. Jane Harrison, *Ancient Art and Ritual* (London: Oxford University Press, 1913), 119–152.

11. Anne Barton, *Shakespeare and the Idea of the Play* (London: Chatto and Windus, 1962), 20.

12. Quoted in Barton, 23–24.

13. Quoted in Barton, 24.

14. Wickham, *The Medieval Theater*, 183–184.

15. Wickham, "Medieval Comic Traditions and the Beginnings of English Comedy" in *Comic Drama: The European Heritage* (London: Methuen, 1978) perceptively discusses this aspect of the medieval theater.

16. Vincent Hopper and Gerald B. Lahey in introduction to *Medieval Mysteries, Moralities and Interludes* (New York: Barron's Educational Series, 1962), 9, presents a helpful description of the term "mystery:"

In discussions of medieval drama, the student constantly encounters the terms *mystery, miracle,* and *morality* as words descriptive of distinct types of plays. This verbal distinction between *mystery* and *miracle* was little known during the centuries in which medieval drama flourished. It appears to have been introduced in the middle of the eighteenth century to formally distinguish between religious plays based on Biblical stories and factual narratives (the *mystery*) and plays based upon the lives and legends of the saints (the *miracle*). . . .Notwithstanding, there was in France some evidence of a tradition of calling Biblical plays mystery plays. The French *mystere* derived neither from the Greek *mysterion*, referring to secret or clandestine religious ceremonies, nor was it related to the English term *myster* as descriptive of a specialized trade or craft. It is supposedly derived from the late Latin *ministerium*, referring to Church service. Whatever be the truth of the matter, the distinction observed is convenient.

17. *The Concise Oxford Companion to the Theater*, ed. Phyliss Hartnoll (London: Oxford University Press, 1972), 375.

18. See Stanley J. Kahrl, *Traditions of Medieval English Drama* (Pittsburgh: University of Pittsburgh Press, 1975), 16: "It is now generally agreed that 'N' stands here for the Latin *nomen*, 'name', meaning that the bann-criers were to insert the appropriate name of a town at this point."

19. Chambers in Volume II gives an entire list of forty-eight plays with its appropriate guild in one cycle from the *Ashburnham MS.*, 410–11.

20. The performance of several mystery plays which I saw in the courtyard of Southwark Cathedral in London on Shakespeare's birthday, April 23, 1972, used a wagon for the stage.

21. Quoted in Hopper and Lahey, 15.

22. Wickham, 61.

23. Eleanor Prosser vividly makes the point about the amount of community involvement: "There is clear evidence of at least a dozen full cycles in Britain by the middle of the fourteenth century, indicating a state of dramatic activity comparable, say, to an annual production of twelve 'Oberammergaus' in the state of Illinois," *Drama and Religion in the English Mystery* Plays (Stanford: Stanford University Press, 1961), 4.

24. Kolve, 271.

25. Kolve, 48.

26. Wickham points out the architecture of the cathedrals with their great distances between the worshippers and the Real Presence meant that the Eucharist needed to be made more visible to the people (*Early English Stages 1300 to 1660*, Volume One), 311–12).

27. Kahrl gives strong evidence that the entire cycle of plays could not have taken place in one day, 44–5.

28. Kolve presents two graphs to indicate the intricate structure of the cycle: the first graph connects episodes which are related as figure and fulfillment (p. 85) and the second graph illustrates the relationship of the cycle to such historical divisions as *The Three Laws and The Seven Ages of the World,* 120.

29. Kolve, 104.

30. Murray Roston, *Biblical Drama in England* (London: Faber and Faber, 1968), 19.

31. Barton, 25.

32. Robert A. Potter, "The Form and Concept of the English Morality Play," (dissertation Claremont, 1965), 190, quoted in Kahrl, 105.

33. Hardison, 28.

Chapter Ten

Shakespeare: All the World's a Stage

The medieval mystery play encompassed all of the reality and affirmed that God is the director of an orderly and harmonious universe. Human action, whether in the Biblical narrative of the Corpus Christi cycle or in the later morality plays, is a response to this divine arrangement. Men and women are therefore actors in a drama in which the central action is that of God upholding the universe and redeeming humankind by being present in the lives of believers. No one questioned the reality of the action on stage. The actions were Biblical narratives or were based on Scriptural ethics and therefore true.

Kent van den Berg in *Playhouse and Cosmos: Shakespearean Theater as Metaphor*[1] perceptively suggests that the Shakespearean playhouse itself incorporated both the medieval and Renaissance perspectives. The stage with its fixed order of hell in the cellarage beneath and its heavens painted on the canopy above represented what van den Berg terms "the medieval cosmic emblem."[2] The circular stage based as the Roman theater, on the other hand, evokes the Renaissance sense of freedom and power.

"This Wooden O," as Frances Yates points out in *Theater of the World*,[3] not only has classical roots from the writings of Vitruvius but also in the well-rounded structure of the Globe was a replica of the order and perfection of God's universe.[4] And the sign associated with Shakespeare Globe Theater, *Totus mundus agit historiorem* (literally, all the world plays the actor), continued to reflect the audience's belief in meaningful correspondence between the various planes of existence.

The very name and shape of Shakespeare's major playhouse reflect the metaphor of life as a play. If the world is a stage, then the theater will be named the Globe simply because that is what it was. In Greek drama, the total openness of the amphitheater and the emphasis on public action reflected the belief that the dramatist sees human action as directly related to the *communitas*, the world of nature, and the arena of the gods. Mystery dramas, also staged outdoors, portrayed the interaction between divine and human history. In contrast to the later drama beginning in the 16th century with its enclosed spaces and emphasis on domestic settings, Shakespeare's theater attempted to be a microcosm of the world itself. Its flat open arena and its large balcony and its second smaller double balcony was a mirror of the universe as perceived by the Renaissance audience and playwright—the divine presence, the court, and the people—three levels, separate yet often intermingling. The theater is indeed a space where Antony's presence dominated "The little O, the earth" and where his voice "propertied/As all the tuned spheres/. . . might shake the orbe" (*Antony and Cleopatra*, V, ii, 80, 84–85, 86).

For Elizabethans to affirm that the king was a lion among beasts or like the sun was to affirm a sense of order and congruence. This sense of order and congruence manifested itself in many dimensions in Shakespeare's drama. Amid the mistaken identities of comedy and the catastrophes of tragedy, a sense that there is meaning in human events continues to prevail. The coincidences which untangle the comic plots and the magnificent speeches of the tragic heroes as they die all point to the belief that a transcendent order is at work in the universe. This belief is encapsulated most clearly in Hamlet's declaration that

> there is special providence in the fall of a sparrow. If it be now, 'tis not to come; if it be not to come, it will be now; if it be not now, yet it will come; the readiness is all. (V, ii, 231–234)

But note the counterpoint: divine providence and human readiness. Providence does not imply that divine control simply causes everything to happen. Rather, amid trust in divine guidance, readiness recognizes and allows and affirms human freedom.

Renaissance thought understood human action to be more important than divine action. God is still the Director (Providence), but the spotlight is on the human stage. Hamlet must decide; he must act. But he knows that he is acting in a cosmic play whose Producer provides directions for the players. So too the Reformation emphasis on the priesthood of all believers, while acknowledging the centrality of God's justifying humankind through grace alone, places more responsibility on the individual believer to play important roles in the church and in daily life.

In an age of increasing historical consciousness, Shakespeare's plays are, in Erich Auerbach's term "creaturely,"[5] that is, aware of the transcendent presence of divine guidance, but rooted in the tangible, in the here and now. As Auerbach points out,

. . . in the drama of the Elizabethans, the superstructure has been lost; the drama of Christ is no longer the general drama, is no longer the point of confluence of all the streams of human destiny. The new dramatized history has a specific human action as its center, derives its unity from that center, and the road has been opened for an autonomous human tragedy.[6]

In theatrical terms, the protagonist is now the maker of his own plot. The tragic character continues to construct his life until the denouement of death. In comedy, the heroes and heroines instigate actions which will move them toward festive rituals, often marriage. But in either form, the protagonist has constructed actions which are deliberately and carefully initiated by the characters themselves.

I

The metaphor of *theatrum mundi*, the theater of the world, a common image in Renaissance writers,[7] is transformed within Shakespeare's plays into a complex mode of expression which sees human actions as most significant within the cosmic drama. Thus "All the world's a stage . . ." is one of Shakespeare's most obsessive images. He delights in the use of words such as act, perform, part, scene, tragedy, play, pageant, shadow, and counterfeit.[8] Such terms not only refer specifically to elements of drama, but also evoke in the audience the theatrical nature of human action with the world as a stage.

The Chorus as it begins *Henry V* invokes both the stage as world and the world as stage:

O for a Muse of fire, that would ascend
The brightest heaven of invention,
A kingdom for a stage, princes to act,
And monarchs to behold the swelling scene.

(Prologue, 1–4)

The Chorus in this play opens our vision to the infinite, all of which will be presented with the finite space of the Globe:

Can this cockpit hold
The vasty fields of France? Or may we cram
Within this wooden O the very casques
That did affright the air at Agincourt?
O, pardon! since a crooked figure may
Attest in little place a million,
And let us, ciphers to this great account,

On your imaginary forces work.
Suppose within the girdle of these walls
Are now confined two mighty monarchies,
Whose high upreared and abutting fronts
The perilous narrow ocean parts asunder.
Piece out our imperfections with your thoughts . . .

(Prologue, 11–23)

The Globe, as Yates observes,

. . . was a magical theater, a cosmic theater, a religious theater, an actors' theater, designed to give fullest support to the voices and the gestures of the players as they enacted the drama of the life of man within the Theater of the World. His theater would have been for Shakespeare the pattern of the universe, the idea of the Macrocosm, the world stage on which the Microcosm acted his parts.[9]

Theatricality, or the explicit dramatic use of the elements of the theater and of the stage in both the structural and thematic dimensions of a play, provides one of the major implications for the relationship of the dramatic and religious.[10] The theatrical metaphor is not only spoken through the mouths of Shakespeare's characters, as we will see, but also presented in the personal voice of the poet in his sonnet:

. . . this huge stage presenteth nought but shows
Whereas the stars in secret influence comment. (Sonnet 15).

The most well-known passage in the plays is, of course, Jaques' expression in *As You Like It*:

All the world's a stage,
And all the men and women merely players:
They have their exits and their entrances,
And one man in his time plays many parts . . .

(II, vii, 139–142)

Brief passages from the comedies, histories, and tragedies are representative of the pervasiveness of the image. In *The Merchant of Venice*, Antonio speaks of his role as part of the cosmic drama:

I hold the world but as the world, Gratiano,
A stage where every man must play a part,
And mine a sad one. (I, i, 77–79)

York, in *Richard II*, finds the image helpful to describe the King's procession in his downfall:

> As in a theater, the eyes of men,
> After a well-grac'd actor leaves the stage,
> Are idly bent on him that enters next . . .

and York adds the belief that

> . . . Heaven hath a hand in these events,
> To whose high will we bow our calm contents . . .
>
>   (V, ii, 23–25, 37–38)

In the tragedies, the image moves to one of futility and complete illusion, as in Macbeth's soliloquy:

> Life's but a walking shadow, a poor player
> That struts and frets his hour upon the stage
> And then is heard no more. (V, v, 24–26)

Lear echoes the sad emptiness of the world as a theater of folly:

> When we are born, we cry that we are come
> To this great stage of fools. (IV, vi, 186–187)

In *Julius Caesar*, Brutus directs the conspirators to model themselves as players:

> Let not our looks put on our purposes,
> But bear it as our Roman actors do,
> With untir'd spirits and formal constancy.
>
>   (II, ii, 225–227)

And in *Othello*, a misuse of the theater, a failure of the spectator to respond with both eyes and ears, becomes the dramatist's image for Othello's dilemma pitted against the false acting of Iago.

Dramatic art itself—its language, its conventions, its relationship to truth and social order—provides the images and themes for Shakespeare's drama. In both tragedy and comedy, the metaphor was integral to the dramatist's act. Two of his plays, the tragedy of *Hamlet* and the comedy of *The Tempest*, will be explored in order to trace more fully Shakespeare's dramatic employment of the images and actions of the theater. Such exploration will provide a base from which to make further observations on Shakespeare's artistic use of theatricality and its implications on the dramatic and the religious.

II

The images of theatricality reach a crescendo in the play about playing, *Hamlet*, for as William Hazlitt already noted: "Hamlet is the prince of philosophical speculations."[11] Hamlet, the actor par excellence with self-awareness, puts on various masks, and instead of following the assigned role of obedient and docile prince, begins to ask fundamental questions: Of what play am I a part? Am I an actor in a play of revenge? Am I part of a drama of moral punishment? Or, am I merely grappling with shadows and wrestling with illusions? In brief, how shall I act? As Maynard Mack writes in his well-known essay, "The World of Hamlet": "Hamlet's world is pre-eminently in the interrogative mood "and he adds: "Hamlet's world is a world of riddles."[12]

Hamlet not only participates in the action, but he assumes himself to be a somewhat detached observer of the action as he puts "an antic disposition on." (I, v, 172) In a deliberate change of roles, Hamlet moves from actor to spectator to playwright-producer-director of the play within the play. Not until Act V when he leaps into Ophelia's grave to meet the actor, Death, and cries, "This is I,/Hamlet, the Dane" (V, i, 280–281) does he remove the last of his masks. By the end of the play, he has accepted his humanity. He realizes that he, as all others, is, in his earlier words, one part godlike, or angelic, and "noble in reason," in the other part merely "quintessence of dust." (II, ii, 316, 322)

The play deliberately places itself within the broadest possible setting of the world as stage. The worlds of *Hamlet* begin in the castle and the court, reach out to Denmark, and then extend to Norway, Poland, Germany, France, and England and far beyond these countries to the realms of Purgatory, Hell, and Heaven. At the same time, all of the action resides within the inner self of Hamlet as his spirit is torn between heaven and hell.

Not only geographically, but also socially, the range is wide in Hamlet. First is the royal court with the King and Queen, Prince Hamlet, Prince Fortinbras as well as the chief counselor, Polonius, and assorted ambassadors, courtiers, and gentlemen. The scholar Horatio and the priest who buries Ophelia represent a second estate. And the play is filled with common people: gravediggers, soldiers, sailors, and the players. All orders, both natural and supernatural, inhabit the stage of Hamlet.

Within these large dimensions, ceremonies and rites dominate the action. From the changing of the guard in the very first scene continuing with the entire court in attendance at "The Murder of Gonzago" and concluding with the fencing battle between Laertes and Hamlet and the final changing of the leadership within the kingdom, the participants act within proscribed order and ritual expectation. As Thomas Stroup writes, ". . . the play as a whole can be regarded as one single procession . . ."[13]

And that procession is simply full of actors. Polonius who in his university days has acted the part of Julius Caesar waits behind the wings to see how Ophelia and Hamlet will interact. He performs the same approach in the closet scene with fatal consequences. Claudius is a player-king, "a king of shreds and patches." (III, iv, 102) If he and Gertrude are, as Hamlet says, "hypocrites," then we should remind ourselves that this is the Greek word for actors. Rosencrantz and Guildenstern by their own admission are playing a part, and Ophelia somewhat unwilling comes on in her part with a book of devotions in her hands.

The vocabulary of the participants in the action reflects the difficult, if not impossible, task of discerning the real amid illusion and appearance. Such words and phrases as apparition, seems, assumes, puts on, and most of all, show, act, and especially play,[14] heighten the metaphor of theatricality and contribute to the on-going tension between truth and falsity. As fiction, plays mask the truth, but by the same token, the plays "hold as t'were the mirror up to nature" (III, ii, 25) and show life its true image. As mirrors, they "show virtue her own feature, scorn her own image, and the very age and body of time his form and pressure." (III, ii, 22–24) It is this mingling of truth and illusion amid the actions of rites and ceremonies which Hamlet expresses.

For many of the ceremonies are in actuality "maimed rites." (V, i, 242) Marriages are false, funeral rituals are truncated, entertainments which as deliberate strategies to determine guilt are interrupted, and fencing matches are in reality vehicles to poison and destroy. Within these distorted rituals, Hamlet must find his way.

The play begins in the dark and the audience as well as the guards are surrounded by the unknown and the uncertain: "Who's there?" (I, i, 1) This initiating action, the appearance of the Ghost, immediately raises questions: Is this a message of evil? Is this apparition a prophetic emissary to spur Hamlet to revenge? If the ghost is honest, is Claudius dissembling and false, someone who can "smile and smile and be a villain"? (I, v, 108) The Ghost forces Hamlet to discern what is real and what is not. As Jean Howard comments on the opening scenes of *Hamlet*:

> The orchestration of the whole moment keeps the audience searching for a stable point of reference, for a voice of true authority to separate out from those whose certitude masks guile or signals complacence We search, like Hamlet, for a perspective we can trust.[15]

Hamlet in his first appearance is playing the role of a grieving son: an "inky cloak," a suit of "solemn black," "forc'd breath," and a "dejected . . . visage." (I, ii, 77–81) He explicitly asks the question whether this costume denotes him "truly" or whether they only "seem" to be "actions that a man can play," "the trappings and the suits of woe." (I, ii, 83–86) Hamlet is already insisting that no performance can adequately express the self, yet he will find himself trying on many new roles during the course of the play, for he must continue to perform actions which set aright the disordered state of affairs within the kingdom.

Hamlet struggles throughout the entire play with what it means "to act." Clearly, he is conscious of the doubleness of the term: to do something with sincerity and meaning or to feign, to pretend only. And as important, who is acting in the world around him? Is his mother in real grief or only going through the motions? When she inquires about his grief ("Why seems it so particular with thee?"), he responds vehemently: "Seems, madam! Nay, it is; I know not 'seems'." (I, ii, 75–76) Later, is Claudius really praying? Does Ophelia truly love him? In such a world, whom can he and we trust? In fact, as Hamlet puts "an antic disposition on," (I, v, 172) he himself is engaged in pretending. Not only the others around him, but he himself is duplicitous as he takes on various roles.

Within this constantly changing world, everyone tries to discover ways to control the action, or in theatrical terms, to be the director and write the script for others to follow. Indeed, as Wendy Coppedge Sanford perceptively notes,

> The surface action of *Hamlet* develops as a series of encounters between the characters, structured in explicit theatrical terms—'scenes' arranged by the characters themselves as dramatists and directors.[16]

Various persons manipulate others and place them within a play to suit their own ends. At Elsinore Castle, everyone is being watched, and most play the part of actor or spectator, whether willing to do so or not. Thus, many scenes consist of audiences who did not intend or expect to see the play presented before them: the ghost appearing before the guards and Hamlet and later to Gertrude, the King and Queen coming upon Hamlet reading a book, Hamlet observing Claudius at prayer, Polonius discovered too late behind the arras, the King belatedly aware of Gertrude's poisonous cup, and Laertes' recognition that he has been "justly kill'd with mine own treachery." (V, ii, 317)

No scene encapsulates all of these motifs of dramatists and directors more fully than Hamlet's staging of the play, "The Murder of Gonzago": ". . . the play's the thing/Wherein I'll catch the conscience of the King." (II, ii, 633–634) Earlier in the same scene, Hamlet had described the players as engaging "in a fiction, in a dream of passion." (II, ii, 578) He is admitting that theater is distinct from reality, but in his desire to produce the play before the king, he now sees drama as an instrument to influence and even shape reality.

All plays within plays tend to blur the distinction between the imagination and the actual. But "The Murder of Gonzago," the turning point in Hamlet, dissolves this difference even more so, for everyone knows the Player King is acting, but Claudius disguised as the Player King has not yet been unmasked. As Anne Barton observes, "the Player King and Queen [within 'The Murder of Gonzago'] reach out to threaten the reality of their audience."[17] On stage are Claudius and Gertrude who are spectators of this play. Watching them is Prince Hamlet who is now playing a producer-playwright role. Surrounding the king and the prince are members of the court—Polonius, Rosencrantz and Guildenstern and others—who have also been directing and playing roles. Finally, there is the audience who is keenly observing all of these audiences. "Where," Maynard Mack rightly asks, "does the playing end? Which are the guilty creatures sitting at a play? When is an act not an 'act'?"[18] *Hamlet,* it would seem, should only be played in the round.

But Hamlet interrupts his own play. Instead of allowing the drama to work its way into Claudius' conscience so that he might reveal his guilt, Hamlet blurts out the rest of the story:

> He poisons him i' th' garden for his estate; his name's Gonzago, the story is extant, and writ in very choice Italian; you shall see anon how the murderer gets the love of Gonzago's wife. (III, ii, 272–275)

Herbert Coursen catches the scene:

> The indelible impression both in the spectators of the larger play, who have been playing Hamlet's play, and the 'spectators' on stage, who have not, is that something in Hamlet—not Claudius—forces the play's premature closing. Hamlet is unable to maintain his role as spectator . . .[19]

Neither does Hamlet sustain his role as playwright-producer, but again becomes actor in a play in which he did not intend to participate, the murder of Polonius.

Not only in his staging of the play before the court, but in all his actions, Hamlet's most difficult question is: Is there an order in the universe by which he can proceed? or in more theatrical terms, is there a Director in charge of the cosmic order? The presence of the Ghost was ambiguous; the signs Hamlet has attempted to perceive from others have not been convincing; his inner self as revealed in the soliloquies has been wrestling with this search for certainty.

But gradually Hamlet becomes more aware of the ways of the divine. In his first soliloquy, he rejects suicide since "The Everlasting" has forbidden it. (I, iii, 131) He continues to recognize the ethical implications of human action: "Thus conscience does make cowards of us all." (III, i, 83) Hamlet's self-reproaches about his failure to act are theological:

> Since He that made us with such large discourse,
> Looking before and after, gave us not
> That capability and god-like reason
> To fust in us unus'd . . . (IV, iv, 36–39)

In Act V, Hamlet begins to accept more fully that he is part of a larger whole, that Providence, and not he himself, is in control of all. S. F. Johnson puts the matter directly: "In Act I, he was a student prince; in Act V he is the ordained minister of providence."[20] In the opening scene of Act V, Hamlet speaks of a skull he unearthed as "one that would circumvent God." (V, i, 88) Now that he has confronted death, he realizes that he is not to play God, but is to accept his own finitude and to know that all human plots fade:

> . . . let us know
> Our indiscretion sometimes serves us well
> When our deep plots do pall; and that should learn us
> There's a divinity that shapes our ends,
> Rough-hew them how we will— (V, ii, 7–11)

Hamlet now is ready for what may happen, attempting neither to control nor to avoid, as he recalls the well-known Biblical passage concerning Providence:

> . . . there is special providence in the fall of a sparrow. If it be now,
> 'tis not to come; if it be not to come, it will be now; if it be not now,
> yet it will come; the readiness is all. (V, ii, 231–234)

He is aware, in the words of A.C.Bradley of the "Other Director."[21] Within the cosmic drama in which Providence rules (Thomas McFarland calls it "the Christian matrix of the tragedy"[22]), Hamlet is a human actor, no more and no less.

In the staged rapier contest with Laertes, Claudius is attempting to perform the trick that Hamlet had earlier successfully tried on him. But, as one commentator suggests,

> Hamlet has an ally, a providence who takes charge of the play and gives it an
> unexpected twist. Laertes fails to come in on his cue, and Gertrude, who has not

been admitted to the producer's confidence, makes the wrong move and spoils the show.[23]

Hamlet in dying acknowledges they have all been taking part in a play:

> You that look pale and tremble at this chance
> That are but mutes or audience to this act,
> Had I but time—as this fell sergeant, Death,
> Is strict in his arrest—O, I could tell you—
> But let it be. (V, ii, 345–349)

For a moment, Hamlet harks back to his role as director-playwright as he is surrounded by the deaths of Gertrude, Claudius, and Laertes. He attempts to communicate some final message, some interpretation of the past action, but he lets it be as Death lowers a curtain, silence.

And that is Hamlet's final word: "The rest is silence." (V, ii, 369) That is most appropriate as his last witness, that after all the action and inaction, after all the plots and counterplots, after all the directing and observing, that the playwright and the actors and the audience are silent. And just as at the beginning of the play a soul from Purgatory appears, so at the end, Horatio requests "flights of angels may sing thee to thy rest." (V, ii, 371)

Horatio and Fortinbras are in charge of the concluding rituals of the play. They gather the remaining with drum roll and flourish. Horatio instructs his audience that there is one more play to perform:[24]

> . . . give order that these bodies
> High on a stage be placed to the view;
> And let me speak to th' yet unknowing world
> How these things came about . . . (V, ii, 388–391)

Robert Egan describes the scene:

> By way of explicating what has transpired in the play, Horatio, in effect, convenes an audience for a repeat performance of that play. Instead of opening out to disclose some revelation akin to that attempted by Hamlet at the moment of his death, the play turns back upon its own artificial sphere as the ultimate explanation of its meaning.[25]

Perceptive as this observation is, the adjective "artificial" is not accurate. At no time does the play suggest negative judgments about the truth that drama is the mirror of actuality. To pretend to direct—that is presumption. To assume that one has no part to play—that is abdication. But to see and live one's life as a significant actor among other players within the divine order, such knowledge Hamlet dramatizes as appropriate and meaningful.

III

The Tempest is a journey into a world of suspended reality and revelatory illusions. If Hamlet is actor, producer, director and script writer, Prospero is all of these and more. Here the theatrical image is the play itself. As we enter Prospero's world, we are participating in "a most majestic vision" (IV, i, 118) in which the whole earth is turned to theater. The imaginative masque which Prospero presents to the lovers, Ferdinand and Miranda, is staged by magic and illusion. The play and reality have become one. Hence the play does not attempt to catch the conscience, but our imaginations, our dreams. *The Tempest* is a dazzling theatrical revelation of the total identification of stage and life.

The entire action takes place between two actions: the sinking of the ship and Prospero's return to Milan. The action between these two frames is Prospero's pageant in which the natural and the supernatural are interwoven. In fact, as Jan Kott observes, "All that happens on the island will be a play within a play, a performance produced by Prospero."[26] Reality dissolves; dreams and shadows are dominant, for the stage is inhabited by spirits, as Prospero himself insists:

Spirits, which by mine art
I have from their confines call'd to enact
My present fancies. (IV, i, 120–122)

"Spirits" describe not only the participants in the masque in Act IV, but many of the actors: Ariel as Prospero's guardian angel and stage manager and Caliban as evil spirit incarnate. Miranda even addresses Ferdinand as "spirit" as they come together in a magical world of love and enchantment:

What is 't? A spirit?
Lord, how it looks about! Believe me, sir,
It carries a brave form. But 'tis a spirit. (I, ii, 409–411)

The action of the play is a contest between spirits; the forces of good and evil are pitted against each other: Ariel/Caliban, Prospero/Antonio, Alonzo/Sebastian.

Three planes of existence are presented simultaneously: the cosmic, the theatrical, and the human, as we discern even from the setting of the island. The island is a microcosm of the entire cosmos, it is the stage of Prospero's dramatic powers, and it is the place where the interaction between the various characters takes place. And where is this island? Jan Kott's answer is accurate:

> Prospero's island is either the world, or the stage. To the Elizabethans it was all the same; the stage was the world, and the world was the stage.[27]

The concentric circles are all present; beginning with Prospero's inner imagination, we move to the love relationship of Miranda and Ferdinand to the international repercussions of the usurpation in Milan and finally to the spirit world beyond. All are set within one another so that like the regression of Chinese boxes, we are absorbed in both the finite and the infinite at the same time.

Presiding over all these worlds is Prospero who is playwright, director, actor, and spectator of the entire action. He is surrounded by a spirit world which he conjures up at will. Omniscient, omnipotent, he is indeed the father of Paradise (IV, i, 123–124). His divine power has two aspects: one of harsh severity and the other of forgiveness and love. He asks Ferdinand whether he has "too austerely punish'd [him]" (IV, i, 1) and later comments that "the rarer action is/In virtue than in vengeance." (V, i, 27–28)

Prospero attributes the landing on the island to "Providence divine" (I, ii, 159) and in his role as teacher and director, he continues to work with the assumption that divine Providence rules all.[28] He instructs Ferdinand that

> All thy vexations
> Were but by trials of thy love, and thou
> Hast strangely stood the test. (IV, i, 5–7)

He presses Alonzo, Antonio, and Sebastian to see their true condition. Having recognized their plight, they make restitution. Most of all, he educates Caliban not only to hear the heavenly music of the spheres but also to follow a visionary ideal. Caliban, crude and earthy as he is, is now spouting forth effusive poetry:

> The isle is full of noises,
> Sounds and sweet airs that give delight and hurt not.
> Sometimes a thousand twangling instruments
> Will hum about mine ears; and sometime voices
> That, if I then had wak'd after long sleep,
> Will make me sleep again; and then, in dreaming,
> The clouds methought would open and show riches
> Ready to drop upon me, that, when I waked,
> I cried to dream again. (III, ii, 144–152)

Out of these reformative processes, Caliban confesses that he'll "be wise hereafter/And seek for grace." (V, i, 294–295) When Prospero works with others, he does not focus on their limitations, but on their possibilities.

But this very god-like power and status prompts the audience to question not only the reality of the man and his magic but also his motives. Are his great powers capable of great evil as well as great good? Although his name in English has nuances of victorious and flourishing, we should be aware that *prospero* is the Italian for *faustus*.[29] Who is the real Prospero? Is he a charlatan or a benevolent ruler who wishes to purge the island of evil? Until the very end of the play, Prospero's ambiguous role as necromancer or obedient servant of Providence is kept in tension.

It is through music, sleep, and dreams that all are transformed, having undergone "a sea-change." (I, ii, 400) From potential tragedy, the action of the play moves toward comedy. The harmony within nature is reflected in the love, acceptance, and forgiveness within the human world of Ferdinand and Miranda and even the grotesque world of Caliban. All the worlds of *The Tempest* have undergone an amazing metamorphosis: from jealousy to unity, from power to love, from war and rebellion to peace, all reflected in the change from tempest to calmness. Not only has Ariel and Caliban's slavery been changed to freedom, but each of the other characters (except Antonio) has also experienced a rebirth, as Ferdinand expresses it: ". . . of whom I have/Received a second life." (V, i, 194–195) The reigning elements of comedy—rejoicing, reconciliation, reunion, and resurrection (what was thought to be dead is alive)—are all part of Gonzalo's final commentary:

> O, rejoice
> Beyond a common joy, and set it down
> With gold on lasting pillars: in one voyage
> Did Claribel her husband find at Tunis,
> And Ferdinand her brother found a wife
> Where he himself was lost, Prospero his dukedom
> In a poor isle, and all of us ourselves
> When no man was his own. (V, i, 206–213)

Prospero, in contrast with most other protagonists in Shakespeare's plays, regains his dukedom. His inner journey is revealed most fully in the Epilogue but also in his well-known observations after the masque has concluded:

> Our revels now are ended. These our actors,
> As I foretold you, were all spirits and
> Are melted into air, into thin air;
> And, like the baseless fabric of this vision,
> The cloud-capp'd towers, the gorgeous palaces,

The solemn temples, the great globe itself,
Yea, all which it inherit, shall dissolve
And, like this insubstantial pageant faded,
Leave not a rack behind. We are such stuff
As dreams are made on, and our little life
Is rounded with a sleep. (IV, i, 148–158)

To interpret this passage as a cynical dismissal of life and a renunciation of imagination is to miss the obvious fact that Prospero himself confesses in the immediate lines following that he is "troubled" and speaks of his "weakness" and "infirmity" (IV, i, 158–160). Prospero's now realizes, as Thomas Van Laan has observed:

that just as the masque is an unsubstantial fiction in contrast to the higher reality of the actual life encompassing it, so also is this actual life itself a kind of unsubstantial fiction in contrast to the even higher reality that encompasses it . . . Our reality can legitimately be compared to the masque because it too is ultimately no more than a kind of 'pageant' or play, whose dramatist, since he must exist on a level of a reality higher than that of his play, can be identified as God.[30]

This experience is a foreshadowing of what Prospero explicitly acknowledges in the Epilogue, that he is merely and nevertheless, wholly human. The great dreamer is giving up the magic world and forswearing illusion. In theatrical terms, he is not the director nor playwright of his life or the life of others, but the actor who is requesting not applause, but prayer and mercy:

Now I want
Spirits to enforce, art to enchant,
And my ending is despair
Unless I be reliev'd by prayer,
Which pierces so that it assaults
Mercy itself and frees all faults,
As you from crimes would pardon'd be,
Let your indulgence set me free. (Epilogue, 13–20)

The use of explicit religious terms such as prayer, mercy, and indulgence points to the request as one of Christian charity, that is, love and forgiveness. He is imploring his audience to make his vision their own and in so doing, they will be participating in an act of prayer. Such acts will result in mercy and pardon. He challenges the audience to free themselves by freeing him, to be forgiven by forgiving him. The various images of the theater, which this play and many of Shakespeare's earlier plays had presented (mirror, diversion, dream), are overshadowed by the awareness that only prayer grants mercy and frees one from all faults.

Hamlet desires to become a playwright but is an actor trapped inside a tragedy. Prospero, the artist as theatrical magician, creates the play within himself, a dream-world. As Leslie Fiedler suggests, Prospero creates ". . . the brave new world in which love is a thing of innocence and law, and death is dead—in short, a new world for redeeming the Fall."[31]

The earth, the great globe itself as well as the little O, the Globe in London, may dissolve, but what is crucial is that true freedom lies in being related to one's Maker through prayer. Therein lies the divine comedy.

IV

The cosmic nature of Shakespeare's drama, as we have seen in *Hamlet* and *The Tempest*, manifests itself in at least two dimensions: the concentric and the linear. In the concentric sphere not only is the protagonist the microcosm of the universe, but also the action is all-encompassing. Human action ranges outward from the individual to a small group of intimates (for example, a court), to society, to the state, to the world and finally to a metaphysical or divine force beyond. The movement is from the sphere of internal struggle within to the public sphere of national and international affairs to the sphere of spiritual powers, and often coming full circle, for the inner conflict becomes identified with the cosmic and the infinite.

The complete range of human society—the noble and the lowborn, kings and fools—all are on Shakespeare's stage. Still more crucially, the whole spectrum of human experience—political, psychological, religious, and all else—is dramatized. If all the world's a stage, this microcosm only catches a small view, but it is representative of and symbolic of the whole of reality. Anything that takes place on stage in the little world of the play reflects the universe in which each creature has its ordered place.

Time in Shakespearean drama, presented as linear, also reveals the cosmic perspective. Scenes within the Elizabethan playhouse were presented as part of a continuum. A character or a group of characters enters the open stage as if on the way somewhere; they stop and converse or take an action and then move on.[32] Stroup accurately describes the effect:

> What the audience sees is really a parenthesis cut out of infinity . . . In one sense every scene is set within another, a part of an eternal continuum.[33]

While order and coherence are inherent in the theatrical metaphor, it would be unwise not to emphasize the openness and versatility present in the image. To perceive the world as stage is to become more and more self-conscious of multiple possibilities. Baroque music with its endless variations on a single theme parallels the development of Elizabethan drama. If the stage is a mirror and the world is a mirror of the stage, then the person offstage as well as onstage has both the freedom and the necessity to choose which roles to fill.

But the multiplicity of possibilities also raises at least two questions, questions which clearly have both dramatic and religious implications: Where is the true self? and still more fundamentally: What is real? For if all the men and women are merely players, who are they actually and is all action meaningless illusion?

The question for both the audience and the persons on stage and especially for the protagonist himself is: Which of all the selves I see myself playing is the true self? Dramatically, the phrase "to play the part" becomes the crucial decision. In comedy, this versatility shows itself in the disguises and ruses which lovers and their accomplices take on in order for true love to triumph. In tragedy, characters such as Edmund and Iago, as Barton notes, are "artists in deceit."[34] Through their play-acting, they blind others and accomplish their overthrow. In both the histories and the tragedies, the Player King is dominant; Henry IV, Richard III, Claudius, and Lear each suffer from a contradiction between true kingship and flawed leadership.

These themes are all interwoven in *Richard II* as the king attempts but does not succeed in comparing his prison to a world. He then says:

> Yet I'll hammer it out.
> My brain I'll prove the female to my soul,
> My soul the father; and these two beget
> A generation of still-breeding thoughts;
> And these same thoughts people this little world,
> In humours like the people of this world,
> For no thought is contented. (V, v, 5–11)

And a little later his world becomes a stage on which "Thus play I in one person many people/And none contented." (V, v, 31–32) Such attempts to discover the true self amid all the masks imposed by both self and others is part of the tragic self-destruction of many of Shakespeare's participants.

The process of questioning the possibility of a true self leads almost inevitably to the very basic question: What is real? Lear's perception of his world, for example, moves from that of tyrannical control of everyone at the beginning to his lonely mad world on the heath to a gentle and broken shell holding his dear Cordelia at the end. The question for Lear is: amid all turmoil, within and without, what is real?

The key term is, of course, illusion. Its etymology (*illudere*), that is, to mock, to play with, implies that supernatural forces as well as other persons may be deceiving the protagonist. And added to this is the protagonist's own distortion of reality. Through imagination, hallucination, and delusion which haunt the protagonist, he finds it impossible to know what is real. The tragic characters begin to ask: is it all a meaningless farce, a kind of game which the gods or God are playing? If we are merely players, are we only part of a puppet show?

The Renaissance theater by holding the mirror up to nature, by dramatizing the *theatrum mundi* metaphor, and by beginning to raise doubts about the nature of the self and of reality, nurtured the seeds which encouraged the modern theater to begin with the hypothesis: If the stage is all the world there is . . .

NOTES

1. Kent T. van den Berg, *Playhouse and Cosmos: Shakespearean Theater as Metaphor* (Newark: University of Delaware Press, 1985), 48–50.

2. van den Berg, 48.

3. Frances A. Yates, *Theater of the World* (Chicago: University of Chicago Press, 1967), 168.

4. See Harriett Bloker Hawkins, "'All the World's a Stage': Some Illustrations of the Theatrum Mundi," *Shakespeare Quarterly*, 3 (1966):174–78 for three examples of the pictorial image in writings of the 16th and 17th centuries.

5. Eric Auerbach, *Mimesis,* tr. Willard R. Trask (Princeton: Princeton University Press, 1953), 313.

6. Auerbach, 232.

7. See Thomas B. Stroup, *Microcosmos: The Shape of the Elizabethan Play* (Lexington: University of Kentucky Press, 1965) for a thorough survey of the image in both prose and poetry of the Renaissance.

8. Anne Barton in *Shakespeare and the Idea of the Play* (London: Chatto and Windus, 1962) traces these terms carefully through Shakespeare's drama, 81–6.

9. Yates, 189.

10. The terms "theatricality" or "metatheater" or "metadrama" have been variously employed. Several writers have focused primarily on Shakespeare: van den Berg, Barton, Stroup, James L. Calderwood, *Shakespearean Metadrama* (Minneapolis: University of Minnesota Press, 1971), Robert Egan, *Drama Within Drama: Shakespeare's Sense of His Art* (New York: Columbia University Press, 1975), Sidney Homan, *When the Theater Turns to Itself: The Aesthetic Metaphor in Shakespeare* (Lewisburg: Bucknell University Press, 1986), Jean E. Howard, *Shakespeare's Art of Orchestration* (Urbana: University of Illinois Press, 1984), and Thomas F. Van Laan, *Role-Playing in Shakespeare* (Toronto: University of Toronto Press, 1978). Other writers explore various periods of drama in the light of this image: Lionel Abel, *Metatheater: A New View of Dramatic Form* (New York: Hill and Wang, 1963), and Robert J. Nelson, *Play Within a Play* (New Haven: Yale University Press, 1958). I am indebted to each of these writers and have learned much from them.

11. William Hazlitt, *Characters of Shakespeare's Plays,* (1817).

12. Maynard Mack, "The World of Hamlet" in *Tragic Themes in Western Literature*, ed. Cleanth Brooks (New Haven: Yale University Press, 1955), 33–4.

13. Stroup, 100.

14. Mack perceptively explores these words in the play, 39–46.

15. Howard, 151.

16. Wendy Coppedge Sanford, *Theater as Metaphor in Hamlet* (Cambridge: Harvard University Press, 1967), 7.

17. Barton, 146.

18. Mack, 46.

19. Herbert R. Coursen, Jr., *Christian Ritual and the World of Shakespeare's Tragedies* (Lewisburg: Bucknell University Press, 1976), 120–121.

20. S. F. Johnson, "The Regeneration of Hamlet," *Shakespeare Quarterly*, 3, (1952), 206.

21. Quoted in Sanford, 21.

22. Thomas McFarland, *Tragic Meanings in Shakespeare* (New York: Random House, 1966), 23–24.

23. Harold Fisch, *Hamlet and the Word: The Covenant Pattern in Shakespeare* (New York: Frederick Unger Publishing Co., 1971), 163–164.

24. Charles K. Cannon, "As in a Theater: Hamlet in the Light of Calvin's Doctrine of Predestination," *Studies in English Literature*, 1500–1900, 11 (Spring 1971): 203–22, observes the pattern of circles within circles at this point in the play: "Horatio . . . speaks what sounds . . . like the prologue to a new play based upon the play about to continue . . . [T]his new play must conclude with another Hamlet's requesting another Horatio to tell his story, and on and on" 201.

25. Egan, 12.

26. Jan Kott, *Shakespeare Our Contemporary*, tr. Boleslaw Taborski (Garden City: Doubleday, 1966), 244.

27. Kott, 253.

28. One commentator (Fisch, 217–222) draws parallels between Prospero and the biblical Joseph, both of whom have been driven into exile by brothers and now rule over a strange land. Fisch also observes that *The Tempest* evokes the Garden of Eden, the story of the enmity between the brothers Cain and Abel and the account of the Flood.

29. Egan, 97.

30. Van Laan, 250.

31. Leslie A. Fiedler, "The Defense of the Illusion and the Creation of Myth," in *English Essays*, ed. D. H. Robertson, Jr. (New York: Columbia University Press, 1944), 94.

32. See Leslie Hotson, *Shakespeare's Wooden O* (London: Rupert Hart-David, 1959), chapter 3, for a full discussion of pageant in Shakespeare's day.

33. Stroup, 89.

34. Barton, 88.

Chapter Eleven

Modern Drama: If the Stage is All the World There Is

Down our streets is a building. We sit down in Row G, Seats 3 and 4, we are put in the dark, the curtain rises, and before us is the theater: an illumined box with objects in it, floating in the darkness.

The proscenium arch, the curtain, the fourth wall removed, and most of all, the experience of an audience being boxed inside in the same space as the action—these specific characteristics of the modern theater reflect the drama which is presented on the modern stage.

Already in 1798, Diderot, the influential French literary critic, was advising the dramatist and the actors:

> Think no more of the audience than if it had never existed. Imagine a huge wall across the front of the stage, separating you from the audience, and behave exactly as if the curtain had never risen.[1]

In the 19th century, Richard Wagner insisted that the house lights should be darkened (gaslights were first used in 1849) so that the audience's complete focus would be on the stage action. He also abolished box seats from which members of the audience had observed each other for three hundred years. Now every chair was turned toward the stage. His conception of the stage was that every aspect should be used to heighten the attention on what happens with the immediate confines of the stage.

The advertisement which Squire Bancroft used to describe the renovated Haymarket Theater in London in 1800 echoes this focus on the stage:

> A rich and elaborate gold border about 2 ft. broad, after the pattern of a picture-frame, is continued all round the proscenium, and carried even below the actors' feet—there can be no doubt the sense of illusion is increased.[2]

To look at a picture within a frame such as the proscenium stage is to encourage detachment, to observe the action with objectivity. The play becomes a little world that the audience is permitted to observe and to participate imaginatively through the willing suspension of disbelief. The action is set apart in a magic box and in another world, separated from the audience by a world of darkness.[3] Modern dramatists of the late 19th and early 20th century perceived the relationship of the stage to the world as a complete reversal of what the medieval audiences and Shakespeare drew from this image. The emphasis is on the here and the now, the immediate and the direct. The narrowed focus is on the finite space and on immediate time. The stage is all the world there is.

Medieval and Renaissance drama shared a common assumption, the presence of order, the belief that the universe has coherence. The medieval drama with its setting within the church and later in the streets reflected the conviction that the actions portrayed were part of a larger infinite cosmic structure. And the Elizabethan stage, as was noted in the previous chapter, with its metaphorical imagery of Heaven and Hell within the Globe, continued to assume that human action was located within the cosmic order.

More specifically, space, time, and action were totally unrestricted in medieval drama. Theatrical space was the whole cosmos, time all of salvation history, and action the relationship of God, human beings, angels and devils. By the very nature of its vastness, the medieval play was designed as larger than life or even nature; it was quintessentially non-representational and cosmic. The plays represent a continuity between a temporal world (ours) and a timeless world (God's), as V. A. Kolve describes this relationship:

> . . . time is displayed as an artifact shaped by God whose patterns express His eternal truth. Time concerns us because we are alive in it and because God's plan for man's redemption can be worked out only in its terms. But man's real business is eternity, and the drama exists to remind us of that.[4]

In the mystery, miracle, and morality plays, God's intervention in human history prompts men and women to respond to such divine action. The finite temporal human world therefore is subservient to the infinite timeless divine order.

Shakespeare affirmed both the divine and the human worlds and saw one as the reflection of the other. The temporal domain gains in importance in the Renaissance, and thus value is placed within the human world as well as within the divine order, as George Poulet suggests:

> Temporality then no longer appeared solely as the indelible mark of mortality; it appeared also as the theater and field of action where despite his mortality, man could reveal his authentic dignity and gain a personal immortality.[5]

Even though both Hamlet and Prospero affirm that they are within God's providence, what each does and how each decides to act makes all the difference. Divine guidance and human action are deliberately balanced within Shakespeare's vision. Given the religious and dramatic situation that all the world's a stage, the finite space of a theatrical stage is truly a microcosm of the fullness and richness of human existence.

Already in the late 17th and early 18th century, the religious and dramatic imagery is becoming more impersonal: deity as detached clockmaker now objectively observes his handiwork. Impersonal laws of nature are believed to govern human action. The theatrical counterpart is the comedy of manners, a drama which has its roots in the inflexible rigidity of the laws of society. The wearing of masks (hypocrisy) and the artificial conventions of society provide a stage of comic puppets and a plot of intricate entanglements. Only the occasional saucy servant of Moliere or the exuberant vitality of a character or two in Wycherley or Sheridan can break through the facade of this rigid world.

Meanwhile deity smiles benignly on all the hustle and bustle on the stage of the world. The actors are beginning to identify more and more with the role of godly spectator. We are looking at ourselves looking at ourselves.

This sense of self-consciousness is evident in a play as early as 1798, *Die Verkehrte Welt* by Ludwig Tieck. At the end of Act III, the following scene transpires:

Scavola.	Look, friends, here we sit as spectators and watch a play; spectators sit in that play and watch a play, and then yet another play is performed in this third play before those actors now thrice metamorphized.
Wachtel.	Just to put my mind at rest I'd gladly be an actor in that last comedy. The farther from the spectator, the better.
The other man.	Consider this, friends: maybe we ourselves are actors in some play, and someone else is watching this completely mixed-up stuff. Then we'd be the first play. Maybe this is the way the angels see us.[6]

What is happening is that the theater is assuming that its art is the art of illusion or pretending. In the modern theater no reality exists outside the confines of the stage. If the action on stage is not part of a larger whole as it was for the Greeks and the medieval and Elizabethan audiences, then to what may the dramatist look for ways to portray human action? If the stage is all the world there is, then what does the dramatist create in order for the audience to identify with the stage?

The dramatists of the late 19th and early 20th century pursued at least three directions on answering this question and the result is the great era of modern drama.

One direction, of course, is realism, that followed by Henrik Ibsen, the towering 19th century figure who is often called the father of modern drama. Ibsen wrote in a letter to a friend: "The illusion I wished to produce is that of reality. I wished to produce the impression on the reader that what he was reading had really happened."[7] Such a theater is set in the here and now; its living room looks as if it were located in a Norwegian house just down the road. The power lies in the immediacy and in the way the spectators identify themselves with the characters. If the art of theater is pretending, then we may, as Tom Driver notes, "compound the pretense basic to all theater by pretending that the pretense is not going on, which leads to realism."[8] If the stage is all the world there is, then according to realism, the stage will present a photograph of our visible and sensible world.

A second direction is expressionism which August Strindberg pursued with intensity and deep passion. As Strindberg described in his note to *A Dream Play*, "a single consciousness holds sway over them all [the characters in the play]."[9] Subjectivity is central; irrationality and madness reign supreme. The dark underside of life is exposed and the result is distortion and grotesqueness. If the stage is all the world there is, then according to expressionism, the stage will present a world of fantasy and dream, more likely nightmare.

The final direction is theatricalism which Luigi Pirandello explored with dazzling creativity. Earlier dramatists had employed the metaphor of this theatrical image, but Pirandello pressed the image of forcing the audience to ask not only "Where is the real self?" but "Is there a real self?" In his introduction to *Six Characters in Search of an Author*, Pirandello expressed a credo appropriate for all his plays:

> . . . And so let them go where dramatic characters do go to have life: on a stage. And let us see what will happen. That's what I did. And, naturally, the result was what it had to be: a mixture of tragic and comic, fantastic and realistic, in a humorous situation that was quite new and infinitely complex, a drama which is conveyed by means of the characters, who carry it within them and suffer it, a drama, breathing, speaking, self-propelled, which seeks at all costs to find the means of its own presentation; and the comedy of the vain attempt at an improvised realization of the drama on stage.[10]

Pirandello made theater out of the dramatic process itself; he created drama out of the very elements of theater: mask, role, costume, plot, and all the rest. The strategy was to employ deliberate use of specifically theatrical technique. If the stage is all the world there is, then according to theatricalism, the stage will present multiple worlds, all flowing from self-reflection.

Each of these three directions will now be probed more fully, both by describing the theatrical style and by looking closely at a specific play by each of the three dramatists.

I

In Ibsen's notes about his great play, *Ghosts* (1881), the first sentence states: "The play is to be like a picture of life."[11] Such a credo implies that value and significance are to be found within the visible world. Thus Ibsen's plays were appropriately placed within the proscenium stage as if one were viewing a picture within a frame. Since the audience was completely screened off from the play by "the fourth wall," the actors faced upstage whenever they wished, and no actor took any notice of the audience.

Soliloquies, monologues, and asides were clearly unsuited to the new staging, and in the name of realism, Ibsen and his fellow realists in the latter half of the 19th century did not employ such devices. Such conventions not only were inappropriate on the realistic and naturalistic stages but still more, their absence indicated a widening gap between actors and audience, for such devices imply a complicity between actor and audience in the pleasure of putting on a play. The aside and soliloquy serve the purpose of sharing with the spectators what is transpiring within the character. The devices therefore engage the audience directly; they ask the audience to agree or disagree; they remind both actors and audience that a play is in progress. In the 19th century, the actors stay within the proscenium frame and do not violate the boundary between themselves and the audience.William Archer, the influential dramatic critic of the turn of the century, describes the change in detail:

> Take, for instance, the soliloquy and the aside: When an actor, in a huge theater, entered between a pair of profile wings, or through a canvas door with no handle, into a room with a window and three chairs painted on the back cloth, and proceeded to walk right out of this primitive scene to a spot on the projecting "apros," so far forward that the occupants of the stage-boxes had a full view of his back, the thing was from the outset so absolutely unreal and conventional that no further convention could trouble or shock the audience . . . But when a man enters a room absolutely indistinguishable in proportions, fittings and furniture from the rooms which the audience inhabit every day, the case is at once altered . . . If a gentleman enters this room, advances to the footlights, and proceeds to talk to himself, kindly expounding to himself his own character, motives and situation, our instincts at once cry out against the absurdity — the intrusion of the conventional into the real, or, if you prefer it, the clash of two different conventions.[12]

Thus the audience only eavesdrops on the action on stage.

Ibsen's plays concentrate on the here and now. All action is confined to the interior of the house, and in *Ghosts*, to one room. This enclosed "garden room," the illusion of an outdoors indoors, becomes a trap which compresses the actions and crushes all who enter it.

Although an action such as the burning of the orphanage takes place off-stage, the center of attention is the single room in which everyone meets and all encounters and conflicts take place. Within this limited space, all that is significant will take place, for as any realist affirms, one finds the great within the small. Tragedy in this perspective can and does happen not only within the palaces and courts of the noble and the aristocratic, but also within the living rooms of the middle class.

Not only the setting, but also the language deliberately emphasizes the attempt to capture the real. In the same letter to Edmund Gosse cited earlier, Ibsen insisted that not only "the illusion [he] wished to produce was that of reality," but he also goes on to write about his choice of language: "What I desired to depict were human beings, and therefore I would not make them talk the language of the gods."[13] Although Ibsen experimented with verse at times in his artistic career, the major plays—*Brand* (1866), *Peer Gynt* (1867), *A Doll's House* (1873), *Ghosts* (1881), *An Enemy of the People* (1882), *The Wild Duck* (1884), *Rosmersholm* (1886), and *Hedda Gabler* (1890)—are all written in prose. Though Ibsen wished to avoid verse as well as elevated affectation, his prose is not that of tape-recorder flatness. It is prose, but not at all prosaic. Rather, the language has psychological density, and is composed of a mesh of implications, hints, cross references, silences, and guarded metaphors. Ibsen, along with Chekhov, made the term "subtext" meaningful to modern readers and viewers.

Contemporary subject matter dominates Ibsen's plays. He wrestled with many socio-ethical issues: euthanasia, syphilis, illegitimacy, and feminism. The plays were about what was actually going on in the world, not historical subjects or narratives of ideal deeds. The large intellectual forces of the late nineteenth century—Marx with the struggles of classes, Freud with our roiling inner desires and most of all, Darwin with the survival of the fit and the importance of heredity and environment—this was the air Ibsen breathed.

The detached scientific perspective encouraged artists to present as empirical a representation of reality as was possible. The horizontal relationship between the individual and society and between human beings and nature determined the action, not the relation of Fate or God or other transcendental powers. To define the real as only that which is visible, as the modern stage did, is to drastically transform the scope of the dramatic action. Anything which is transcendental or supernatural such as the gods in Greek drama and Providence in Shakespeare is by definition not part of the world of the play. Thus symbols such as a wild duck or a cherry orchard or demons or ghosts become the means to convey the larger dimensions of the action.

Realism symbolizes, as Driver suggests, "the latent intention of all modern drama," an intention he identifies as "a quest for reality."[14] When this quest

involved controversial social issues, as it did for Ibsen, these new topics in-
cited many critics and members of the audience to charge that the theater had
become little better than a sewer. Copies of *Ghosts* sold so badly that whole
bales of it were returned to the publisher. No acting company in Scandinavia
dared to perform it.[15] The *Norse Morgenbladet* described Ibsen as "a fallen
star," buried in "the black abyss where dwell horrors and poison, worms and
vermin."[16]

The English were even more vindictive when the play was performed in
London in 1891: "Scandinavian humbug," "Ibsen's putrid play," "as foul
and filthy a concoction as has ever been allowed to disgrace the boards of
an English theater."[17] Clement Scott wrote in *The Daily Telegraph*: ". . . this
so-called master . . . seems, to our judgment, to resemble one of his own
Norwegian ravens emerging from the rocks with an insatiable appetite for
decayed flesh."[18] Others compared *Ghosts* to "an open drain; a loathsome
sore unbandaged; a dirty act done publicly; a lazar-house with all its doors
and windows open."[19]

To such charges of immorality and decadence, Ibsen replied that the plays,
as truthful depictions of life, were moral since truth is the highest form of morality, and that to present an idealized picture of life would be to avoid truth
and to become truly immoral. Furthermore, if viewers rejected the picture of
the human condition presented on stage, they should employ their energy to
change the society around them rather than to denounce the dramatist. What
Ibsen set forth, according to Robert Brustein, was a "Theater of Revolt"
which repudiates the "subjective heroic mode . . . The action itself is a form of
rebellion, being an assault on the abuses of the time."[20] Ibsen himself insisted
he employed such themes not simply to document the surfaces of dramatic
life but to penetrate them. Later, he wrote, "Zola descends to bathe into the
sewer, I, to cleanse it."[21] He employs the same image of cleansing in a letter
written during the composition of *Ghosts*:

> The work of writing this play has been to me like a bath which I have felt to
> leave cleaner, healthier, and freer. Who is the man among us who has not now
> and then felt and acknowledged within himself a contradiction between word
> and action, between will and task, between life and teaching on the whole?[22]

This contradiction between word and action, the presence of hypocrisy, is
one of the major themes in Ibsen's drama. *Ghosts* underlines this motif with
its revelations and secrets, with suppression of truth, with its life-lies[23] which
are unmasked. The past therefore haunts Ibsen's plays. Out of the struggle
either to bury the past or escape into it frequently comes a sacrificial death.
If one has found no meaningful way to live, then the ritual of dying may
give significance to the present. Or, is the act of dying another false game of

illusion rather than a meaningful sacrificial ritual? Ibsen in his major plays, including *Ghosts*, leaves this question ambiguously open at the conclusion of his drama.

The title of *Ghosts* itself, linguistic scholars observe, points directly to the presence of death and the dead. *Ghosts*, states F. L. Lucas, "is not quite an adequate rendering of the *Norse Gengangere* 'those who gang again,' 'the dead who walk,' . . . 'the dead who return.'" Lucas adds they are "phantoms that walk our earth and haunt the living."[24] In *Ghosts*, the primary action consists of a desperate but futile attempt (by means of a monument to the dead) to keep the dead buried in their graves.

But the ghost of Captain Alving will continue to haunt the family, not only in the secrets uncovered by his wife and Pastor Manders, but also in the heredity of his son Oswald and Alving's illegitimate daughter, Regine. Each of these two offsprings' weaknesses and strengths is appropriate, as Brian Johnson writes: "Regine healthy in body but disastrously lacking in mind, Oswald intellectually creative but crippled physically . . ."[25] The house of the Alvings is a fallen and infected house.

Mrs. Alving's one-word utterance "Ghosts"[26] at the end of Act I is her acknowledgement that what she had experienced earlier when her husband had his love affair with the maid (the offspring of which is Regine, their current servant), is being repeated in Oswald's seduction in the next room. The often-quoted passage at the opening of Act II elaborates Mrs. Alving's fears:

Mrs. Alving:	You have to understand what I mean by that. I'm anxious and fearful because of the ghosts that haunt me, that I can't get rid of.
Manders:	Because—what did you say?
Mrs. Alving:	Ghosts. When I heard Regina and Oswald in there, it was as if I was seeing ghosts. But I almost believe we are ghosts, all of us, Pastor. It's not only what we inherit from our father and mothers that keeps on returning in us; but they hang on all the same, and we can't get rid of them. I just have to pick up a newspaper, and it's as if I could see the ghosts slipping between the lines. They must be haunting our whole country, ghosts everywhere—so many and thick, they're like grains of sand. And there we are, the lot of us, so miserable afraid of the lights. (p. 236)

A few moments later, she adds:"I go around here struggling with ghosts, inside and outside both." (p. 239)

Thus the symbolic title possesses several dimensions: (1) biological: the genetic disease now present in Oswald; (2) psychological: the sexual desires passed on from parents to children ("the sins of the fathers are visited up the children"(p.250); (3) intellectual: the specters of belief which continue to prevail long after they have lost their meaning; and (4) spiritual: the spirits of the dead inhabit the bodies of the living, controlling their future. The play centers not only on the external manifestation of an evil heritage but still more, on the struggle with ghosts within.[27]

In the presence of such fears and doubts, the great human dilemma is overwhelming guilt. How can one escape the ghosts, within and without, which bring guilt?

To expiate her sin and guilt, Mrs. Alving will pour her energy into the memorial to her husband. From this fallen and infected house will now come another house, an orphanage. But when the orphanage burns, Captain Alving's home will now be perpetuated in another house, Engstrand's brothel, an appropriate inheritance from this family of entangled culpability.

This conflict between guilt and the joy of life (*livsgeden*[28]) finds its parallel in the play's imagery of light and darkness. The ghosts cannot stand the light and in this setting of a gloomy landscape streaming with rain, they obviously flourish. Light is what is needed to expose the truth, but it does not prevail. The two catastrophes are both instances of too much light: the burning of the orphanage and Oswald's pathetically mad request to his mother at the end of the play: "Mother, give me the sun."(p. 275) But even the source of light cannot pierce the darkness which overwhelms this house.

The plot of the play, therefore, as with many other dramas of Ibsen, is essentially a gradual exhuming of the buried past. Like the families in Greek drama, a net of past evil encompasses all.

Several critics have observed the Greek quality of *Ghosts*. Almost as soon as the work appeared, the classical Danish scholar P.O. Schjott saw in the play a modern version of the heredity curse of Greek drama.[29] G. Wilson Knight has suggested that the heritage of guilt in *Ghosts* "is like the curse on the house of Atreus in the *Oresteia* . . ."[30] The entire work, insists Francis Fergusson, is constructed on the pattern of *Oedipus*, beginning at a point just before the catastrophe, proceeding like a detective story by digging up the past, and spiralling toward a terrible and inevitable conclusion.[31] Finally, several parallels between *Ghosts* and *The Bacchae* (see Part Three, Chapter 1) are striking. In Euripides' play, the god of wine and joy-of-life, Dionysus, revenges himself upon the family that attempts to deny his divinity. As the play ends, Agave is confronted by the mutilated body of her own son whom she had killed—a terrible testimony to the power of the god she had offended. In *Ghosts*, Mrs. Alving has set herself against the force of the joy-of-life and has constructed a triumphant lie to overcome this force. *Ghosts* ends with the mother confronting the wreckage of the son whom her crime helped to destroy.

Throughout the play therefore the Greek sense of inevitability haunts the action. The uncertain present of Act I leads to the ghostly revelation of the past in Act II. Only a hopeless future faces not only Oswald but also his mother at the conclusion of Act III. Too late—always the sign of tragedy—Mrs. Alving has recognized that she has listened to Pastor Manders in choices in which she did not really believe and that she has followed the strict conformity of society with its stern call to Duty. Such falsity blinded her to the realization that her husband had truly incarnated the joy-of-life. She now experiences deep love for him, but she has already destroyed him. The *Moment*, what commentators associate with Soren Kierkegaard, *Oieblikket*, is now before Mrs. Alving. One critic observes:

> The consideration is that *Oieblikket* (the *Moment*) or a refracted image thereof is the tour de force of an Ibsen play. It is the heart of the play. Crisis and/or climax, terms often used to describe the most intense part of a play, are not sufficient to describe the condition of the *Moment* because they lack the significance of the individual existential act. With the category of the *Moment*, the choice, the leap, and repetition are brought into perspective . . . This little *Moment*, brief as it is, is the action that unties the knot. It is the leap, because existential choice is the leap . . . Only by leaping across the chasm through the leap of faith (by virtue of the absurd) can the *Moment* be had.[32]

Mrs. Alving is now confronted with the choice of whether to aid her son to live or to die. The situation is hideously ironic for Oswald now asks his mother to do consciously what she unconsciously has done to his father—destroy him. But we know there is really no choice. Oswald is already, as he described himself earlier in the play, "It's like a living death;" (p. 249) he is the ghost of his former self. There is no escape for either Oswald or his mother. All have lived a lie. Ghosts, as they do in *Hamlet*, may come from a supernatural world, but Ibsen's ghosts are creations of human making. No external force can or will save the Alving house. Their actions, set in place by past decisions, are limited to the here and now. Ibsen's stage of realism is all the world there is.

II

Words for August Strindberg were means to create and to exorcise. And he wrote many; the standard collected edition of his works in Swedish has fifty-five volumes in addition to a dozen volumes of letters. During his prolific lifetime, he wrote fifty-eight plays and fifteen novels as well as three volumes of poetry and over a thousand short fictional pieces and essays.

Almost every new play was another experience, a search to find the appropriate focus and style for his artistic vision. He experimented with poetic plays, naturalistic tragedies, boulevard comedies, fairy plays, historical chronicles, and in his later years, chamber plays in sonata form.

No matter what the particular mode, however, his literary work is highly autobiographical. As Robert Brustein comments:

> More than any other dramatist who ever lived, Strindberg writes himself, and the self he continually exposes is that of alienated modern man, crawling between heaven and earth, desperately trying to pluck some absolutes from a forsaken universe.[33]

Every work Strindberg wrote was rooted in an intensely personal experience: his constant need for money, his marital difficulties, and particularly his highly ambivalent attitude toward women. Therefore, it is not uncoincidental that the epitome of Strindberg's writing and that for which his literary reputation and influence have been most important are his expressionistic dream plays. If Ibsen's characters are known for their self-revelation and Pirandello's for their self-reflection, Strindberg's people on stage are obsessed, as their creator was, by self-expression.

The term "expressionism" is almost as elusive as romanticism. Strindberg probably never heard the term used, for it was first employed to describe European painters at the turn of the century who were taking new directions in the graphic arts.[34] In the decade 1910–1920, a number of German dramatists—Paul Kornfeld, George Kaiser, Franz Werfel, and Ernst Toller—permeated with a spirit of radicalism were placed under the umbrella term of expressionism.

What the theorists described was what Strindberg had already created in his drama. Thus historians of aesthetics saw Strindberg as the precursor of this movement in the arts.

Expressionism centers on inner experience and gives it objective form in art. It emphasizes feelings, not the object. Truth is primarily subjective based on intuition. The expressionist artist therefore turns into the self, turns the gaze within the ego. Two particularly rich terms in German, the *Ausstrahlungen des Ich*[35] (the radiation, expression, and unfolding of the ego) and *Einfühlung*[36] (literally, one-feeling) catch the nuances of expressionism.

The external world in such a perspective is presented as if by a dream: episodic, fragmented, with fluid space and fractured time. The logic of the play is the logic of a dream state, an irrational world. Expressionism objectifies a state of mind and presents the experience of the inner anguish of its creator.

Strindberg wished to lead his audiences beyond the surface appearances, as he himself notes: "I struggle upwards but go downwards."[37] Believing the naturalist's commitment to externals was false to inner truth, the expressionist sought to express the ecstasy, pathos and terror that exist on the underside of reality. Strindberg discovered that the form of dreams was the one form capable of adequately expressing both his own concerns and those of his audience.

If human motivations are located within emotional depths, then the dramatist must probe and present the subconscious and the unconscious. If we are torn inside by irreversible impulses and are victims of deep conflicts and desires, then the Dionysian path rather than the Apollonian way will be the one to follow.[38] Such a world of madness will possess dissonance, distortion, and the demonic.

The result will be drama with little or no plot, but rather a mosaic-like blend of dream images. Stage design and lighting will be exploited to present a distorted stage which mirrors the troubled, even unbalanced, perspective of the characters.

Since a basic failing of traditional theater, according to Strindberg, is its commitment to consistent characterization, the expressionist presents persons who engage in contradictory behavior and sometimes speak incoherently. Instead of focusing on the individual who possesses a proper name, the characters are identified only as the Schoolmaster, the Gentleman, the Poet. Such use of the generic, the abstract, the allegorical, the symbolic indicates, according to Maurice Gravier, "a quest for the common substratum of all humanity. [Such expressionists] want to probe to the very roots of existence; they thirst for the absolute."[39]

Strindberg attempted to portray characters who reveal both the human idiosyncrasies and contradictory impulses as well as the universal characteristics of humankind. Such a quest reflects Strindberg's own life in which he was aware of the tempestuous uniqueness of his experience but at the same time believed that his inner history was the reservoir out of which art is to be created. Thus Strindberg was always seeking the form which would allow the maximum opportunity to objectify inner experience.

Yet it must be insisted that although all art is subjective, there is a profound difference between the creative ego that expands and seizes upon the given order of its cultural world and the ego through which the debris of a cultural chaos is filtered. Before the 19th century, the cultural world was still sufficiently intact that the artist could assume a direct and recognizable relationship between the external world and human innermost motivations and feelings. The nineteenth century believed that human nature is so fluid that hidden impulses and duties cannot be controlled. The cultural world became progressively so disorganized that the artist felt deep estrangement and could not affirm that coherence exists within a larger cosmic whole. The artist was forced to create his own universe and the expressionist looked within to do this task. Strindberg's credo is clear:

> . . . it seems to me that the psychological process is what interests people most today. Our inquisitive souls are no longer satisfied with seeing a thing happen; we must also know how it happens. We want to see the wires themselves, to watch the machinery, to examine the box with the false bottom, to take hold of the magic ring in order to find the join, and look at the cards to see how they are marked.[40]

The image of careful observation of the wires, the machinery and all the rest is an accurate description of Strindberg's dramatic approach in his expressionistic plays. When Strindberg looked within, having been immersed in rigid religious beliefs earlier in his life, to no one's surprise, he recognized that one of the major occupants of his inner life was guilt. The exploration of *A Dream Play* illustrates what powerful theater Strindberg created from the texture of his inner self in relation to the inner lives of the people on his stage. For, in Strindberg's theater, the interior life is all the stage there is.

A Dream Play which Strindberg wrote in 1901–02 has been both damned ("utterly incoherent")[41] and praised ("there is nothing in the modern theater to surpass it"[42]). Strindberg himself revealed his own ambivalence when he described the play as his "most beloved dream, the child of my greatest pain."[43]

The pain presumably reflected Strindberg's own life, for several commentators[44] have traced the many autobiographical elements in the drama, especially the dramatist's love-hate relationship with his third wife, Harriet Bosse. Strindberg's attachment to the play was rooted in the same source, for here again life and art were inextricably intertwined.

The author's famous note to the play, written several years after the drama was completed, has created as many difficulties as it has provided insight into the play. Strindberg wrote that he had

> sought to reproduce the disconnected but apparently logical form of a dream. Anything can happen; everything is possible and probable. Time and space do not exist; on a slight groundwork of reality, imagination spins and weaves new patterns made up of memories, experiences, unfettered fancies, absurdities, and improvisations. The characters are split, double, and multiply; they evaporate, crystallize, scatter, and converge. But a single consciousness holds sway over them all—that of the dreamer.[45]

The seemingly simple question: "Who is the dreamer?" has provoked a host of different responses from commentators; the student, the Daughter of Indra, and the Poet[46] have all been cited. Where readers do converge is that one's experience of entering the play is that of sinking into a dream. A series of vignettes loosely related bring us scenes as strange as a castle which bursts into a huge chrysanthemum and an organ which metamorphizes into a grotto. The characters in the play also have almost no individuality. They are identified only by sex, professional, family, or social status: the Father, the Glazier, the Teacher. All glide like figures in a vision. The Officer shades into the Lawyer who in turn changes into the Poet. For the expressionist, reality cannot be apprehended except as distortion. Dream and nightmare, exaggeration and hallucination therefore are the appropriate modes for presenting human existence.

Walter Sokel perceptively notes that the Expressionist dramatist and the dreamer have much in common for both

> concentrate entirely on the purpose of expressing an inner world and refuses to let conformity to external reality divert him from his purpose . . .The scenery of the Expressionist stage changes with the psychic forces whirling about in it . . . .Landscapes reflect the emotional situation of the characters . . . the entire stage becomes a universe of mind, and the individual scenes are not replicas of three-dimensional physical reality, but visualized stages of thought.[47]

Although one could quibble with the phrase "stages of thought" (the phrase seems alien to Strindberg's art), the centrality of the visual is absolutely accurate. The text on the page never adequately represents a dramatist's vision; in this play, from its opening to its strange ending, the eye and the imagination are crucial.

The scenic description of the Prologue indicates that the play begins not on earth but somewhere above it:

> Cloud formations resembling castles and citadels in ruins on crumbling slate hills form the backdrop.
>   The constellations Leo, Virgo and Libra can be seen and among them is the planet Jupiter shining brightly. INDRA'S DAUGHTER is standing in the uppermost cloud.[48]

This perspective of outside the earth does not provide a cosmic view of all the subsequent action as, for example, the appearance of the Ghost at the opening of *Hamlet* prefigures the presence of the supernatural throughout the play. Rather, as Indra's daughter descends to the earth, she sinks into the slough of human existence, achieving complete incarnation as a human being. This existence, she and we soon discover, is an illusion.

The pivotal scene is the gathering of the Chancellor and the Deans of Theology, Philosophy, Medicine and Law who are present to open a door. The door is both a door to the Opera House[49] and a symbolic door which will reveal, as the Dean of Theology states, "the solution of the riddle of the universe." Finally the door is opened and what is concealed behind the door? "Nothing." (p. 78)

In the midst of such disillusionment, how can the mystery of suffering be faced? Is the suffering a punishment for past deeds? The conversation of the Daughter and the Lawyer supports such an explanation:

DAUGHTER   Aren't there any pleasant duties?

LAWYER   They become pleasant when they're fulfilled . . .

DAUGHTER   When they don't exist any more . . . So duty is everything unpleasant! What's pleasant, then?

LAWYER   What's pleasant is sin.

DAUGHTER   Sin?

LAWYER   Which is to be punished, yes! If I've had a pleasant day and evening, I have the pangs of hell and a bad conscience the next day. (p. 61)

With such pervasive guilt, the refrain of the play "Human beings are to be pitied" is most appropriate. The play's characters are constantly torn between the craving for joy which enslaves them and the desire for suffering which liberates them.

"We begin," writes Austin Quigley about *A Dream Play*, "by seeking to see and understand the play in terms of our world, our inherited assumptions, but we end by seeing our world in terms that the play provides."[50] Having experienced the world of this play, as if sinking into a dream, we now awaken. But what was seen and felt and heard on Strindberg's stage has permeated us.

Anthony Abbot accurately points out "the deepest meaning" of the title: "It is this life that is the dream, and the dream may be pierced only by suffering."[51] In this play, according to John Peter, "Strindberg has created a world which is not only wretched but also beyond redemption; its inhabitants suffering constantly and its creator is absent."[52]

As the Daughter prepares to leave the earth, she describes the life of suffering here below:

So the halves of the heart are torn apart,
And feelings are torn as between horses
By contradiction, indecision, disharmony . . . (pp.85–86)

This stage of suffering, Strindberg implies, is all the world there is.

III

Luigi Pirandello wrote many volumes of poetry as well as many works of fiction, but drama provided him with a literary genre which combined the fixed and the ordered with the improvisational and the spontaneous. Fascinated by the multilayered nature of theater, Pirandello played with the paradoxes the genre offers. A play is a fixed work of art brought to life by human beings who assume roles. Although the script is set, the process of presenting the play is never exactly the same. Drama moves and is fixed. This relationship between theater and life is the very stuff out of which Pirandello forged his art, for life and art can join and engage in counterpoint in the interplay between text, audience, and stage.

The self-reflective and uncertain hold on truth and reality is illustrated by the titles of many of Pirandello's plays: *Cosí é (se vi pare)*, *Right You Are (If You Think So)*; *Ciascuno a suo modo (Each In His Own Way)*; and *Sogno, ma forse no (A Dream But Perhaps It Isn't)*. The audience is confronted in each of his plays with a multitude of possibilities. No absolute certainty can be established because life is change, change in the observer as well as the observed; there can never be any fixed truth.

No Pirandello play reflects this paradox more fully than *Enrico IV (Henry IV)* written in 1922. The well-known drama just preceding this play, *Six Characters in Search of An Author*, explored the image of life as theater and *Henry IV* developed the metaphor in still greater force and richness.

The action of the play takes place in several different times and places. The curtain opens in the court of the German Emperor Henry IV in the 11th Century, the Henry known in history for his excommunication by Pope Gregory VII and being forced to walk barefoot to Canossa to do penance. Several of the king's counselors are instructing a new recruit when suddenly one of them lights a cigarette. We are jolted into the present and our experience with this hall of mirrors has begun.

Gradually, it is revealed that the whole villa is an elaborate stage set, constructed for the benefit of an Italian nobleman who remains nameless. He begins and ends the play as Henry; he has no other identity. Some twenty years earlier, the nobleman on his way to a masquerade ball costumed as the medieval emperor fell from his horse and was knocked unconscious. Later, we discover that the accident was caused by his rival, Belcredi. Upon gaining consciousness in his psychotic state, he believed himself to be Henry IV; the masquerade had become his reality. "I shall never forget that scene," recalls his former mistress, Donna Matilda, "all our masked faces hideous and gazing at him, at that terrible mask of his face, which was no longer a mask, but madness, madness personified!"[53] His sister decided not to institutionalize him, but to sequester him in a villa where his entire surroundings, both place and persons, reproduced the medieval court. Thus the opening scene is one of actors playing young men who are playing valets for a player king.

A group of acquaintances, including Belcredi, costumed in medieval clothes, come to visit to attempt to cure Henry of his madness. A doctor, comparing Henry to a watch that has stopped at a certain hour, decides to get the mechanism going again through a violent trick. A young man will be costumed as the young Henry, and the daughter of his lover of twenty years ago, who is a striking image of her mother, will put on the dress her mother had worn to the masquerade ball. Both will take the place of life-size portraits in the throne room and stand within the portrait frames. As the young girl calls to Henry, her mother will appear and Henry confronted with his love as she was then and as she is now will realize (according to the doctor) that twenty years have passed and return to his senses.

Meanwhile, Henry confesses to us and to his courtiers that eight years ago, his sanity returned. But he adds that he made a conscious decision to continue to play his role and to maintain his mask. Only as Henry IV can he defeat time and live with intensity. As Robert Brustein comments, "The actor had turned madman; now the madman would turn actor, in revolt against existence itself."[54]

In Act III, the *coup* prepared by the guests takes place; the young girl calls to Henry as he enters the hall. The effect on Henry is that of absolute terror. At first he leaps back, his entire body trembling, but when the others enter the hall, he sees with rage that all has been a trick. He now shares with his guests that for the last eight years, he has lived ". . . with the most lucid consciousness . . ." for as he states: ". . . I can act with the madman to perfection . . ."(pp. 204, 205) Suddenly, he, ". . . laughing like a madman . . ." (p. 207) seizes the daughter. When Belcredi rushes at him, Henry strikes Belcredi, mortally wounding him. While the others shout, "He's mad, mad," Belcredi protests, "He's not mad." Henry, as the stage directions indicate, "terrified by the life of his own masquerade which has driven him to crime," ends the play: ". . . here we are . . . together . . . for ever!" (p. 208)

He will now keep the mad mask forever. As he stepped out of his role for a moment in order to gain revenge, he is forced back into it permanently. Committing an act which can only be justified within the former masquerade, he now will never be able to take off his costume. The bitter irony is that his action has proved his madness.

But persisting questions are: When is Henry mad and when is he not? Is not the decision to continue the masquerade one of a distorted mind? Is it sane to make a conscious acceptance of illusion? Further, as Eric Bentley asks: "On whose authority do we have it that the nameless one was ever cured?"

Bentley's accurate answer: "Only his own."[55] Other questions rise. Is it not a mark of a disordered personality to kill someone in revenge? And most of all, what kind of madness is it to make a decision to be a play-actor for all of one's life? The more he insists on his sanity, the more it appears he is mad.

The very structure of the drama, plays within plays, intensifies the audience's uncertainty of what is actual and what is illusory. A man plays Henry IV within a play. A cast of characters around him plays the part with him. Another play may be within the other; Henry states that he is aware of playing the role of the king.

What is the only difference between Henry and his friends? Henry wears his mask, and insists he is always consciously aware of the mask. His mask, he states, is not a mask to himself. Henry was content in his role as Holy Roman Emperor until they come to cure him. He explains to them that he is already cured, "because I can act the madman to perfection here, and I try to do it very quietly. I'm only sorry for you that you have to love your madness so agitatedly, without knowing it or seeing it." (pp. 205–206)

Earlier in the play Henry alludes to the masks of others, particularly his lover. He asks her if she has ever found ". . . a different self in yourself? Have you always been the same?" (p.169) Throughout the play, Pirandello asks the audience: Is it not true that we have a different face for each person that we meet? Henry tells us, "But we, all of us, cling tight to our conceptions of ourselves, just as he who is growing old dyes his hair." (p. 169)

This image, the dying of hair to make one appear young, reflects the understanding of humor which Pirandello dramatized in his plays and described in his long essay, *L'umorismo*. He asks us to imagine an elderly lady toward whom we might feel an immediate inclination to be sympathetic. But, then, he asks us also to imagine her as overdressed, with a heavily painted face and hair dyed like a girl's. Of course, he adds, we shall find such a figure to be funny, and we will be ready to laugh. Yet, says Pirandello, suppose she is aware of the figure she is cutting, and is behaving in this way in order to hold the affections of her husband; then we shall be sobered. Again the old woman will strike us as pathetic, and, paradoxically, the comic will appear to be no laughing matter at all.[56] The appropriate response is pain "where every feeling, every thought, every impulse which arises in the humorist unfolds itself in its opposite: every yes into a no, which eventually comes to acquire the same value as the yes."[57] Or, in more theatrical terms, Pirandello describes the human situation:

I see, as it were, a labyrinth where our soul wanders through countless, conflicting paths, without ever finding a way out. In this labyrinth I see a two-headed Hermes which with one face laughs and with the other weeps; it laughs with one face at the other face's weeping.[58]

Henry IV is a *scena delle beffe*, a play of jokes.[59] Pirandello asserted that contradictions and opposition pervade both life and art. Comedy and tragedy are inherent in any one experience. Only humor perceives the tragic within the comic, the comic within the tragic.

The humorist, according to Pirandello, perceives the false nature of who and what we are:

> Let us begin with the construction that illusion builds for each of us, that is, the construction that each of us makes of himself through the work of illusion. Do we see ourselves in our true and genuine reality, as we really are, or rather as what we should like to be? By means of a spontaneous internal device, a product of secret tendencies and unconscious imitation, do we not in good faith believe ourselves to be different from what we essentially are? And we think, act, and live according to this fictitious, and yet sincere, interpretation of ourselves.[60]

Thus Pirandello understands the human self not as a static and fixed reality, but as fluid and relative, what Joseph Wood Krutch calls "the dissolution of the ego."[61] "What," comments Krutch, Pirandello seems to ask, "can a 'self' be except what it is being from moment to moment?"[62]

In the midst of such flux, what human beings do is to create their own reality, to construct the inner and outer world in such ways that each of us can bear the pain and suffering. But Pirandello warns us of the difficulty:

> I think that life is a sad piece of buffoonery; because we have in ourselves, without being able to know why . . . the need to deceive ourselves constantly by creating a reality (one for each and never the same for all) which, from time to time, is discovered to be vain and illusory . . . .[63]

Such are the dilemmas of Henry IV, for each person's illusions become one's reality. As Thomas Bishop states:

> The historically accurate surroundings in which [Henry] is placed are illusion, because they are contrived. And yet for Enrico they are the only reality for twelve years of delusion—so real in fact that, when he regained his senses, the illusion became reality, and reality mere illusion, because the outside world had lost all meaning for him.[64]

The result of creating one's reality through what the mind believes may well be madness.

The image is one of all of us wearing masks at a masquerade in a hall of mirrors.[65] *Maschere nude*—naked masks—Pirandello called the collected edition of his plays. *Maschere* in Italian denotes masks of cloth or wood which are worn by people who want to disguise themselves. But the term also points to the stereotypical characters of the *commedia dell' arte* such as Harlequin and Pantalone. If such characters remove their masks, they will be naked, and yet they will still wear masks, the masks that conceal their real selves from themselves. Martin Esslin accurately summarizes the effect:

> Thus, our existence is essentially one of multiple realities that mutually undercut and relativize each other. If the theater is a house of multiple illusions, so is the internal theater within ourselves: the roles we play in society toward others, and the roles we play toward ourselves within ourselves.[66]

In contrast to Ibsen in which characters wear masks of social and moral uprightness but falsity and hypocrisy are hidden underneath, Pirandello's characters wear masks which underneath the present mask is another. Each mask invalidates the next as well as the previous one. His plays move between the conflicting actions of masking and unmasking. The characters attempt to find meaning and significance through the role-playing and various disguises, roles and disguises sometimes assumed from within but frequently imposed from without. Henry discovers that he cannot live without his mask, but at the same time, he cannot live if he has no identity but the mask.

"Masks, masks," Pirandello exclaims, "They disappear in a breath, giving way to others . . . Each one fixes his mask up as he can, the exterior mask. Because inside them is another one, often contradicting the one outside. Nothing is true."[67] In the midst of such relativity what Pirandello desires to do, in the words of Walter Sorrell, is "to unmask all masks."[68]

Pirandello's theater has been called the *teatro dello specchio* (theater of the looking glass).[69] The image of the mirror occurs in almost all his plays, for example, in *It Is So (If You Think So)* when Laudisi, examining his image in a glass reflects:

> As for me, I say that here, right in front of you, I can see myself with my eyes and touch myself with my fingers. But what are you for other people? What are you in their eyes? An image, my dear sir, just an image in the glass! They're all carrying just such a phantom around inside themselves, and here they are racking their brains about the phantoms in other people; and they think all that is quite another thing! (p. 106)

It is as if Pirandello's characters live their lives in the continuous play of reflecting mirrors. When they look at each other, it is for the purpose of watching themselves watch the others who watch them.

In an essay in the London *Evening News*, Pirandello elaborated another characteristic of the image of mirror:

> I have had the audacity of placing a mirror in the very center of the stage. It is the mirror of Intelligence. Man, while alive, lives but does not see himself.

Sentiment by itself is blind: I have therefore so managed that this blind man at a certain moment should open his eyes and should see himself in that mirror and should stand as if frozen by the thought of an image of his own life.[70]

What Henry experienced when he saw the portrait of his lover come to life is that of being confronted as if frozen by the thought of an image of his own life. He has, in Eric Bentley's words, "applied himself to the Pirandellian task of constructing himself."[71]

Henry has become a great actor; he has become in his madness, a magnificent, terrifying actor. He is not only actor par excellence, but also director and playwright who has constructed, amid the setting in which he has been placed, his own play. The additional role of spectator is intensified in Henry's drama by his adopting the role of critic who judges his own performance. Pirandello's self-reflective theater presents the modern tragic flaw of self-consciousness, to be locked in the "I." For Pirandello, as Driver indicates, "consciousness is a prison. One cannot escape from it, cannot be sure of reality outside it, and cannot know by means of it the contours and substance of the 'real' world."[72]

Pirandello's art, paralleling the advent of psychology, recognized that inner contradiction within the human personality. The modern theater, exemplified in Pirandello, is extremely conscious of consciousness. Pirandello's artistry testifies to the aesthetic power of such a perspective. The stage, this arena for acting in the play of life, is all there is.

IV

The modern stage is boxed in; the actors and the audience are placed together in a confined space. We as members of the audience have also transformed our role. Instead of sharing with the actors the sense that the cosmos is meaningful in ever-larger concentric circles from the stage we are viewing, modern audiences hear actors express an urgent need to confirm their existence. What the audience experiences with the actors is therefore a sense of shared solitude. As Henry IV states at the end of his play: "Here we are . . . together . . . for ever!" We as audience say those words through him and with him.

Among others, de Toqueville recognized the terrifying effects which the nineteenth century made upon Western civilization. The revolutionary idea of democracy brought much good, but it also shattered the sense of communal and cosmic participation, as de Toqueville noted:

Not only does democracy make every man forget his ancestors, but it hides his descendants and separates his contemporaries from him. Each man is forever thrown back on himself alone, and there is danger that he may be shut up in the solitude of his own heart.[73]

The individual feels little connection with others, let alone to larger circles of meaning.

From the Greek theater through Shakespeare, the action on stage could clearly and meaningfully be related to eternity—that is, to some value or idea such as the gods, Fate, Heaven or Hell—which transcends the human condition and which is affirmed by the dramatist, the audience, or both. Irving Howe in his description of *The Idea of the Modern* puts the dilemma for the modern theater directly: "The problem of belief becomes exacerbated, sometimes to the point of dismissal."[74]

The result, as Gottfried Benn, the German poet at the turn of the century, describes the crisis of belief in transcendent realities, is that "there is no outer reality, there is only human consciousness, constantly building, modifying, rebuilding new worlds of its own creativity."[75] Modern drama subordinates all of external reality to the internal reality of the psychological self. As the Manager states in the opening of *Six Characters in Search of An Author*, ". . . you who act your own part become the puppet of yourself. Do you understand?" The leading man's reply suggests the inherent self-destruction in such a position: "I'm hanged if I do." We have become entangled in the strings of our own making; each of us imprisoned in the I. Introspective self-consciousness may lead to self-knowledge but also to solipsism as well as paralysis or even madness. We are the children of Freud, and our forebearers are Descartes and Hamlet. Meanwhile, we dangle from our own self-consciousness; we are too often, as the phrase says, "hung up on ourselves." We are in the words of the Father in *Six Characters*, "suspended, caught up in the air on a kind of hook" (p. 231). The self-reflection of the modern theater possesses its own entropy.

Not only are the actors trapped in their roles, but they have gone or can go nowhere. Instead of moving from darkness to light, from problem to solution, from unmeaning to meaning, drama from Chekhov to Beckett makes real the sense of stasis. Modern plays end in irresolution; Henry's final words are echoed in Mrs. Alving's haunting indecision: "No—No, no, no!—yes,—no, no!"

Medieval drama traversed the seven ages of the world during its portrayal of the *Corpus Christi* cycle[76] while the Renaissance theater, as in Shakespeare's *As You Like It*, (II, 139–166) dramatized the seven ages of the individual. Modern drama, however, makes vivid this present time, the present space, for the stage is all the world there is. W. B. Yeats responded strongly to the notorious performance of *Ghosts* in London in 1891: "All the characters [in *Ghosts*] seemed to me less than life-size; the stage, though it was but the little Royalty stage, seemed larger than I had ever seen it. Little whispering puppets moved here and there in the middle of that great abyss."[77] Yeats concludes his comments with the paradoxical dilemma of drama since Ibsen: "Certainly they [the characters] were all in prison, and yet there was no prison."[78]

NOTES

1. Quoted in Tom F. Driver, *Romantic Quest and Modern Query, A History of the Modern Theater* (New York: Delacorte Press, 1970), 38.

2. Quoted in J. L. Styan, *Drama, Stage, and Audience* (Cambridge: Cambridge University Press, 1975), 170.

3. John Gassner and Ralph G. Allen in *Theater and Drama in the Making* (Boston: Houghton, Mifflin, 1964), 592, note that London theaters were already enlarged in the 18th century. "In 1791, for example, the intimate Drury Lane . . . was torn down. It was replaced three years later by a much larger Drury, seating 3,700 . . ."

4. V. A. Kolve, *The Play Called Corpus Christi* (Stanford: Stanford University Press, 1966), 122–123.

5. George Poulet, *Studies in Human Time*, tr. Elliott Coleman (Baltimore: Johns Hopkins University Press, 1956), 10.

6. Ludwig Tieck, *Die Verkehrte Welt* (original version, 1798) quoted in Lewis White Beck, *The Actor and the Spectator* (New Haven: Yale University Press, 1975), Epigraph.

7. Letter to Edmund Gosse, quoted in Brian Johnson, *To The Third Empire: Ibsen's Early Plays* (Minneapolis: University of Minnesota, 1980), 225.

8. Driver, 426.

9. August Strindberg, Note to A *Dream Play* (1902), quoted in Toby Cole, *Playwrights on Playwriting* (New York: Hill and Wang, 1960), 183.

10. Luigi Pirandello, *Preface, Six Characters in Search of an Author*, tr. Eric Bentley, *Naked Masks* (New York: E. P. Dutton and Co., Inc., 1952), 366.

11. Letter to Sophus Schandorf, quoted in Maurice Valency, *The Flower and the Castle: An Introduction to Modern Drama* (New York: Grosset and Dunlap, 1963), 159.

12. William Archer, *The Old Drama and the New* (New York: Dodd and Mead and Company, 1929), 20–21.

13. Johnson, 225.

14. Driver, 95.

15. F. L. Lucas, in *The Drama of Ibsen and Strindberg* (London: Cassell, 1962), 168, notes that *Ghosts* was "first performed (much to their credit) in the United States, by a Danish-Norwegian company in Chicago and elsewhere, in 1882" and adds, "Yet when a performance was given in 1887 at the Residenztheatr in Berlin, there were some 14,000 applications for the 670 places available."

16. Quoted in Lucas, 168–169.

17. Quoted in Lucas, 169.

18. Quoted in Raymond Williams, *Drama From Ibsen to Eliot* (London: Chatto and Windus, 1954), 41.

19. Quoted in Williams, 41.

20. Robert Brustein, *The Theater of Revolt: Studies in Modern Drama from Ibsen to Genet* (Boston: Little, Brown and Company, 1964), 24.

21. Quoted in Michael Meyer, *Ibsen: A Biography* (Garden City, NY: Doubleday and Company, 1971), 489.

22. Quoted in Robert W. Corrigan, *The Theater in Search of a Fix* (New York: Delacorte Press, 1973), 108.

23. Lucas, 154.

24. Lucas, 154.

25. Brian Johnston, *The Ibsen Cycle, Boston Cycle,* (Boston: Twayne Publishers, 1975), 181.

26. All quotations from *Ghosts* are from *Henrik Ibsen: The Complete Major Prose Plays*, tr. Rolf Fjelde (New York: Penquin Books, 1978), 232.

27. The noted Ibsen scholar, Evert Sprinchorn, insists that Pastor Manders "is as much the prey of those ghosts as Mrs. Alving is," *Ibsen News and Comments*, Number 2 (1981). 5.

28. Johnston, *Cycle*, notes that this term is "an untranslatable word which means something much more profound such as life impulse itself," 170.

29. Johnston, *Cycle*, 166.

30. G. Wilson Knight, *Henrik Ibsen* (New York: Grove Press, 1962), 51.

31. Francis Fergusson, *The Idea of a Theater* (Garden City, NY: Doubleday and Company, Inc., 1949), 161–165.

32. Jane Ellert Tammany, *Henrik Ibsen's Theater Aesthetic and Dramatic Art* (New York: Philosophical Library, 1980), 214.

33. Brustein, 88.

34. According to one commentator, the term "expressionism" was coined at an exhibition of Matisse in France in 1901, cited in Carl Enoch William Leonard Dahlström, *Strindberg's Dramatic Expressionism* (New York: Arno Press, 1980), 5.

35. Dahlström, 49.

36. Dahlström, 14.

37. Strindberg, *Brev* (October 4, 1905), pp. 222–223, quoted in "Introduction," *Strindberg*, edited and with introduction by Otto Reinert (Englewood Cliffs: Prentice-Hall, Inc., 1971), 9.

38. Joseph Wood Krutch, "Modernism" in *Modern Drama* (Ithaca, NY: Cornell University Press, 35.

39. Maurice Gravier, "The Character and the Soul," quoted in Reinert, 88.

40. Strindberg's Foreword to *Miss Julie* in Cole, 178.

41. Sprinchorn, "The Logic of a Dream Play," quoted in Reinert, 88.

42. Valency, 343.

43. Strindberg, *Brev* (April 17, 1907), p. 229, quoted in Reinert, 11.

44. Lucas, 441–447, and Brustein, 87–134, among many others specifically tie Strindberg's plays to particular events in the dramatist's life.

45. Strindberg, *Note to A Dream Play* in Cole, 182–183.

46. "The student is coming out of his own dream, the dream of the play," Corrigan, 123; "Strindberg uses the complex character of the Daughter of Indra to thematize, and thus integrate the play," Austin E. Quigley, *The Modern Stage and Other Worlds* (New York: Methuen, 1985), 125; *A Dream Play*; in a strict sense, is the Poet's dream," Valency, 331.

47. Walter Sokol, *The Writer in Extremis: Expressionism in Twentieth-Century German Literature* (Stanford: Stanford University Press, 1959), 38.

48. All quotations of *A Dream Play* are from *A Dream Play* and *Four Chamber Plays*, tr. Walter Johnson (Seattle: University of Washington Press, 1973), 19–20.

49. Valency identifies the door as that which Strindberg waited for Harriet Bosse after her performances: "the unhappy plight of one who spent a lifetime, as it seemed, waiting in theater corridors for a lady who never came," 338–339.

50. Quigley, 140.

51. Anthony S. Abbot, *The Vital Lie: Reality and Illusion in Modern Drama* (Tuscaloosa: University of Alabama Press, 1989), 32–33.

52. John Peter, *Vladmir's Carrot: Modern Drama and the Modern Imagination* (Chicago: University of Chicago Press, 1987), 312.

53. All quotations of Pirandello's plays are from *Naked Masks: Five Plays by Luigi Pirandello*, ed. Eric Bentley, tr. (New York: E. P. Dutton & Co., Inc. 1952) 159.

54. Brustein, 297.

55. Eric Bentley, *Theater of War: Modern Drama from Ibsen to Brecht* (New York: Viking Press, 1973), 40–41.

56. Pirandello, *On Humor*, tr. Antonio Illiano and Daniel P. Testa (Chapel Hill: University of North Carolina Press, 1974), 113.

57. Pirandello,*On Humor*, 125.

58. Quoted in Walter Starkie, *Luigi Pirandello* (Berkeley: University of California Press, 1965), 32.

59. Valency, *The End of the World: An Introduction to Contemporary Drama* (New Schocken Books, 1983), 156.

60. Pirandello, *On Humor*, 132.

61. Krutch, 66ff.

62. Krutch, 82–83.

63. Pirandello, quoted in Luigi Barzini, "How Pirandello Became Pirandellian (and Other Things), *New York Times*, 25 March 1975, Section 2, 1.

64. Thomas Biship, *Pirandello and the French Theater* (London: Peter Owen, 1961, 26.

65. June Schleuter notes that "the central symbol of this fluidity and multiplicity of identity is the masquerade," *Metafictional Characters in Modern Drama* (New York: Columbia University Press, 1979), 22.

66. Martin Esslin, "A Hole Torn in a Paper Sky: Pirandello and Modern Drama," in a *Companion to Pirandello Studies*, ed. John Louis DiGaetani (New York: Greenwood Press, 1991), 264.

67. Pirandello quoted in Walter Sorrell, *The Other Face: The Mask in the Arts* (Indianapolis: Bobbs-Merrill, 1973), 76.

68. Sorrell, 76.

69. Brustein, 288.

70. Pirandello, "Life in a Looking-Glass," London *Evening News*, 24 June 1925, quoted in A. Richard Sogliuzzo, *Luigi Pirandello, Director* (Metuchen, NJ: Scarecrow Press, 1982), 12.

71. Bentley, 42.

72. Driver, 393.

73. Alexis deTocqueville, *Democracy in America*, tr. George Lawrence, ed. J. P. Mayer (New York: Doubleday, 1969), 508.

74. Irving Howe, ed., *The Idea of the Modern in Literature and the Arts* (New York: Horizon Press, 1967), 26.

75. Gottfried Benn, quoted in Howe, 15.

76. Kolve elaborates the seven ages of the world, 88–106, 120.

77. Quoted in Johnson, *Cycle*, 80.

78. Quoted in Johnson, *Cycle*, 80.

Chapter Twelve

Contemporary Theater: Glimpses of the Transcendent

Post-World War II drama in both its multiple styles and themes reflects both a discontinuity with the past and a deep indebtedness to the dramatic tradition. To speak about the drama of any period is necessarily to oversimplify. When one discusses drama of the past, one is discussing not the average but the exceptional work; only the outstanding plays have survived and have been considered representative of the time. But the more closely one comes to the present, the more one recognizes not the individual trees but the huge forest.

To select so-called representative plays is always hazardous. Yet without specific evidence, summary observations are even more precarious. Thus this chapter will be even more deliberately inductive than the previous essays in its examination of seven plays.

The seven plays represent one work from each decade since World War Two as well as American, British, and European authors.[1] My hypothesis is that each play is both rooted in a past theatrical tradition as well as exploits a particular dramatic element:

T. S. Eliot, *The Cocktail Party* (1949)—indebted to medieval drama and concentrating on ritual

Samuel Beckett, *Endgame* (1957)—indebted to Strindberg concentrating on time and space

Tom Stoppard, *Rosencrantz and Guildenstern Are Dead* (1967)—indebted to Shakespeare and Pirandello and concentrating on theatricality

Peter Shaffer, *Equus* (1973)—indebted to Biblical imagery and concentrating on mask

David Mamet, *Glengarry Glen Ross* (1982)—indebted to Ibsen and concentrating on language

Tony Kushner, *Angels in America* (1992)—a fusion of dramatic styles concentrating on spectacle
Mary Zimmerman, *Metamorphoses* (2001)—indebted to Greek drama and
concentrating on myth

My hypothesis is that while focusing on the particular theatrical elements
and on the play's connection to the tradition, we will recognize, as Pinter has
reminded us, that "life is much more mysterious than plays make it out to
be."[2] Each of the playwrights wrestles with deeply human questions which
probe spiritual depths. The search for meaning is made vivid in multiple ways
within the contemporary theater.

A couple engage in the idle gossip and chatter of a cocktail party, a doting
servant hovers about his feeble master while two elderly people peer out of
ashcans, two nobodies from *Hamlet* wander around looking for meaning, a
very troubled boy and a doctor lost in his professional world wrestle together in
words and actions, a greedy set of real estate salesmen destroy themselves, an
apocalyptic fantasy combines Mormonism, Aids, and much else, and a cluster
of people from Greek mythology romp and splash in a large pool of water.

The temptation, in view of the images we have just experienced, is to dis-
miss the contemporary theater as a degeneration of the heroic, a deterioration
of the amoral. Certainly, the subject matter has changed. What is the vision
that both reflects and illumines those stages? The question which is dramatized, made real, in these theaters is: Wherein lies our hope? And that inquiry
is a religious question, an ultimate question, one of those points at which
theological and aesthetic considerations merge.

The contemporary theater speaks not only from us and for us but also to
us. Its stage, like the Greek and Elizabethan acting area, reveals in its strange
settings and unconventional plots the form and shape of who we are.

George Bernard Shaw's famous statement that "the theater is really the
week-day church" was echoed by Gordon Craig, the influential producer and
playwright of the early twentieth century: "Art is not a pick-me-up; it is a
communion . . . The theater is not a bar; it is a famous temple." The theater
and its near relative, the movie complex, have become the places where we
congregate to experience insights and to find meaning in our lives. These
spaces become spaces which Eugène Ionesco, French experimental playwright, accurately describes as the search for hope; our "true vocation . . .
[is our] quest for the imperishable."[3] Our theater is surely a metaphor of our
uncertainties, our groping for light and our search for meaning.

The contemporary playwright thus invites us to see within the here and
now, the presence of the mysterious and the unfathomable. The contemporary
audience, as John Lahr suggests, can and does

accept the inconceivable. They are open to the universe and to themselves . . .
And the stage, by allowing and structuring those moments of imaginative deeds,
becomes a mode of the sacred.[4]

The stage by becoming a mode of the sacred grants the audience glimpses
of the transcendent. Glimpses, yes, but nevertheless, glimpses.

NOTES

1. Another criterion was that I had not published criticism on the plays. Thus the
plays of Albee, O'Neill, Miller, and Ionesco as well as Beckett's *Waiting for Godot*
were not eligible.

2. Quoted in John Russell Taylor, "Accident," *Sight and Sound* (Autumn 1966):
184.

3. Eugène Ionesco, *Notes and Counter-Notes*, tr. Donald Watson (London: John
Calder, 1964), 265.

4. John Lahr, *Astonish Me: Adventures in Contemporary Drama* (New York: Viking Press, 1973), 140.

Chapter Thirteen

T. S. Eliot, *The Cocktail Party*

As will be true for each play selected from the decades from World War Two to the present, many plays other than *The Cocktail Party* vie for consideration. The American theater, particularly in Tennessee William's *The Glass Menagerie* (1945) and *A Streetcar Named Desire* (1947) and Arthur Miller's *Death of a Salesman* (1940), finally achieved world-wide attention. Sartre's *No Exit* (1944) as well as the plays of Brecht, especially *Mother Courage* (1949), clearly are strong candidates for discussion.

Yet *The Cocktail Party* first presented at the Edinburgh Festival in 1949 which led to well-received productions in London and New York, confirms that in the twentieth century, the dramatic uses of myth and ritual are still viable. Not only the explicitly Christian framework in the drama of Graham Greene, Christopher Fry,[1] Charles Williams, Dorothy Sayers, Ronald Duncan, and W. H. Auden, among others, but also such plays as Anouilh's *Becket*, MacLeish's *J.B.* and Bolt's *A Man for All Seasons* substantiate the claim that narratives from the past can be powerfully retold with effective audience response.[2]

Eliot's interest in and knowledge of myth and ritual and its presence in his poetry has been well-documented. "The Wasteland," "The Love Song of J. Alfred Prufrock" as well as the "Four Quartets" reflect the intricate mosaic of Eliot's art as well as his consistent themes of renewal and rebirth. What Eliot already wrote in 1923 about J. G. Frazer's *The Golden Bough* was still guiding him in his major writings in the 40's and 50's, including *The Cocktail Party*: "It [the mythical method of *The Golden Bough*] is, I seriously believe, a step toward making the modern world possible for art . . ."[3] Eliot also followed closely the Cambridge School of Classical Anthropology (Gilbert Murray and Jane Ellen Harrison) and especially Francis Cornford's *The Origin of Greek Comedy* which outlines the pattern of comic ritual. Eliot's conviction that "the drama was originally ritual . . ."[4] clearly influenced his first full-blown play, *Murder in the Cathedral* (1935). The Chorus of Women, the four tempters as if figures from a medieval morality play, and the ritual structure of a worship service all became part of the historical myth of the life and death of Thomas Becket told within the narrative frame of the passion of Christ.

Eliot continued to wrestle with the dilemma of how to make secular audiences understand and be open to spiritual experience. *The Family Reunion* (1939) with its ghostly Furies set within an Agatha Christie murder mystery confused both the public and the critics.

When Eliot constructed his next play, *The Cocktail Party*,[5] he sensitively interwove three myths, three structures of meaning: Euripides' Alcestis, particularly in the character of Henry Harcourt-Reilly as Hercules; secondly, the sacrificial life of Jesus, portrayed especially in the ritualistic ending of Celia's life; and thirdly, the medieval mystical description of the two paths by which to come to God: The Way of Affirmation with its emphasis on Creation and Incarnation (all created things are to be accepted in love as images of the Divine) and the Way of Negation, focused on the sacrificial death of Christ, through which God may be reached by detaching the soul from the things that are not God, and by experiencing the dark night of the soul. The drama could be viewed as a medieval morality play in modern dress.

Eliot subtitled the play: *A Comedy*. And what could be more comic than to open the play with the inane chatter of a cocktail party? The tangled love affairs of Edward, Lavinia, Celia and Peter possess the characteristics of comedy present from the Greeks through Shakespeare to the latest romantic farce. The hopeful, if not happy, ending of the play echoes Dante's *Divine Comedy*, for all lovers first experience the *Inferno* ("Hell is oneself,/Hell is alone . . ." (p. 98) through *Purgatorio* (the workings of Harcourt-Reilly and his accomplices) to *Paradiso* (Celia's meaningful sacrifice and the reconciliation of Edward and Lavinia).

Thus both terms, ritual and comic, are crucial in understanding Eliot's play. Ritual characteristics of ceremonial actions, incantation of word, deliberate gestures, all within a structural pattern of action, may be perceived in many dimensions of the drama: the banal conversation of a cocktail party takes on the meaning of a communion fellowship; Harcourt-Reilly's psychiatric office becomes the confessional for Lavinia and Celia; the intrusive friends, Julia and Alex, are called Guardians, both angels and purveyors of fate who chant purification rites for Celia as they raise their glasses at the end of Act II:

Alex: The words for those who go upon a journey.

Reilly: Protector of travellers.
          Bless the road.

Alex: Watch over her in the desert
       Watch over her in the mountains
       Watch over her in the labyrinth
       Watch over her by the quicksand.

Julia: Protect her from the Voices
       Protect her from the Visions
       Protect her in the tumult
       Protect her in the silence. (*They drink*)

(p. 150)

The play as a whole follows a ritual sequence. Act I presents the boredom and loneliness of all the guests at the cocktail party. Each wishes to overcome the isolation of the self but even the party food is scarce, a suggestion of spiritual starvation. Harcourt-Reilly as the Unidentified Guest (with allusion to Jesus as the Unknown Guest in every home, the Stranger who is always present) begins to plant seeds so that the distorted love of self can grow to a love for others and even for God. His presence is indeed divine.

Sir Henry's meetings with the Chamberlaynes and Celia in Act II force each of them to confront the deep despair which results from the lack of love directed toward others and God. One of the ways to achieve true humanity is through laughter and awareness and acceptance of one's foolishness. "Resign yourself to be the fool you are" (p. 31), Harcourt-Reilly advises Edward in Act I. "I don't mind at all having been a fool" (p. 135), Celia confesses to Sir Henry as she begins to undertake her spiritual journey. Acceptance of human finitude, symbolized by laughter, is the path to spiritual growth. Laughter in *The Cocktail Party,* as Ann Brady observes, is "the key to redemption" and "the method is humor, whose alchemy transforms humiliation into humility, judgment into mercy."[6]

Act III dramatizes the outcomes of the decisions made in the previous act: the Chamberlayne's renewed marital love (even to the extent of a little spat over the inconsequential straightening out of a picture on the wall) and Celia's martyrdom for, as Carol Smith notes, "Celia has chosen to conduct her love affair with God . . ."[7]

The group gathers for another cocktail party but this time the event is not one meaningless game after another, but rather a meaningful ritual of sharing communion. They have a hopeful future together. The Chamberlaynes are left to themselves and in Lavinia's closing words, "Oh, I'm glad. It's begun." (p. 190), Eliot has dramatized as medieval drama and Shakespeare[8] did before him that within human action is cosmic order. The play affirms that the infinite indeed works within the finite, the so-called "ordinary." God is at work in this world and the renewed relations with one another is the testimony to this presence. The audience has undergone the experience, in Eliot's own words, of "eliciting some perception of an order in reality, to bring us to a condition of serenity, stillness, and reconciliation; and they leave us, as Virgil left Dante, to proceed toward a region where that guide can avail us no longer."[9]

NOTES

1. Fry has reshaped Biblical material in several of his plays including his most famous drama, *The Lady's Not for Burning*. See my discussion in *The Drama of Comedy: Victim and Victor* (Richmond: John Knox Press, 1966), 74–99.

2. Musicals have also been successfully adapted from past traditions including the Biblical narratives: *Jesus Christ Superstar*, *Godspell*, and *Joseph and the Amazing Technicolor Dreamcoat*.

3. T. S. Eliot, "Ulysses, Order and Myth," *Dial*, LXXV (November 1923): 182.

4. Eliot, "The Beating of a Drum," *The Nation and Athenaeum*, XXXIV (October 6, 1923):12.

5. All quotations are taken from T. S. Eliot, *The Cocktail Party* (New York: Harcourt, Brace, and World, Inc, 1950).

6. Ann P. Brady, "The Alchemy of Humor in *The Cocktail Party*," in *Approaches to Teaching Eliot's Poetry and Plays*, ed. Jewel Spears Brookes (New York: Modern Language Association of America, 1988), 181, 179.

7. Carol H. Smith, *T. S. Eliot's Dramatic Theory and Practice* (Princeton: Princeton University Press, 1963), 173.

8. Eliot writes *On Poetry and Poets* [New York: Farr, Strauss and Cudahy, 1957, 80) that in Shakespeare's plays he discovers "a kind of musical design . . . which reinforces and is one with the dramatic movement."

9. Eliot, *On Poetry*, 94.

Chapter Fourteen

Samuel Beckett, *Endgame*

Samuel Beckett's *Endgame* (1957) is a closed world. Time is frozen and space is totally circumscribed. Beckett throughout all his plays broke radically with the classical unities in order to create a world with a different kind of time and space. To create a fragmented and disoriented universe, Beckett inverted the image of the theater as "a place of seeing." In *Endgame*, instead, as one commentator has observed, "space and time conceal—from a being whose deepest need is to see."[1]

And yet to probe, amid the complexity of the play,[2] more fully the dimensions of space and time in *Endgame* may not only illumine the drama's action but may also provide amid the bleakness a glimpse of what it means to be human.

The play's opening description, "*Bare interior. Grey light*" (p.1)[3] accurately foreshadows the action. We see a figure "*covered with an old sheet*" as well as two ashbins also "*covered with an old sheet.*" (p.1) Following a long series of movements using a ladder for a look out each window, the second figure, Clov, removes the sheets from the two elderly people peering from ashbins and from Hamm who is seated in an armchair. It is as if in this action the practice of uncovering the set for the next performance is taking place. One observer puts the matter theatrically: "*Endgame* will indeed begin again tomorrow, before a different audience, with slight variations in its performance and reception, taking as its point of departure the announcement of its ending."[4] The cyclic sense of time of this world is already dramatized.

Thus there is no rising action, climax or falling action, for all has fallen before the play's opening. There is no linear movement; the first tableau is the final one except that Clov is at the end dressed for a trip he may or may not take. An oft-repeated ritual is being acted out. "The end is in the beginning," Hamm tells us but adds significantly, "and yet you go on." (p. 69) In that observation, both the futility of human action and the necessity to carry on are affirmed.

The first lines of the play by Clov focus on time: "Finished, it's finished, nearly finished, it must be nearly finished."(p. 1) Variations of the words, finish and end, permeate the play as well as a litany of no mores: no more bicycle wheels, no more pap, no more nature, no more sugar plums, no more tides, no more navigators, no more rugs, no more pain-killers, no more coffins.

The form and content of the play convey the impression of a world which is in gradual decline where everything and everyone is weakening, winding down. All the characters suffer some physical deterioration: Hamm is blind and cannot use his legs; Clov sees but his eyes are bad, walks with great difficulty, and cannot sit; Nell and Nagg in the ashbins have long ago lost their legs and will probably die during the play. No doubt, things are running down and people have lost movement.

The apocalyptic tone of the play is documented by many critics. In fact, James Robinson entitled his essay on *Endgame*, "Samuel Beckett's Doomsday Play: The Spaces of Infinity."[5] Robinson comments that "the characters of Beckett at the edge of Doom remain bound, bound to their dying, bound to each other or to themselves, bound to the consciousness of their unconsummated existence."[6]

In the first textual image in the play, Beckett conveys how time has both ended and is endless: "Grain upon grain, one by one, suddenly, there's a heap, a little heap, the impossible heap." (p. 1) Like Beckett, the Greek philosopher, Zeno, was concerned how finite beings exist in time and space. Finite human beings possess a sense of infinity, both of time and space. This rift, this chasm, Zeno demonstrates by a heap of millet. If one takes a finite quantity of millet and first pours half of it into a heap, and continues this way until all the millet is brought into a single pile once again, one will discover that, although in an infinite universe the heap could be completed, this will never happen within the limitations of the finite. For the closer the heap approaches to completion, the slower it actually increases.

The characters in *Endgame* wait paradoxically for time to end, realizing the impossibility of it. Their lives are accumulated seconds which will never be completed, just as Zeno's heap of millet, continuously divided in half and added to the heap, can never be completed within the limitations of the finite world. Hamm later reflects

Moment upon moment, pattering down, like the millet grains of. . . . (*he hesitates*) that Old Greek, and all life long you wait for that to mount up to a life. (p.70)

Time is a diminishing but never-ending progression of same, yet different, moments leading to no identifiable goal.

Time therefore in *Endgame* is the endless present; there is only a very uncertain future and the past has faded. No one can remember prior events. The term "yesterday" seems almost meaningless. Clov says in response to Hamm's evocation of yesterday: "That means that bloody awful day, long, long ago, before this bloody awful day."(pp. 43–44) Time appears to have slowed to a stop, so that Hamm when asks the hour, Clov replies: "The same as usual."(p. 4) All are imprisoned within an external now.

As in *Waiting for Godot*, the elapsed time in the action of the play consists of waiting—in *Godot* for Godot's promised arrival and in *Endgame*, for Clov's promised departure. What Hamm realizes is that waiting is the final losing game but nevertheless the endgame he is playing is meant to end the waiting. But one cannot simply *stop* waiting anymore when one can overcome a lack of air by stopping breathing. One solution is to make every goal empty, to accompany every wish by a wish for the opposite, to wait for nothing, for zero.

For *Endgame* takes place in the zone of zero. Clov's answer to Hamm's question early in the play ("What time is it?") is zero. (p.4) When later Clov turns the telescope out the window, his observation is "Zero . . . (*he looks*) . . . zero . . . (*he looks*) and zero." (p.29) Hamm speaks of "an extraordinarily bitter day . . . zero by the thermometer" (p.51) and later in the same speech of "an exceedingly dry day . . . zero by the hygrometer." (p.53) And the paradox again is that zero conveys both nothingness and infinity.

If time is reduced to zero in *Endgame*, the sense of space is even more confined. We are in a dim room with only two small windows with curtains down. Nagg and Nell are in ashbins able only to peer out and mutter words now and then. Hamm several times states clearly the dimension of the space:

Outside of here it's death. (pp. 9,70)
Beyond is the . . . other hell. (p. 26)
That here we're down in a hole. (p. 39)

What is conveyed about the play's space are images of skull and womb, as one writer notes, "the conscious and unconscious waiting-rooms to living itself."[7] We seem to be inside an immense skull with the two small windows seeing as eyes attempting to behold the outside. An early theater critic of New York's Cherry Lane production in 1958 projected a vision of the play as foetus: "Imagine a feotus, doomed to be stillborn, suspended in darkness in the amniotic fluid, to life-not-to-be leaking away through the fontanelle—the membranous gap at the top of the skull of every human embryo."[8]

And yet Hamm refers to the room as his kingdom. Ruby Cohn, one of Beckett's most perceptive readers over the years, comments:

> In production, his armchair looks like a mock throne, his toque like a mock crown. He utters high-handed orders to Clov, a servant who is intermittently good and faithful. Both Hamm and Clov suggest that the world perished by Hamm's will.[9]

Imperially, Hamm issues continuous commands to Clov. No one of Hamm's instructions is more specific than that he be located in the exact center of the room. Hamm not only wants to be director of the *theatrum mundi*, but he also needs the reassurance that his position is *axis mundi*:

HAMM:
   Back to my place!
   (*Clov pushes chair back to center.*)
   Is that my place?

CLOV:
   Yes, that's your place.

HAMM:
   Am I right in the center?

CLOV:
   I'll measure it.

HAMM:
   More or less! More or less!

CLOV (*moving chair slightly*):
   There!

HAMM:
   I'm more or less in the center?

CLOV:
   I'd say so.

HAMM:
   You'd say so! Put me right in the center!

CLOV:
   I'll go and get the tape.

HAMM:
   Roughly! Roughly!
   (*Clov moves chair slightly.*)
   Bang in the center!

CLOV:
> There!
> (*Pause*)

HAMM:
> I feel a little too far to the left.
> (*Clov moves chair slightly.*)
> Now I feel a little too far to the right.
> (*Clov moves chair slightly.*)
> Now I feel a little too far back.
> (*Clov moves chair slightly.*) (pp. 26–27)

In this space, the characters are self-consciously aware their world is a stage. When Clov insists that he will leave Hamm, and adds, "What is there to keep me here?" Hamm responds: "The dialogue." (p.58) Later, Hamm angrily informs Clov that he is speaking "an aside, ape. Did you never hear an aside before?" and, after a pause, adds: "I'm warming up for my last soliloquy." (pp.77–78) Hamm responds to Clov's discovery of a small boy within the telescope's sight with the words: "Not an underplot, I trust." (p. 78) When Clov finally decides to leave, he explains: "This is what we call making an exit." (p.81) And in the closing moments of the play, Hamm performs his own farewell by discarding his whistle and his dog and by again covering his face with the bloody handkerchief. The grandeur of man the actor, John Sheedy has noted, "has shrunk to a single possibility: the ham actor."[10]

But Hamm is also the director and god in his little world. The room, shabby as it is, is the world, the theater of the world, both literally and figuratively. The space and the action can be seen as a very structured game of chess, observes Hugh Kenner:

> The king is hobbled by the rule which allows him to move in any direction but only one square at a time; Hamm's circuit of the stage and return to center perhaps exhibits him patrolling the inner boundaries of the little nine-square territory he commands. To venture further will evidently expose him to check ('Outside of here it's death.') His knight shuttles to and from, his pawns are pinned.[11]

And such an observation underlines the fact that the form of the play is the progressive stripping away of all elements within this enclosed space. Hamm's "dominion," as J. R. Moore suggests, "is truly wretched—infinite poverty in a little room."[12]

Thus Hamm's final words "Me—to play" (pp. 68, 82) which are repeated twice during the play implies not only Hamm as actor but Hamm as player, as the player king in an absurd drama moving to the endgame.

Roger Blin, the original director of the play in Paris, and to whom the play is dedicated, has commented: "*Fin de partie* is a tragic play, but Beckett denies that there is a drama there, he believes that the public is alerted from the first to the fact that nothing takes place."[13] Richard Goldman affirms this assessment:

> . . . while *Endgame* is devoid of event—the putative departure of Clov is a non-event, and despite a few critical attempts to suggest that its possibility is a source of the play's 'suspense,' its impossibility is stressed repeatedly ('there's no one else'—there's nowhere else'), and suspense is a dramatic virtue which one imagines Beckett would be unlikely to hang on.[14]

Endgame makes nothing real; we experience the reality of Nothingness. One critic observes that this "extinct world rolls through nothing towards nothing . . ."[15] and adds later ". . . the opponent is not human but time and against the latter one seeks to lose, to be eliminated into Nothing, not to win and continue a perverse encounter without hope."[16]

For the end is not checkmate but stalemate. Hamm is unable to go on yet also unable to finish. He covers his face with the large blood-stained St. Veronica handkerchief and remains motionless. Against time, this stalemate can last for eternity.

Hamm's closing words "You . . . remain" (p. 84) are addressed to us, the audience. We will remain. And having experienced the abyss, we can now step back from it with new awareness deeply imbedded within us.

NOTES

1. Lawrence E. Harvey, *Samuel Beckett: Poet and Critic* (Princeton: Princeton University Press, 1970), 427.

2. The play has evoked a myriad of interpretative approaches. Among many others have been analogies to Shakespeare's *Hamlet:* Stanley Clavell, *Ending the Waiting Game*: A Reading of Beckett's *Endgame;* in *Must We Mean What We Say? Book of Essays* (London: Cambridge University Press, 1976), 154 and to *The Tempest*: Michael Robinson, *The Long Sonata to the Dead: A Study of Samuel Beckett* (New York: Grove Press, 1958), 266–267 and Ruby Cohn, *Samuel Beckett: The Comic Gamut* (New Brunswick, NJ: Rutgers University Press), 236–237. A second cluster of interpretations are Biblical, particularly Genesis: Charles Lyons, "Beckett's *Endgame;* An Anti-Myth of Creation," *Modern Drama* (September, 1964): 204–209. Two critics explore the Noah/Ham allusions: Jane Alison Hale, *The Broken Window: Beckett's Dramatic Perspective* (West Lafayette, Indiana: Purdue University Press, 1987), 48–49; and Clavell, 138–146. Cohn discusses extensively the Biblical imagery, 227–236.

3. All quotations from the text are from Samuel Beckett, *Endgame* (New York: Grove Press, 1958).

4. Hale, 56.

5. James E. Robinson, "Samuel Beckett's Doomsday Play: The Space of Infinity," in *The Theatrical Space*, ed. James Redmond (Cambridge University Press, 1987), 215–221.

6. James Robinson, 215.

7. Bell Gale Chevigney, "Introduction," in *Twentieth Century Interpretations of Endgame* (Englewood Cliffs, NJ: Prentice-Hall, Inc., 1969), 3.

8. Jerry Tallman, *The Village Voice*, 5 February 1958, 7.

9. Cohn, 230.

10. John Sheedy, "The Comic Apocalpse of King Hamm," *Modern Drama*, IX (December 1966): 315.

11. Hugh Kenner, *Samuel Beckett: A Critical Study* (Berkeley: University of California Press, 1968), 157–158.

12. J. K. Moore, "Some Night Thoughts on Beckett," *Massachusetts Review*, VIII (Summer 1967): 533.

13. Roger Blin, *Beckett in the Theatre,* eds. Dongol McMillan and Martha Filsenfeld (London: John Calder, 1980), 169.

14. Richard M. Goldman, "Endgame and Its Scorekeepers," in Chevigny, 34.

15. Michael Robinson, 262.

16. Michael Robinson, 264.

Chapter Fifteen

Tom Stoppard, *Rosencrantz and Guildenstern Are Dead*

In the playful mood of the drama itself, one ventures to submit sub-titles for Tom Stoppard's *Rosencrantz and Guildenstern Are Dead* (1967): Waiting for Hamlet and Two Characters in Search of a Plot. No doubt about it, Stoppard forages the tradition for various elements of his plays: to Shakespeare for his characters and general framework, including several full scenes;[1] to Pirandello for the theatrical concept of giving the characters self-conscious awareness of their role-playing;[2] and to Beckett for the interchangeability of the two non-characters as well as many of their routines.[3]

Yet Stoppard's play is distinctive. While Beckett's two earthy tramps appear almost resigned to their world-weary waiting, Stoppard's two courtiers intensely engage in witty repartee to demand clarity and explanation of their situation. In Stoppard's art, Pirandello's role-playing of being condemned to remain on stage and of giving dramatic life to imaginative characters becomes an infinite regression of plays within plays. Shakespeare's two rather cold and calculating time servers are transformed into what Stoppard calls "a couple of bewildered innocents."[4] Shakespeare's religio-philosophical belief of a cosmic order in which every fall of a sparrow is within special providence becomes in Rosencrantz's desperate words: "Incidents! All we get is incidents! Dear God, is it too much to expect a little sustained action?!"[5] In brief, Stoppard's eye and ear have interwoven dramatic elements from other playwrights into an original play of dazzling intensity.

The strand most dominant in the play which is also found in Shakespeare, Pirandello, and Beckett is theatricality, the use of the elements of drama to construct the play itself. Like Beckett, Stoppard demonstrates that theatrical action can be created out of inaction. Obscure philosophical questions counter-pointed with slapstick vaudeville give Rosencrantz and Guildenstern, like Vladimir and Estragon in *Waiting for Godot*, freedom to play directly to the audience. Like Pirandello, Stoppard recognizes the multiplicity of selves each person possesses, for as Guildenstern exclaims, "Give us this day our daily mask!" (p. 39) Like Shakespeare, Stoppard exploits the play-life metaphor with countless references to acting, plays within plays, advice of actors and reminders to the audience that they are watching a play. For, as Norman Berlin puts it, the play "intellectually confronts and theatricalizes the condition of man the player and the world as theater."[6]

If life is a play, Rosencrantz and Guildenstern do not know the plot. They have roles in a drama which are not defined; they have not read *Hamlet*. The result of all this uncertainty is Guildenstern's desperate plea: "But we don't know what's going on, or what to do with ourselves. We don't know how to *act*." (p. 66)

Yet the play sets boundaries for the two players; they have prescribed roles within the Elizabethan revenge-tragedy of *Hamlet;* in William Babula's description of the play, "Script is Destiny."[7] Stoppard in a *New York Times* interview at the opening of his play in New York in 1968 acknowledged that he "had written about two people on whom Shakespeare imposed inevitability," but he adds, "I haven't got a philosophy figured out for you. If I had worked it out, I probably wouldn't have written a play about it."[8]

No actual world exists offstage; the only reality surrounding their confined stage is an on-going performance of *Hamlet*. Thus all of their world's a stage, and the production being performed is Shakespeare's tragedy. The Players and the members of the Court intersect the lives of Rosencrantz and Guildenstern suddenly and unexpectedly; indeed, as the Player comments, ". . . every exit [is] an entrance somewhere else," (p. 28) one could add, an entrance into *Hamlet*. Helene Keyssar-Franke observes, "Stoppard's strategy is to juxtapose scenes in which Rosencrantz and Guildenstern operate outside of their roles in Hamlet to scenes in which they do enact them; this creates a sense of the possibility of freedom and the tension of the improbability of escape."[9]

In Shakespeare's and even in Pirandello's dramas, the life-stage image focused upon the relationship of a real world and a play world. Stoppard has intensified the theatrical metaphor by having two play worlds collide: Hamlet's world and interwoven between it, Rosencrantz and Guildenstern's own imaginative world.[10] An added complexity is that, in Richard Corballis' view, "Rosencrantz and Guildenstern are portrayed as an extension of the audience and therefore as 'real' people; the Hamlet characters, by virtue of the onstage audience (added to the offstage one) are made to appear all the more stagey, 'clockwork' and 'unreal'."[11]

Such multiple worlds mean that Rosencrantz and Guildenstern are not only actors, but also spectators of other plays. They observe scenes from *Hamlet* and comment to one another about what they saw and heard. They

are audience also to the traveling tragedians; as the Player in his first words
"joyously" says to them: "An audience!" (p. 21) Later, when the play *The
Murder of Gonzago* is performed before the Court, two characters are added
who are mirror images of Rosencrantz and Guildenstern. As Robert Egan
states, "What began as their dress rehearsal of *The Murder of Gonzago* has
metamorphised into the playing to *The Life and Death of Rosencrantz and
Guildenstern.*"[12] But the two courtiers as spectators fail to recognize themselves. Although here art mirrors reality, they do not see that it does:

> . . . under their cloaks the two SPIES are wearing coats identical to those worn
> by ROS and GUIL, whose coats are now covered by their cloaks. ROS ap-
> proaches "his" SPY doubtfully. He does not quite understand why the coats are
> familiar. ROS stands close, touches the coat, thoughtfully. . . .
>   ROS: Well, if it isn't—! No, wait a minute, don't tell me—it's a long time
> since—where was it? Ah, this is taking me back to—when was it? I know you,
> don't I? I never forget a face—(he looks into the SPY's face) . . . not that I know
> yours, that is. For a moment I thought—no, I don't know you, do I? (p. 82)

As players, Rosencrantz and Guildenstern do not know how to act; as spectators, they do not know how to see.

Rosencrantz and Guildenstern only gradually recognize the truth of the title
of the play. Babula's dictum, "Script is Destiny" about this play is nowhere
more obvious than in the words spoken by the Ambassador in the final scene
from *Hamlet*:

> The ears are senseless that should give us hearing,
> To tell him [Hamlet] his commandment is fulfilled,
> That Rosencrantz and Guildenstern are dead (V, ii, 380–382)

But the larger question is: When did they die? Based on the play itself, the
possible answers to that question are many: (1) they die at the end of the play:
"Now you see me, now you . . .". . . *and disappears* (p. 126); (2) they are
already dead at the opening of the play: ". . . the fingernails grow after death
. . ." as Rosencrantz cuts his nails (p. 18); (3) they die at each performance of
the play; (4) they never died; they exist only in Shakespeare's and Stoppard's
imagination and thus they never lived.

Paradoxically, each of the four hypotheses is accurate.[13] Stoppard's play,
as Thomas Whitaker suggests, is "the modern theme. . . : consciousness of
consciousness."[14] Modern painters paint paintings about paints; modern poets
make poetry out of the process of poetry; and modern playwrights make plays
out of playing. And no play does this more intricately, even about dying, than
Stoppard's play.

But does this self-reflexive playing by Rosencrantz and Guildenstern point, as many commentators suggest, toward a meaningless universe? Perhaps, but perhaps not. As Whitaker observes, *"Rosencrantz and Guildenstern Are Dead* cancels itself very neatly. If plays were statements, it would be a phony statement that everything is phony. Stoppard has dramatized the paradox of the Cretan liar . . ."[15]

From the opening scene in which Guildenstern has tossed a coin ninety-five times which comes up heads, Stoppard introduces elements of mystery and the inexplicable within the play.[16] We as an audience begin to question our empirical and positivistic assumptions, just as the Elizabethan audience did at the appearance of the Ghost in opening scene of *Hamlet.* Such a phenomenon does move us "to re-examine [one's] faith" (p. 12) and certainly causes us to consider whether "we are now within un-, sub- or supernatural forces." (p. 17) It is important to note that the world of the play requires some kind of faith, a faith that attempts to respond to happenings which defy reason. Stoppard describes what he does is to proceed by

> A series of conflicting statements by conflicting characters, and they tend to play a sort of infinite leap-frog. You know, an argument, a refutation, then a rebuttal of the refutation, then a counter-rebuttal, so that there is never any point . . . at which I feel *that* is a speech to stop it on, *that* is the last word.[17]

Stoppard's tentativeness may be the first step to reject our time's reigning positivism and to open the possibility for options of belief and trust.[18]

Rosencrantz and Guildenstern do not heed the Player's wise advice: "Everything has to be taken on trust . . ." (p. 67) Hamlet in his play gradually learned to put his trust in that which was beyond him, "a divinity that shapes our ends." (V, ii, 10) Not until he acknowledged that "This is I, Hamlet the Dane" (V, i, 280–281), is he able to see himself truly. But when Guildenstern asks, "Who are we?" the Player responds: "You are Rosencrantz and Guildenstern. That's enough." (p. 122) But the Player's assertion is rejected; skepticism, not trust, blindness, not acceptance of one's own selfhood mark Rosencrantz and Guildenstern.

Yet the very metaphor of theatricality inherently points to larger worlds. As the tragedians are performing their play, they are being observed by Rosencrantz and Guildenstern; Rosencrantz and Guildenstern's in turn are being watched by us. Are we not then perhaps personae in a larger all-encompassing drama?

For what Guildenstern says about their lives is also true of ours:

> We can move, of course, change direction, rattle about, but our movement is contained within a larger one that carries us along as inexorably as the wind and the current . . . (p. 122)

We, like Hamlet and Rosencrantz and Guildenstern, find "our movement is contained within a larger one." For the theatrical image inherently reflects back on itself.

The inexplicable amid the witty rationality of Rosencrantz and Guildenstern, the tension between freedom and inevitability, trust amid unknowing—all these indeed cause one "to re-examine one's faith." Stoppard challenges his audience to move beyond the empirical to the non-rational and perhaps even to a leap of faith. Amid the paradoxes Stoppard dramatizes, Christopher Fry's advice may be words of wisdom for Stoppard's audience: "Rest in the riddle, rest; why not?"[19]

NOTES

1. William Babula's "The Play-Life Metaphor in Shakespeare and Stoppard," *Modern Drama, XV*, (December 1972): 279–282 notes the theatrical images in the two dramatists.

2. Susan Ruskino, *Tom Stoppard* (Boston: Twayne Publishers, 1986, 35), among many other readers, points out the Pirandellian echoes, especially in relation to *Henry IV*.

3. Ronald Hayman, *Tom Stoppard* (London: Heinemann, 1977, 36), explicates the similarities to *Waiting for Godot*.

4. Quoted in Tim Brassell, *Tom Stoppard: An Assessment* (New York: St. Martin's Press, 1985), 38.

5. All quotations from *Rosencrantz and Guildenstern Are Dead* are from the edition, New York: Grove Press, 1967, 118.

6. Norman Berlin, "*Rosencrantz and Guildenstern Are Dead*, Theatre of Criticism," *Modern Drama, XVI* (December 1973): 276.

7. Babula, 279.

8. Quoted in an interview with Patricia Lewis, "See the Father . . .," *New York Times*, 24 March 1968, D3.

9. Helene Keyssar-Franke, "The Strategy of *Rosencrantz and Guildenstern Are Dead*," *Educational Theatre Journal*, 27 (1975) :87.

10. June Schleuter, *Metafictional Characters in Modern Drama*, (New York: Columbia University Press, 1977, 99) perceptively observes the similarities and differences between the inner play and the outer play.

11. Richard Corballis, *Stoppard, The Mystery and the Clockwork* (New York: Methuen, 1984), 36.

12. Robert Egan, "A Thin Beam of Light: The Purpose of Playing in *Rosencrantz and Guildenstern Are Dead*," *Theatre Journal* (March 1979): 65.

13. Stoppard has said, "I write plays because dialogue is the most respectable way of contradicting myself," quoted in Kenneth Tynan, "Withdrawing with Style from the Chaos," *New Yorker*, 53 (December 19, 1973): 44.

14. Thomas R. Whitaker, *Fields of Play in Modern Drama* (Princeton: Princeton University Press, 1977), 12.

15. Whitaker, 15.

16. Douglas Colby (*As the Curtain Rises: On Contemporary British Drama 1966–1976,* Cranbury, N. J.: Associated University Presses, 1978, 29), comments that Stoppard employs the opening image of coin-tossing as "a multi-layered metaphor which encompasses the . . . major themes of the play."

17. Stoppard in "Ambush for the Audience," quoted in Ian Mackenzie, "Tom Stoppard: The Monological Imagination," *Modern Drama,* XXXII (December 1989): 575.

18. Victor L. Cahn (*Beyond Absurdity: The Plays of Tom Stoppard,* (Cranbury, NJ: Associated University Presses, 1979), 39, elaborates on this step beyond absurdity in this play:

> "Rosencrantz and Guildenstern are not trapped in some nondescript void. Theirs is essentially the predicament of the individual trapped in a world where the powers in charge carry on as though all events had purpose, but where that purpose nonetheless eludes the individual citizen. This is a significant step in absurdist theater. The majority of plays from that tradition contain not even a semblance of order or purpose. The world simply runs riot."

19. Christopher Fry, *The Lady's Not For Burning* (London: Oxford University Press, 1949), 56.

Chapter Sixteen

Peter Shaffer, *Equus*

"One's outer life passes in a solitude haunted by the masks of others; one's inner life passes in a solitude haunted by the masks of one's self," wrote Eugene O'Neill in 1932 in his "Memoranda on Masks."[1] Such a psychological insight reminds us that masks, both actual and figurative, are inherent in drama. The masks of comedy and tragedy, emblematic of the whole history of theater, force the spectator, as do all masks, to look into rather than only look at. As audience we recognize the doubleness both of ourselves and the actors wearing a mask, the inner and the outer self.

Did the Greek and Roman actors wear masks so that, owing to the great size of their theaters, they could be seen more distinctly? Or, did they wear masks to amplify their voices? Such pragmatic theories have generally been rejected; instead, just as is true of all drama, the power of the mask is what prompted the making and the wearing of the covering of the face.

To wear a mask is to imitate, to take on the role of another, whether divine, human, demonic, or animal. The masked person then is believed to possess the powers of that which the mask portrays. To wear a mask is to reveal another aspect of the self. At the same time, to wear a mask is to hide from others and even from ourselves or to engage in disguise, either in jest or deception. The French language uses the telling phrase "*jouer du masque*,"[2] to play the mask. It best indicates the playfulness in presenting a face other than one's actual one to the world while we continue to doubt whether the wearer knows his real face or is at all aware of the one which he is showing to us. The mystery of the human self is intensified by wearing and observing masks; deep within the unconscious, we both love and fear the mask.

To be masked or unmasked is the essence of the dramatic impulse. If one unmasks, openness and confession may follow, often by also encouraging the other to unmask. But the intense vulnerability which results from unmasking and especially from being unmasked may lead to the destruction of the self behind the mask.

The mask is the symbol of all metamorphoses, the illusion of another reality, the disguise by which we reach for another identity. We have great difficulty living with our own masks as well with the masks of others, but we know we would be unable to live without masks.

British playwright Peter Shaffer has dramatized both the creative and destructive power of mask in *Equus* (1973).[3]

Tonight we are in the theater. Total darkness. Silence. Within a circular spot of bright light in the center of the stage appears a young man completely dressed in chestnut brown. Realistically, majestically, he lifts a mask, a mask of great beauty and strength and places it on his head. Human becomes horse and almost a god before our very eyes.

Central to the play are the horses played by actors who stand upright on four-inch-high coiled springs set on metal horse shoes and who walk as if the whole body of the horse extended invisibly behind them. The airy stylized masks of intertwined leather and silver wire convey heiratic dignity and beauty. Shaffer in his note with the play advised that "great care must also be taken that the masks are put on before the audience with very precise timing—the actors watching each other, so that the masking has an exact and ceremonial effect." (p. 3) When the actors mask, they are transformed into wondrous creatures, the stage now charged with mystery and awe.[4] The slightest turn of the neck evokes ballet-like softness; the sound of all the metal hooves on the wooden stage conveys terror indescribable. In the horses are found strength, ecstasy, power, and obedience as well as malevolence or, as Shaffer himself described the horses as "an ambiguous presence—both conquering and submissive, both judging and accusing on the one hand and accepting and gentle on the other."[5]

Religion and sensuality merge. Alan, the young boy who worships the horse, confesses: "They sort of pulled me. I couldn't take my eyes off them. Just to watch their skins. The way their necks twist, and sweat shines in the folds." (p. 47) Immediately following, he describes the white horse of Revelation: "He that sat upon him was called Faithful and True. His eyes were as flames of fire, and he had a name written that no one knew but himself." (pp. 47–48) Instead of the traditional *Agnus Dei*, Shaffer boldly proposes *Equus Dei. A Christian Century* writer puts the matter directly: "Equus is not really a horse, however—neither the boy's favorite mount named Nugget nor the horsiness of horsehood. Equus is the image of God."[6] Without the mask, such a statement would not be credible; the half man/half horse creatures convey the presence of mystery and awe.

But the relationship between Alan and Equus is not one of distance; the religious and sexual are one: "The horse isn't dressed. It's the most naked thing you ever saw!" (p. 48) and at the end of Act I as he prepares for his orgasmic ride of Equus, Alan chants: "Equus the Godslave, Faithful and True. Into my hands he commends himself—naked in his chinkle-chankle." (p. 71)

Within the entire play, nakedness becomes the image of unmasking and being unmasked. As Martin Dysart, the psychiatric doctor in charge of Alan, proceeds to uncover why Alan committed this strange act of blinding six horses, he employs a series of devices: a tape recorder, hypnotic pencil-tapping, a truth placebo. But none of these would be effective were it not for the mutual unmasking both consented to in an earlier scene:

Dysart: Do you dream often?

Alan: Do *you*?

Dysart: It's my job to ask the questions. Yours to answer them.

Alan: Says who?

Dysart: Says me. Do you dream often?

Alan: Do you?

Dysart: Look—Alan.

Alan: I'll answer if you answer. In turns.

Pause.

Dysart: Very well. Only we have to speak the truth.

Alan: *[mocking]* Very well. (pp. 35–36)

Dysart has now removed the disguise of professional detachment; he is willing to be vulnerable as one human being to another. Although the forces inside Alan and Dysart have opposite charges, like a magnet, they are attracted to one another. In their common nakedness, the two begin to trust one another.

Others involved in the play's action also unmask and are unmasked. Alan's mother keeps her strict decorum as a loving parent until she blurts out: "Whatever's happened has happened because of Alan . . . I only know he was my little Alan, and then the Devil came" (p. 77) Alan's father, opposed to his wife's religious upbringing of Alan, clutches his mask of upright middle-class materialistic values until Alan observes him at the pornographic theater. He continues to insist that he has entered the theater for "business purposes" to discuss posters for his printing trade. (p. 92) But Alan sees his father in a new way with his mask removed:

Poor old sod, that's what I felt—he's just like me! He hates ladies and gents just like me! Posh things—and la-di-da. He goes off by himself at night, and does his own secret thing which no one'll know about, just like me! There's no difference—he's just the same as me—just the same! (p. 95)

The only character who keeps the mask seemingly in place is Hesther Salomon, the magistrate in charge of Alan's case. As Dysart's sounding board and confidant, she displays, according to Dennis Klein, the characteristics of her two Biblical names: Esther's compassionate justice and Solomon's balanced wisdom.[7] Is there more than friendship between her and Dysart? This question and many others about her role are unanswerable, for she is hidden behind her detached but smiling face.

At the end of Act I, Alan has moved from unmasking to re-enactment. At Dysart's invitation, Alan performs the ritual of riding Equus naked in the wind and the mist. He mimes a symbolic ride on his god, echoes of Christ's ride on the white horse in Revelation. In passionate joy and agony, Alan cries: "Mane on my legs, on my flanks, like whips!" (p. 72) As if possessed, Alan experiences not only sexual climax but also union with Equus:

I want to be *in* you!
I want to BE you forever and ever!—
Now! Equus, I love you!
Now!
Bear me away!
Make us One Person! (p. 72)

This frantic chant is from a soul possessed with passion. Combined with intense body language ("he twists like a flame"), Alan creates grace out of desperation and hysterics.

In the climactic scenes of Act II, Dysart is again unmasking Alan as the boy re-enacts the events of the horses' blinding. After the traumatic scene at the pornographic theater, Jill Mason, Alan's friend, leads him to the stables, "into the Temple, the Holy of Holies." (p. 97)[8] Jill gently says: "Take your sweater off . . . I will, if you will" (p. 99). She is willing to begin the unmasking. The two mutually agree to be nude before one another.[9] The two stand in silence for a few moments as they face one another. The image is of two classic statues, as if Venus is being met by her lover. We see both a reflection of a sensuous Renoir painting, the innocence of Adam and Eve before the fall, and first adolescent romantic love—all at the same time. Alan is ready and willing to be united with another human being, flesh and blood, rather than with an intangible deity who casts him as a humble servant.

Suddenly the noise of Equus fills the place! Alan now feels naked, stripped, totally vulnerable, for he believes Equus as jealous god sees his betrayal. Although Alan puts on the mask of macho male ("I put it in her! . . . All the way. I shoved it. I put it in her all the way" (p. 100), we recognize Alan's impotence in the presence of his god. Revealed to Alan is the awful consuming power of Equus, a power that calls him a failure and an unworthy servant. Alan cannot see Jill. Equus has masked her, making Alan's passion impossible to share.

Alan must now blind the horses who have seen him:

Dysart: The Lord thy God is a Jealous God. He sees you. He sees you forever and ever, Alan: He sees you! . . . *He sees you!*

Alan: *[in terror]* Eyes! . . . White eyes—never closed! Eyes like flames—coming—coming! . . . God seest! God seest! . . . NO! . . . Equus . . . Noble Equus . . . Faithful and True . . . God-slave . . . Thou—God—Seest—NOTHING! *He stabs out Nugget's eyes.* (p. 103)

As Dysart attempts to heal Alan, he himself begins to realize that he is masking himself from his own humanity. His opening monologue describes the need for a Kierkegaardian leap of faith: "All reined up in old language and old assumptions, straining to jump clean-hoofed on to a whole new track of being I only suspect is there." (p. 18) His dream in which he is chief priest in Homeric Greece wearing a wide gold mask while officiating at the rite of carving up children, accurately describes his professional life. He is hiding behind professional detachment: "My face is going green behind the mask. Of course, I redouble my efforts to look professional—cutting and snipping for all I'm worth . . ." (p. 24) He does not want the two assistant priests, also wearing masks, to see his inner doubts: "And then, of course—the damn mask begins to slip." (p. 24) The slipping of Dysart's mask becomes the on-going action of the play. The dream reveals that he both understands his work in religious terms, with the religion he serves consisting of obedience to the god Normal, and that his work is murderous, that the normality desired by society is only an illusion maintained by the forceful containment or elimination of the inner life. Like Oedipus, he knows that he will be destroyed if his doubts come to light.[10]

Alan's persistent questioning of Dysart's personal life "aims at [his] area of maximum vulnerability." (p. 59) Dysart's lack of passion,[11] his "antiseptic proficiency" (p. 60), his professional menopause all point to a physician who cannot heal himself. He is a priest without worship and "Without worship you shrink, it's as brutal as that . . . I shrank my *own* life." (p. 81) As Ebner comments, "Dysart has neither sex nor worship but society's tame substitutes for each."[12]

Dysart gradually realizes that he has both healed and eviscerated Alan. In the final scene, Dysart as a gentle father carries the bruised Alan in a blanket. Both are now stripped and naked. What will Alan now see? Only the Normal; the divine and the demonic have now been driven out. Alan, in Dysart's words, will not "gallop anymore." (p. 108) He is now bare, but he will not be born again. But out of Alan's dying sacrifice, Dysart is beginning to be reborn; he is seeking to go beyond the darkness to a whole new track of being:

> In an ultimate sense I cannot know what I do in this place—yet I do ultimate things. Essentially I cannot know what I do—yet I do essential things . . . I need—more desperately than my children need me—a way of seeing in the dark. What way is this? . . . *What dark is this?* . . . I cannot call it ordained of God: I can't get that far. I will however pay it so much homage. There is now, in my mouth, this sharp chain. And it never comes out. (p. 106)

As Calvin Seerveld says:

> Dysart comes to see, fearfully, that what he does professionally is bigger than what he himself does . . . He gives homage to this unknown God who hounds men with the bit and bridle of suffering stuck in our mouths. Dysart wants to deeply believe in more than meets the professional eye.[13]

Dysart is now chained to Equus, willing to be led.

Dysart had no god except the great god Normal, and he now desires a true deity. Dysart has seen what he cannot explain; he has experienced what he cannot understand. He, like Alan, is on, what one commentator observed, a "quest for being."[14] Beneath the various masks lies a passion that yearns to be fed. He is searching for connection; his spiritual hunger is rooted in a deep need for transcendence. One commentator has commented that more than being a play about a boy blinding horses, *Equus* is "about God," about "God watching us."[15]

But what is the nature of the god the play portrays? Omnipotent, omni-scient, Equus is a god who judges. Equus is also a god who is in chains, but the suffering neither leads to the possibility of redemption nor to love, trust, and mercy. Shaffer masks God in a caricature. For during the play, the god Equus is unmasked as a jealous, unforgiving, and unmerciful deity.

With such a distant and uncaring deity, the presence of the holy is restricted to occasional moments, once every three weeks as Alan rides Equus. He, like all the others, is condemned to live all the rest of the time in the normal world, a world, according to the play, of dullness, filled with materialistic values. But to equate "Normal" with dullness is to ignore that within the ordinary, the extraordinary can and does take place.

Yet Shaffer has through the action of the play portrayed the cosmos pervaded by the sacred. As Shaffer himself noted in a little-known interview, "To me one of the central themes is the invasion of a very reasonably expert, psychiatrically trained mind, by the idea of what in the 19th century was called 'the Holy.'"[16] Each person is clinging to a substitute for meaning: Alan's father to his movies, Alan's mother to her orphans, Hesther Salomon to her work, and Dysart to his art books. But Alan has been invaded by "the Holy," and Dysart in one of the most powerful moments of the play confesses his jealousy:

> Don't you see? That's the Accusation! That's what his stare has been saying to me all this time. '*At least I galloped! When did you?*' (p. 80)

That direct question penetrates each member of the audience.

NOTES

1. Eugene O'Neill, "Memoranda on Masks," *The American Spectator*, (November 1932), 3, quoted in *Playwrights on Playwrighting*, ed. Toby Cole (New York: Hill and Wang, 1960), 65.

2. Walter Sorrell, *The Other Face: The Mask in the Arts* (Indianapolis: Bobbs-Merrill, 1973), 31.

3. All quotations from the play are from Peter Shaffer, *Equus and Shrivings* (New York:Atheneum, 1976).

4. The Greek world permeates the play, for example, in Dysart's dream of being chief priest in Homeric Greece and his frequent trips to the Peleponnese. Gene A. Plunket in *Peter Shaffer: Roles, Rites and Rituals in the Theater* (Rutherford, N. J.: Fairleigh Dickinson University Press, 1988) 166, points out the Greek elements of the chorus and the dialogue of stichomythia. Another commentator, Dennis Klein in *Peter Shaffer* (Boston: Twayne Publishers, 1979,) 136, suggests that the structure of *Equus* is similar to a classic Greek tragedy with Dysart's opening speech as the prologue, the therapy sessions as the *episodos*, and Dysart's closing speech as the *exodi* which results in a catharsis of pity and fear.

5. Peter Shaffer, "Equus: Playwright Peter Shaffer Interprets Its Ritual," *Vogue*, 175 (February 1975): 136.

6. Samuel Terrien, "Equus: Human Conflicts and the Trinity," *Christian Century*, 94 (May 18, 1977): 472.

7. Klein, 128. Another critic, I. Dean Ebner in "The Double Crisis of Sexuality and Worship in Shaffer's *Equus* (*Christianity and Literature*, Volume 31, Number 2 (1982): 32, disagrees:

> [Hesther Salomon] is a symbol of the double shallowness and of the double crisis of our time. Shaffer places her gently but clearly as a dramatic foil to the rich, real discoveries of body and soul which emerge during Alan's therapy with Dysart.

8. Larry Brouchard in *Tragic Method and Tragic Theology* (University Park: Pennsylvania State Press, 1989) 197, points out that the scene "superficially is like Genesis 3: The gift of autonomous freedom curtails the possibility, even the likelihood of rejecting God for self. The seductress in the barn is the serpent in the garden."

9. Tom Buckley in "Write Me, Said the Play to Peter Shaffer," *New York Times Magazine* (April 13, 1975) 26, vividly describes the way the scene was arrived at:

> It was also Dexter who decided that the climactic stable scene between the boy and the girl should be played in the nude, Shaffer said. 'In rehearsal, they were clothed, he added. Then, one afternoon with only three or four of us in the theater, John, who had told the actors but had not told me, gave a signal and they ran through it without clothes. We were all destroyed by it. The lights came up and there we all were, absolutely, shaking. John looked at us and said, 'That's all I wanted to know.' 'The difference between that boy leaping up and down out of darkness like a fish out of water, striking at those heads, naked or in a sweater and jeans, seems to me like the difference between poetry and prose on stage.'

10. Brouchard comments that "Blinding, of course, is the most visceral image in *Equus*, freighted with illusions to Odysseus and Cyclops, Oedipus, Samson, Gloucester in *Lear*—people whose sight was feared or who despaired to see too much." (p. 197)

11. William Lynch in "What's Wrong with *Equus*? Ask Euripides," *America* (December 13, 1975): 420.

12. Ebner, 31.

13. Calvin Seerveld, "Equus: Two Views," *Vanguard* (May 1976): 72.

14. Terrien, 474.

15. Frederick Sontag, "God's Eyes Everywhere," *Christian Century*, 92 (December 17, 1975): 1162.

16. Glover William, "*Equus* Author Explains Reactions," *Allentown Sunday Call-Chronicle* 9 March 197, E4.

Chapter Seventeen

David Mamet, *Glengarry Glen Ross*

"Words are acts,"[1] David Mamet has said, who later elaborated on this concept which has been so central to his drama: "I am fascinated by the way, the way the language we use, its rhythms, actually determines the way we behave, rather than the other way around."[2]

In *Glengarry Glen Ross* (1982), shark-like salesmen are continually propelled by their language; for them, to talk is to survive. As their words spill out, their behavior attempts to match their language. Action is language, language whose rhythms, tonalities, intensities, and silences reveal the inner self.

Mamet writes for the theater, for the ear. He hears Americans talking with exactitude. In Mamet's drama, the universe of language reflects action. One commentator accurately notes that "Mamet's characters are what they say they are and do what they *say* they do. For Mamet, language . . . is truly symbolic action."[3] Their language is the weapon by which they denigrate, insinuate, and abuse as well as the means by which they cajole, flatter, and seduce their customers and one another. For part of the fascination the audience experiences is that the salesmen are seduced by the sheer exhilaration they conjure up with language.

The title of the play refers to two tracts of land development in Florida: Glengarry Highlands and Glen Ross Farms, the real estate which these Chicago salesman are attempting to sell. Although the names sound mellifluous (perhaps the most serene words in the entire play), the land itself is absolutely worthless. When the play opens, the agency is holding a contest among its four salesmen: first prize is a Cadillac, second prize is, appropriately, a set of steak knives, and the two losers get fired. In such a setting, only the very fit will survive. The men will not only manipulate and exploit gullible customers, but they will also deliberately manipulate and exploit each other. They live by victimizing others, but the most abject victims are themselves. As Anne Dean comments, these men "sell not only real estate but also hope and consolation, as much to themselves as to their hapless clients."[4] These salesmen therefore construct alternative worlds with nothing more substantial than words. They are actors entirely dependent on audiences for survival.

Mamet's play reflects the image of the American salesman of popular and literary culture whose speech bristles, as Ruby Cohn suggests, with "rhetorical questions, calculated repetitions, impatient interruptions."[5] Like their earlier counterparts, O'Neill's Hickey and Miller's Willy Loman, these salesmen thrive on colloquialism and slang. In their monosyllabic words, we hear and feel both their exhilaration and sweaty desperation.

In the opening speech of the play, Shelly "The Machine" Levene, the most desperate of the lot, attempts to appeal to his unsympathetic office manager:

John . . . John . . . John. Okay. John. John. Look: (*Pause.*) The Glengarry Highland's leads, you're sending Roma out. Fine. He's a good man. We know what he is. He's fine. All I'm saying, you look at the *board*, he's throwing . . . . wait, wait, wait, he's throwing them *away*, he's throwing the leads away. All that I'm saying, that you're wasting leads. I don't want to tell you your *job*. All that I'm saying, things get *set*, I know they do, you get a certain *mindset* . . . A guy gets a reputation. We know how this . . . all I'm saying, put a *closer* on the job. There's more than one man for the . . . Put a . . . wait a second, put a *proven man* out . . . and you watch, now wait a second—and you watch your *dollar* volumes.[6]

Here, as in his other plays, Mamet jumps the audience into the middle of a dramatic situation, and lets us piece together the jigsaw of the story from the tantalizing chunks of speech his characters scatter around the stage. Levene builds up a kind of rhythmic litany which he hopes will move the manager to respond. The dialogue manages to maintain the illusion of normal conversation while at the same time cutting beneath the surface to expose deeper layers of meaning. Sentences are stretched and strained, turned back on one another so that we become aware not only of Levene's calculated ingenuousness but also of his growing anxiety. Syntax is broken; grammar is dislocated. Levene's speech, as many others in Mamet's plays, is written rather like a race from the first word to the last, constantly threatening to get to the point and then quickly back-tracking or desperately stumbling on its way.

Mamet's characters talk a kind of aural graffiti—scrawling over words they have barely spoken, scratching out sentences before they are finished, recklessly mangling thought in the process. As a result, every declaration is open to interpretation. In their frenzied pace, they omit words, even whole phrases. In their stutter-speech which Mamet orchestrates with overlapping rhythms, interjected phrases, emotional retreats, and attempted advances, the drama of missed conversation is made transparent. As C.W.E. Bigsby points out, in Mamet's dialogue, "the most common punctuation mark in the printed text is the comma, as mismatched phrases and random ideas are strung together in a protective flow of sound."[7]

Talk becomes the aggressive mode to hide their fears; beneath the verbal facade lurks isolation and tracklessness. The rapid rhythms expose their deep insecurity within; if they would stop talking, the silence they would have to confront would be overwhelming. So long as they can keep the narrative flowing and uninterrupted, they are able to feel at least momentarily safe.

Just beneath the very thin veneer of basic civility, Mamet creates a primitive, almost animalistic, world. This is a play about males in mortal conflict and their speech reflects the role of the conqueror who rules and violates others. As one critic observes, Mamet's language "is written for the muscles, not for the mind."[8]

The alpha-males in this play do not mean what they say. Language is always camouflage or subterfuge. All of these salesmen are as aware as linguistics professors at a gut-level of semantics and its subtexts. Mamet present countless innovations on the words "speak" and "say" and "mean." Depending on when and how they are uttered, these basic monosyllables convey primal shifts in the balance of power: who's up, who's down, who for all practical purposes is heard.

If Mamet's characters in this play are not speaking in the clammy jargon of the trade in which "leads" and "closings" are the holiest of words, they are barking out the harshest four-letter expletives. The profanity and vulgarity no doubt affect some people so that they hear nothing else. The *Time* critic had a point: "Delete the most common four-letter Anglo-Saxonism from the script and his drama might last only one hour instead of two."[9] Yet in the speech and within the scatology itself, the theater-goer hears the desperate cadences of loneliness and fear. Often the foul-mouthed bravado is only desperate bluster, a braggadocio show of power by men who know their true powerlessness only too well. This is street language refined and extended into the baroque, even the lyrical.[10] Thus, Mamet presents something far more complicated than realism while maintaining the external elements of that style. The surface of his plays is usually psychological realism, the Ibsen tradition of photographic naturalism, but underneath, the cauldron of the surreal simmers. His plays are electrically charged with tensions which cannot be explained away with the usual logic.

What *Glengarry Glen Ross* depicts is the raw reality of power. In each of the three scenes in Act I, a series of encounters between pairs of characters portray patterns of dominance and subservience.[11] Levene, as we saw, in the opening scene, tries to shore up his disintegrating world with a manic torrent of words to which the manager replies in laconic monosyllables. Increasingly desperate, Levene attempts to appeal by camaraderie, intimidation, and finally bribery. His shifting strategy is reflected not only in the content of his speech, but still more in the tone, volume, and the rhythm of the exchange.

At the end of the play, Levene has finally run out of words. From his long aria at the beginning of Act II about making the biggest deal of his life, he is now almost totally destroyed. But he is still trying to bribe his way back into his employer's favor. As we watch the dollar bills spill from his pockets on to a desk, we at last see the greenery of the play's title. What we now observe is the abject terror of a life in which all words are finally nothing because it is only money that really talks.

Mamet's characters live in a world of attenuated relationships and disintegrating order. They are seemingly unable to reconstruct the constituent elements of the world which has slipped away from them. In Bigsby's words, they "seem literally demoralized; they find themselves in a context in which their gestures are subverted at the point of origin by their spiritual confusions . . ."[12] Mamet has not only said that his plays are "iconoclastic"[13] but also even more explicitly, he has observed:

> We are spiritually bankrupt—that's what's wrong with this country. We don't take Sundays off. We don't pray. We don't regenerate our spirit. These things aren't luxuries. . . .The spirit has to be replenished. There has to be time for reflection, introspection, and a certain amount of awe and wonder.[14]

This commentary points to the audience's response to Mamet's plays, whether on business as in this play and *American Buffalo* or sexuality (*Sexual Perversity in Chicago*) or any other subject. The members of the audience are exposed to negative examples, and through irony and laughter, they both see beyond the characters the ethical values which are being trampled on and recognize themselves. The *New York Times* critic, Benedict Nightingale, accurately describes *Glengarry Glen Ross*:

> It is a moral play, not a moralizing one. It seeks to 'tell the truth' about the usually invisible violence men inflict on themselves and each other as they grab for gold, not to preach redundant sermons about it.[15]

Earlier in the same review, Nightingale quotes Mamet:

> This is a very violent country full of hate. You can't put a Band-Aid on a suppurating wound. The morality of the theatre is to tell the truth as best you can. When you're not doing that, you're being immoral.[16]

Mamet's dramas, like Ibsen's, dramatize the ethical dilemmas which we struggle with. The particular issues change, but within any society, moral questions challenge the individual to make choices. In *Glengarry Glen Ross*, the drive for power, nourished within a moral vacuum leads to lives of loneliness and fear.

By dramatizing rather than judging, by observing rather than haranguing, Mamet forces us to recognize that our first reaction that these characters are beneath us is not honest. We see a mirror of ourselves as members of a violent and consumer-driven society. For of all ironic twists, Ibsen, among others, would echo Mamet's credo: "Theater is a place of recognition, it's an ethical experience, it's where we share ethical exchange."[17]

NOTES

1. Quoted in John Lahr, "Dogma Days," *The New Yorker*, 68 (November 16, 1992): 121.

2. Quoted in Anne Dean, *David Mamet: Language As Dramatic Action* (Cranbury, N. J.: Associated University Presses, 1990), 16.

3. John Steven Paul, "Big Shoulders," *The Cresset* (October 1984): 20.

4. Dean, 220.

5. Ruby Cohn, "How Are Things Made Round?" in *David Mamet: A Casebook*, ed. Leslie Kane (New York: Garland Publishing, Inc., 1992), 109.

6. All quotations from the play are from David Mamet, *Glengarry Glen Ross* (New York: Grove Press, 1982).

7. Bigsby, C. W. E., *David Mamet* (London: Methuen, 1985), 124.

8. Paul, 19.

9. Christopher Porterfield, "David Mamet's Bond of Futility," *Time* (28 February 1977): 54.

10. See Cohn for a perceptive discussion of Mamet's use of expletives, 117–119.

11. Dean traces the pattern carefully throughout each of the three scenes, 198–207.

12. Bigsby, 60.

13. Quoted in Henry I. Shevey, "Celebrating the Capacity for Self-Knowledge," *New Theatre Quarterly*, 4 (February 1988): 96.

14. Quoted in Hillary deVries, "In David Mamet's Hands a Pen Becomes a Whip," *Christian Science Monitor*, 21 March 1984, 22.

15. Benedict Nightingale, "Is Mamet the Bard of Modern Immorality?" *New York Times*, 4 April 1984, H 5.

16. Nightinggale, H.5.

17. Quoted in Ross Wetzsteon, "David Mamet: Remember that Name," *Village Voice* (5 July 1976): 101.

Chapter Eighteen

Tony Kushner, *Angels in America*

Unfortunately when Aristotle set forth the six elements of drama in his *Poetics*, he did not provide any explication of the final element, spectacle. Our associations with the term are ambivalent: a strange or unusual sight, a remarkable display, a gaudy presentation. But the roots of the word are far less flamboyant: to behold, to make visible, to see. Thus the fundamental nuances of spectacle return us to the *theatron* itself, the place of seeing.

No doubt about it, *Angels in America* is a spectacle. In the seven hours of the two plays, *Part One: Millennium Approaches* and *Part Two: Perestroika* (1992), the stage is filled with fantasy and magic, dead people appearing and long-forgotten ancestors haunting the living. We are bombarded by light and sound, hallucinations, and spiritual visions. One commentator perceptively notes the spectacle of the play:

> And all the mystical moments—feathers falling out of nowhere inexplicably; the *Book of Life* suddenly appearing and disappearing in someone's vision; Prior's ancestors from past centuries appearing to him . . . and finally the pseudo-apocalyptic appearance of the Angel of Death in the final moments—'the theater of the Fabulous', as Kushner calls it . . .[1]

The titles are accurate; the plays are fantasies at an apocalyptic time when old orders, like Perestroika changing the Russian Communist state, are collapsing. The style ranges from political satire to campy humor with scenes as far-out as a beaver gnawing down pine trees in the Antarctic and a diorama of Mormon history. The plays are large, very large, and sprawl from event to event in heaven and on earth.

Yet the plot is quite simple. Two disintegrating couples seem destined from the outset to become intertwined. Joe Pitt, chief clerk to an appeals court judge, finds that his growing alienation from his wife, Harper, has as much to do with sexual ambivalence as with her Valium-induced withdrawal from the world. Louis Ironson, a word processor for the court, finds himself unable to cope when his lover of four years, Prior Walter, discovers the first lesion of AIDS.

The fulcrum on which these two couples are balanced is Joe's mentor, lawyer Roy Cohn, an historical character out of the McCarthy era of American politics. Cohn is poised to fight for his life when he finds out not only that he has AIDS but also that the state is about to begin proceedings to disbar him.

For all their waves of whimsy and fervor, the plays never drift far from the events that will finally bind Joe Pitt and Louis Ironson together in one way, and Roy Cohn and Prior Walter together in another.

The plays reflect the restlessness of the U.S. in the 90's as well as obsession with power. In the second scene of the first play, Cohn is working the phones in multiple conversations. He is orchestrating callers—anxious clients, judges, and Washington contacts—by pushing hold buttons with the finesse of a symphony conductor but at all times manipulating the levers of power. Cohn, as one reviewer comments, is "a smiler with a knife—so monumentally vicious and self-serving as to scream his abhorrence of homosexuals while insisting on his own heterosexuality, even while dying of AIDS."[2] What he says about his heart is true of his entire self: "Tough little muscle. Never bleeds."[3] Later in the second play, Cohn, now pasty and shrunken as he lies in his hospital bed, nevertheless attempts to wield his dominance as a bulwark against change. After he dies, he is still experiencing pretenses of power as he assumes a new position, defense lawyer for deity:

> Yes I will represent you, King of the Universe, yes I will sing and eviscerate, I will bully and seduce, I will win for you and make the plaintiffs, those traitors, wish they had never heard the name of . . . (*Huge thunderclap*) Is it a done deal, are we on? (Part Two, pp. 138–139)

If Cohn and AIDS are images of both power and impotence, destruction as well as rebirth, the titles of the two plays also point to the ambivalent presence of both fear and hope. In *Millennium Approaches*, almost all of the characters articulate apocalyptic statements as Harper does several times:

> It's 1985. Fifteen years till the third millennium. Maybe Christ will come again. (Part One, p. 18)

> Skin burns, birds go blind, icebergs melt. The world's coming to an end. (Part One, p. 28)

Within *Perestroika* (the Russian word for re-building, restructuring), is dramatized the struggle to embrace both loss and change. In the opening scene, the "World's Oldest Bolshevik" asks:

> The Great Question before us is: Are we doomed? The Great Question before us is: Will the Past release us? The Great Question before us is: Can we Change? In Time? And we all desire that Change will come. (Part Two, p. 13)

Much later, the Angel echoes this dilemma:

> What will the grim Unfolding of the Latter Days bring?
> That you or any Being should wish to endure them?
> Death more plenteous than all Heaven has tears to mourn it,
> The slow dissolving of the Great Design,
> The spiraling apart of the Work of Eternity,
> The World and its beautiful particle logic
> All collapsed. All dead, forever,
> In starless, moonlorn onyx night . . .
> We are failing, failing
> The Earth and the Angels.
> Look up, look up,
> It is Not-to-Be Time.
> Oh who asks of the Orders Blessing
> With Apocalyse Descending? (Part Two, pp. 134–135)

Amid these cosmic upheavals, the plays are about love and loss and betrayal of relationships. Everyone abandons someone within the plays. Ghosts from the past, as in Ibsen, come to haunt the living. Ethel Rosenberg, an American who was executed for allegedly being a Russian spy in the 50's, appears to Roy Cohn; ancestors from the 13th and 17th centuries come to visit Prior. The plagues of their times are repeated in the dominant presence of AIDS in our era.

The plays both portray the characters as passive victims doomed by the AIDS virus as well as present ways of living in hope despite the illness. AIDS as the primary metaphor of the plays is both catastrophic ("K. S., baby. Lesion number one. Look it. The wine-dark kiss of the angel of death." Part One, p. 21) but also an opportunity for rebirth and renewal: "History is about to crack wide open. Millennium approaches." (Part One, p. 112)

Angels appear and re-appear in both plays, alternately as messengers of death and messengers of mercy, to warn and encourage persons how to respond to the hurt within and around them. The angel who descends at the end of the first play in "a great blaze of triumphal music, heralding" and "in a shower of unearthly white light, spreading great opalescent gray-silver wings"

(Prior's "awestruck whisper" is "God almighty . . . *Very* Steven Spielberg") speaks:

> Greetings, Prophet:
> The Great Work begins:
> The Messenger has arrived. (Part One, pp. 118–119)

A self-disclosure of an angel is usually associated with light as the Angel in Part Two indicates: "LUMEN PHOSPHOR FLUOR CANDLE!" (Part Two, p. 44). But other commentators have associated the angel with "stasis and death"[4] and with "a bunch of testy, indecisive bureaucrats . . ."[5] Within the plays, the angels anoint Prior as prophet and later a black angel comes to wrestle with him until Prior says: "I . . . will not let thee go except thou bless me." (Part Two, p. 119)

Such a figure appeared to Jacob, but the question within the play is: Are there angels in America? The playwright in talking with the cast of the play at the Mark Taper Forum in Los Angeles in 1992 said: "And how else should an angel land on earth but with the utmost difficulty? If we are to be visited by angels we will have to call them down with sweat and strain."[6] Kushner's angels do not arrive by divine intervention but by human request. Yet the two plays dramatize a precarious balance which avoids the modern temptation of nihilism, but hesitates to affirm the presence of meaning. He mocks Mormonism but at the same time employs religious images such as Bethesda Fountain and the apocalypse as well as the appearance of angels although again undercut by the ironic comment: "Very Steven Spielberg."

The Epilogue of *Perestroika* is set at the Bethesda Fountain in New York's Central Park. The fountain with its statuary angels honors the Civil War dead which a reviewer says could stand for Kushner's play: "They commemorate death but they suggest a world without dying."[7] The name Bethesda was also the name of the pool of healing waters in ancient Jerusalem (John 5:2–9) which one of the characters invokes: "The Fountain of Bethesda will flow again . . . We will all bathe ourselves clean" (Part Two, p. 147). Prior then echoes the same thoughts in the concluding line as the Bethesda angel hovers above: "The Great Work Begins." (Part Two, p. 148)

Perhaps one of the most incisive comments Kushner has made is that "in the Judeo-Christian tradition, the Day of Wrath is both the day of wrath and the coming of the Kingdom of God. The hour of heaven may or may not come. You don't get the answer. You get an absolute maybe."[8] Such a statement echoes Beckett's famous response when asked what was the key word in his plays. One can imagine how his questioner and all of his commentators were awaiting and yet dreading the answer. Beckett replied, "Perhaps."[9]

Clive Barnes ended his review of *Perestroika* by describing it as "one of those plays defining an era, a work of today's imagination and sensibility . . ."[10] Both plays achieve that distinction, for amid the remarkable style and the gaudy spectacle, what is made visible is a spiritual quest, an urgent search for meaning.

NOTES

1. Yale Kramer, "Angels on Broadway," *The American Spectator* (July 1993): 21.

2. Doug Watt, "Angels in America Earns Its Wings," *New York Daily News*, 14 May 1993, 55.

3. All quotations from the plays are from Tony Kushner, *Part One: Millennium Approaches* and *Part Two: Perestroika* (New York: Theatre Communications Group, 1992), Part Two, 27.

4. Frank Rich, "Following the Angel for a Healing Vision of Heaven and Earth," *New York Times,* 24 November 1993, C20.

5. Michael Feingold, "Epic Assumptions," *Village Voice,* 7 December 1998, 93.

6. Quoted in John Lahr, "Angels on Broadway," *New Yorker*, 69 (May 31, 1993): 137.

7. Quoted in Lahr, "Earth Angels," *New Yorker,* 69 (December 13, 1993): 130.

8. Rich, *C20.*

9. Quoted in Tom F. Driver, "Beckett by the Madeleine," *Columbia University Forum*, IV (Summer 1961): 20.

10. Clive Barnes, "Angels' Soars (Sorta)," *New York Post,* 28 November 1993, 37.

Chapter Nineteen

Mary Zimmerman, *Metamorphoses*

I am sitting in the first row of the indoor amphitheater. The audience surrounds the stage on three sides. I can thus see others as they too are involved in the action in shared response. For I am sitting in the Circle in the Square Theater in New York City in the 21st century, A.D. In this space, eight times weekly, some six hundred people see a performance of Mary Zimmerman's *Metamorphoses* (2001). The power of the ancient ritual of Dionyious is still present as it was in the amphitheater in Epidaurus in the fifth century, B.C.

"I ask the help of the gods," the first narrator of *Metamorphoses* begins. "Let one glimpse the secret and speak, better than I know how." (p. 5)[1] For the next ninety minutes, ten stories adapted by Zimmerman from the *Metamorphoses* of the Roman poet Ovid (43 B.C.–17 A.D.) are presented for our contemplation and delight—tales of men and women, gods and goddesses, birds, animals, flowers, trees. Indeed, the scope is, as it was for the ancients, cosmic.

In Book XV, Ovid predicts, "I shall be read, and through the centuries . . . . Through all the ages I shall live . . ."[2] Zimmerman, in the adaptation of his myths which she wrote and directed, makes Ovid's prediction come true in moving and magical action.

A therapist, counseling with Phaeton, son of the sun god, dressed in a stylish black pants suit—*au courant* dress for contemporary psychiatrists—comments on myth and drama:

It has been said that the myth is a public dream, dreams are private myths. Unfortunately we give our mythic side scant attention these days. As a result a great deal escapes us and we no longer understand our own actions. So it remains important and salutary to speak not only of the rational and easily understood, but also of enigmatic things: the irrational and the ambiguous. To speak both privately and publicly. (pp. 67–68)

The irrational, the mythic, dreams — out of these elements from Ovid, Zimmerman has created the play. She has said that the playwright and the audience are "collaborating in a dream"[3] and she has brought some of humanity's oldest dreams — Greek myths — to life.

The stories are timeless, yet contemporary. King Midas resembles a venture capitalist who can do no wrong. Erysichthon, though dressed in a toga, comes across as a greedy mogul unconcerned about the environment who pays dearly for incurring Ceres' wrath. Phaeton's tale is montaged with a full-blown session of Freudian analysis as he whines that his relationship with his father, the Sun, wasn't that great.

Zimmerman envisions the world of drama as a place where public life and private fantasy and imagination merge. The myths, drawing from their archetypal sources, engage our memories and inner lives and appeal to the shadows below the rational. Her approach to myth seems the very embodiment of Francis Fergusson's observation that

one of the most striking properties of myths is that they generate new forms . . . in the imagination of those who try to grasp them. Until some imagination, that of a poet or only a reader or auditor, is thus fecunded by a myth, the myth would seem to exist only potentially. . . .[4]

The new forms which Zimmerman presents melds the tales of the ancients and their gods with modern language and images. It is the theatrical images of the play which make us see more deeply. A door opens to reveal a dead love, alive again, but not quite the same. A woman's body dissolves in mid-embrace into water. A man and woman rise out of the water in unison, arms as if wings, silently and slowly gliding their way to shore. The figure of Narcissus is replaced by his eponymous flower.

Some of the stage devices are elegantly simple. When Zeus creates light, an actor lights a cigarette. To present a fatal storm at sea, a bare-chested thug tosses a bucket of water. Zimmerman in the beauty and power of the play's images and devices has clearly made a break with realism and seeks an almost operatic richness of spectacle. And how does the playwright and the producer and the director make the images so vivid? Through word and gesture, yes, but also in the ways in which space itself is presented.

The space is primal, elemental, cosmic. The heavens, a high platform at the rear with a cloud-flecked screen behind which the gods plot and pity; a 1920's wooden door through which enter mortals and most of all, the thirty-foot-long pool of water which covers almost all the stage. Zimmerman writes in a note on the staging:

> The stage is entirely occupied by a square or rectangular pool of water, of varying depth, bordered on all four sides by a wooden deck approximately three feet wide . . . All scenes take place in and around the pool, with shifts between stories, scenes, and settings indicated by nothing more than a shift in light or merely a shift in the actors' orientation or perhaps a music cue . . . The staging should . . . provide images that amplify the text, lend it poetic resonance, or even, sometimes contradict it. (p. 3)

As one commentator accurately observes, the pool is transformed in "an ocean of imagination."[5] Another critic comments: "The pool almost seems like a character too, with sovereign power to shift symbolic meaning while remaining itself."[6] The water shapes, consumes, and engages those who are in it. Although it is only a few inches deep, the actors sometimes create the illusion that it is as deep as the sea. Characters melt into this pool, galleons are destroyed by storms in this water, and furious passions are depicted by the movement of water. At times, the pool becomes the black and bottomless Styx or a sexy medium for a dark wet dream in which Cinyras ravishes his own daughter. Poseidon in his wrath rains down torrents from a bucket, capsizing a small ship while elsewhere in the pool, a strapping sea spirit drowns Ceyx, the life-size captain, in the breakers. One observer comments that the pool's water is that "into which people melt in despair, upon which they float, suspended in space; out of which they are reborn."[7] The elemental nature of water is thus evoked: it both destroys and purifies; most of all, it transforms.

The mythos of the play, as one observer has commented, is "meditations on mutability."[8] Everything and everyone in the play of *Metamorphoses* is in a state of flux. The playwright has listened well to her source for, as Ovid wrote, "All things change; nothing dies."[9] The playwright's ambition, as stated in the opening invocation, is to catalog transformations on every scale, from the microscopic to the cosmic, from the creation of the world up to this moment when the stories are re-told.

Each myth segues into another with new characters and new dilemmas. The ensemble of actors slips smoothly in and out of numerous characters guided by music, light, and shadow. Everything flows fluidly. There is the pleasure of motion as gods, mortals, and animals keep changing places. The *New York Times* critic comments, "The transformations that ensue—into trees, birds, streams or statues—are by turns curses, blessings, and sometimes, most magically, the natural sign of mercy, of a judgment suspended."[10] In the final tale, that of Baucis and Philemon, for example, the narrator describes an amazing series of transformations:

Suddenly, everything was changing. The poor little house, their simple cottage, was becoming grander and grander, a glittering marble-columned temple. The straw and reeds of the thatched roof metamorphosed into gold, and gates with elaborate carvings sprang up, as ground gave way to marble paving stones. (p. 82)

Transformation here is not merely a theme, but the mystery at the core of existence. There are transformations of things and the body, but also of the mind and the heart, both on stage and in the audience. Props change, costumes change, sets change. Most significantly, we change as we experience the play.

The myths provide order to the chaos of suffering and point to the rebirth and resurrection after death. The tone of the play evolves from scenes of unbearable pain to moments which suddenly overflow with merciful tenderness.[11]

The central subject is love, love of all kinds. At the core of the myths in the spiritual belief that love is the guiding force of the universe. Love of all kinds is dramatized—sacred, profane, taboo, erotic love (Orpheus and Eurydice), self-love (Narcissus), deep marital love (Baucis and Philemon), love of money and for his child (Midas), incestuous love (Cinyra and Myrrha), and adoring love (Alcyone and Ceyx).

A closer look at several of the stories will reveal how love and death and rebirth are intertwined within the narratives.

MIDAS

Midas enters and sits on an armchair in the water, his playful daughter continually interrupting his self-congratulatory exposition about success:

Now, I'm not a greedy man, but it is an accepted fact—a proven fact—that money is a good thing. A thing to be longed for, a *necessary* thing. And my god, I have a lot of it! It wasn't always this way with me—the boats, the houses by the sea, the summer cottages and the winter palaces, the exotic furnishings, the soft clothes, the food . . . (pp. 8–9)

The gods meanwhile grant the king one wish he desires. They bestow the Midas touch with due warning, as Bacchus says: "That's a really, really bad idea." (p. 17) But Midas, after turning various objects into gold, is grief stricken when his daughter jumps on him to give him a hug and unwittingly gilds his own child. Her animated figure stiffens as he beseeches the gods to take away the golden touch. Midas is no longer a king with "net worth: one hundred billion" (p. 8) but a father, crushed. Bacchus offers him one chance at reversal; he must seek the waters of eternal life. Midas wanders offstage in search of his soul.

ORPHEUS AND EURYDICE

The tale of Orpheus and Eurydice is told twice: first with Ovid's emphases on Orpheus' powerful effect on characters inhabiting the underworld, then in the retelling by the early 20th century poet, Rilke, who stresses Eurydice's point of view. They are presented as mirror images of each other on the unanswerable questions about love and time.

Singing and playing his lyre, Orpheus in the first re-telling is an archetype of the human heart's deepest feeling and their expression in poetry and music. When Eurydice dies, he attempts to get her back from the grave. He descends into hell as red lights, music, and sirens envelop the scene. The powers of the underworld propose a deal; she can come back if he does not look back. They gamble on his one weakness. Orpheus, as the mythic god of music, can only move forward in time. Therefore mortal love and feeling can only move forward. As the scene draws to a close, the narrator asks: "Is this a story about how time can only move in one direction?" (p.44) while Orpheus and Eurydice repeat the moment of their parting again and again.

Zimmerman then stages the Rilke's version of the myth. Eurydice, guided by the messenger, Hermes, slowly walks behind Orpheus. He reaches the sunlit portal of earth and turns around. Hermes tells Eurydice that Orpheus has looked back but Eurydice asks, "Who?"—having already forgotten him—and slowly returns to the underworld.

MYRRHA AND CINYRAS

In this tale, the virgin Myrrha is punished for ignoring Aphrodite by being seized with a passion for her own father, Cinyras. She debates with herself what to do: "O gods, I pray you, keep off this wickedness," but then, alternately, "Who would condemn such love as crime?" (p. 53) While her mother is away, she goes to her father's bedroom. Her father has been blindfolded. But after several nights of passionate sex, he insists on seeing her. His instinct, as soon as he removes the blindfold, is to kill his daughter. She flees, crying: "O Gods, I pray you, change me; make me something else; transform me entirely, let me step out of my own heart." (p. 60)

Myrrha dissolves into tears; she steps into a shimmering stream and "her body melted" (p. 61) She slowly disappears beneath the surface of the pool.

PHAETON

In Ovid, Phaeton was born of a brief union between Apollo, the sun god, and Clymene, a mortal woman. In Zimmerman's play, Phaeton as a young man seeks the attention of a remote father figure. The scene is staged so that Ovid's version of the fable and a therapy session at a Hollywoodesque pool setting alternate like film dissolves. Brash Phaeton appears, wearing bright yellow swim trunks as he floats on a bright yellow inflated air mattress and adjusts his Ray-Bans while explaining to his psychobabble-spouting analyst the difficulties he has had with the sun as his father: "But I never knew him, and he wasn't really around. I mean, not *around* around." (p. 62) Phaeton says he finally journeyed to Apollo's realm to claim his birthright: to steer the chariot of the sun across the sky or, in his own words, "Give me the keys to your car." (p. 66) Apollo reluctantly agrees, but he gives this advice: "Don't fly too high." (p. 67) But Phaeton doesn't listen; he sets the earth on fire, and destroys himself.

BAUCIS AND PHILEMON

In the last of the tales, the elderly couple, Baucis and Philemon, welcome strangers as if they were angels come to visit. Because of their generous hospitality, the gods grant them a wish. Their response is that, since they have loved each other their entire lives, they will die at the same moment. When the moment comes, they embrace, sprout leaves and are metamorphosed into trees. As this is happening, the rest of the ensemble surrounds them and whispers:

All:	Let me die the moment my love dies.
Narrator One:	They whisper:
All:	Let me outlive my own capacity to love.
Narrator One:	They whisper:
All:	Let me die still loving, and so, never die. (p. 83).

Reciting those lines, the cast launches small glass vessels with lit candles in them which float on the water. This image calling on another of the elements—fire—in creating a star-filled pool evokes the truth that love has truly conquered death.

It is a beautiful moment, this transformation, but not quite the last. At the end of the Midas tale at the beginning of the play, Bacchus told him that his wish could not be removed, but that Midas should "walk as far as the ends of the earth. Look for a pool of water that reflects the stars at night. Wash your hands in it and there is a chance that everything will be restored." (p. 19) Now as the lights dim and the candles float in the darkening pool, a distracted Midas wanders on, still carrying his daughter's golden jump rope. He kneels at the pool, drops the rope in the water, and dips his hands to wash his face. At that moment his daughter appears, restored.

Such a moment leads one to ask the question one of the narrators raised in the play: "When you see a miracle like that, how can one deny the existence of the gods?" (p. 32)

From the amphitheaters of Greece in the 5th century, B.C. and on through the centuries as we have surveyed drama in Western history, the presence of the holy and the sacred, indeed, of God and the gods, has been central. The *theatron* has been the place of seeing one's self, others, the world, the haunting presence of the gods and the ambiguous working of the ways of God. The stage throughout history has always been the locus where the vertical and the horizontal, the divine and the human meet. In its finite space, the particular actions of human beings and the infinite moments of the eternal are seen in action. Religion and drama continue to be in tension, to intersect and to engage in interplay with one another.

NOTES

1. All quotations from the text are taken from Mary Zimmerman, *Metamorphoses* (Evanston: Northwestern University Press, 2002).

2. Ovid, *Metamorphoses*, Volume II, tr. Frank Justis Miller (Cambridge, MA: Harvard University Press, 1984), 427.

3. Quoted in "Gods in the Wading Pool," *Time* (2 December 2001), 72.

4. Francis Fergusson, *The Human Image in Dramatic Literature* (Garden City, New York: Doubleday and Company, 1957), 162–163.

5. Ben Brantley, "Dreams of '*Metamorphoses*' Echo in a Larger Space," *New York Times*, 5 March 2002, E1.

6. Deborah Garwood, "Myth as Public Dream: The Metamorphosis of Mary Zimmerman's *Metamorphoses*," *Performing Arts Journal* (January 2003): 71.

7. Julia E. Whitworth, "*Metamorphoses* (Theatrical Production)", *Theatre Journal*, Vol. 54, Issue 4 (December 2002): 635.

8. Logan Hill, "Altered Stages," *New York*, 35 (25 February 2002): 72.

9. Ovid, *Metamorphoses*, tr. Samuel Garth (NY: Heritage Press, 1961), 491.

10. Matthew Gurewitsch, "The Theater's Quicksilver Truth is all in Change," *New York Times*, 2 December 2, 2001, Section 2, 1.

11. After being premiered in Chicago in 1998, *Metamorphoses* opened off-Broadway in New York City in early October 2001. The play's themes of death and resurrection resonated with many members of the audience, who, according to early reviews, were highly emotionally responsive to the drama as a reflection on the events of September 11, 2001. In early 2002, the play moved to the Circle in the Square Theater where it continued to attract large audiences.

Coda: Life is a Drama!

The entire experience of drama is a microcosm, an analogy, of our understanding of life itself. To say, for example, life is only a play, a charade, a dumb show, is to suggest that human action is illusory and meaningless. To say that life is a drama is to imply cosmic significance of human action.

Epictetus, Greek Stoic of the first century, A.D., already recognized this relationship between drama and our lives: "Regard yourself as an actor in a play. The poet gives you a part to play and you must play it . . ."[1] Hans Urs von Balthasar, Roman Catholic theologian who has explored more fully than any other scholar the relationship between theology and drama, has said:

> . . . theater owes its very existence substantially to man's need to recognize himself as playing a role. It continually delivers him from the sense of being trapped and from the temptation to regard existence as something closed in upon itself. Through the theater, man acquires the habit of looking for meaning at a higher and less obvious level.[2]

Such a perspective echoes what an early Church Father, Clement of Alexandria, wrote about the truly wise man who "faultlessly plays the role God has given him in the drama of life . . ."[3]

Not all understanding of the relationship of drama and life has been that positive. The Egyptian Pallada suggests: All life is but a stage play; so learn how to act;And put seriousness from you—or endure suffering.[4]

Another Stoic thinker, Marcus Aurelius, speaks of "An empty pageant; a stage play . . . puppets, jerking on their strings—that is life."[5] And Shakespeare's image spoken by Macbeth when he heard of his wife's death is etched in our memory:Life's but a walking shadow, a poor player /That struts and frets his hour upon the stage/ And then is heard no more. (*Macbeth*, V, v, 24-26)

Phrases from the world of theater have entered our world of discourse, especially about human motivations and actions, each of which has ethical implications: to be upstaged, hamming it up, play for the crowd, overacting, having stage fright, missing a cue, the show must go on, you stole my line, use your talent, in the spotlight, and many more.

The word "play" may be especially subject to word-play to suggest how we act: do we play at, play around, play with? What do we play for? The scoreboard? The final game? The grandstand audience? The joy of play? Do we attempt to play God? Or do we let God play through us?

What is apparent in all these words and phrases is that our religious-philosophical commitments determine the way we live our lives as drama. The answer to the fundamental question: Of what kind of drama am I a part? reveals our deepest convictions. Do I discern that I am playing a role in a tragedy, a comedy, a farce, a melodrama? The response reveals our deepest commitments.

An entire series of questions from the world of drama are essentially religious, for they are root inquiries and each response we give will be answers to fundamental questions: What is my role in life? How do I discern my talents in order to follow my true vocation and most of all how shall I act? Such a series might include:

Is there an author? A director? If so, who and how does one learn of them?
What is the scope of the stage?
Is there a plot?
Is there a script? Or, is it mainly improvisation?
Do I (and others) wear masks?
Do the costumes reveal and/or hide the inner person?
What is the role of other characters?—lead characters, supporting roles, bit parts,
walk-ons?
Who is the audience? Spectators or participants?
From where do I enter? And what is the significance of the exit?
Is there anything off-stage?
Are there reviews? If so, who writes them?

Religion and drama have been intersecting and inter-acting throughout this volume: in language, in structure, in history. And the roots of all these relationships are the connections between drama and life itself. Life may be a cabaret, my friend, but it certainly is a drama.

NOTES

1. Handbook 17, quoted in Hans Urs von Balthasar, *Theo-Drama*, Volume I, *Prologomena* (San Francisco: St. Ignatius Press, 1988), 140–141.

2. von Balthasar, 20.

3. *Strom*, VII, 11, 65, quoted in von Balthasar, 56.

4. *Anthl. Palot*, X 172, quoted in von Balthasar, 42.

5. *Strom*, VII, 11, 65, quoted in von Balthasar, 56.